GOD AND TEMPLE

GOD AND TEMPLE

by R. E. CLEMENTS

M.A., B.D., Ph.D.

FORTRESS PRESS
PHILADELPHIA
1965

Library of Congress Catalog Card Number: ~~65-12822~~

65 - 6473

PRINTED IN GREAT BRITAIN

CONTENTS

To My Wife

PREFACE

The foregoing study arose out of a thesis entitled *The Divine Dwelling-Place in the Old Testament* submitted to the Department of Biblical Studies in the University of Sheffield for the degree of Ph.D. in 1961. In its present form, however, a considerable number of changes have been introduced, and the text has been almost entirely rewritten. This has enabled me to take advantage of a more prolonged study of the Old Testament material, and to pay attention to a considerable number of important recent works which have a bearing upon the theme. It is my earnest hope that these changes will make the book a more readable and original contribution to Old Testament studies. For the original thesis I am particularly indebted to the Rev. J. N. Schofield, who suggested the subject, and to Professors F. F. Bruce and A. Guilding who supervised the research. A number of helpful criticisms were made by Principal-emeritus N. H. Snaith.

Professors N. W. Porteous and G. W. Anderson have generously helped with the loan of books and offprints, which has enabled me to give a fuller documentation than would otherwise have been possible. To Professor Anderson in particular a special word of thanks is due for his kindness in reading through the manuscript and offering freely of his advice and help. Without his guidance the book would have been a much inferior composition, whilst for its faults and failings I entirely accept the responsibility.

For simplicity I have transliterated all Hebrew words, although scholars should have no difficulty in recognizing the original. The translations adhere closely, but not entirely, to the Revised Standard Version, as at many points I have thought it necessary to make clear a particular feature of the Hebrew. It is with very real gratitude that I dedicate the book to my wife, whose patience and willingness to sacrifice have contributed in no small measure to its appearance.

New College, University of Edinburgh   R. E. CLEMENTS
May 1964

INTRODUCTION

The purpose of this study is to inquire into the meaning and theological significance of the Jerusalem temple as a witness to the presence of God in Ancient Israel. At a first consideration the notion that God should reserve for himself a special place on earth to be his dwelling-place among men seems strange, and even irrelevant, to the modern Christian. Does not the idea of such a dwelling-place contradict the belief in God as the creator of the entire universe? Is there not in such a notion an implied restriction of the divine presence to one single earthly locality? The answer to both of these questions is in the negative, for it is abundantly clear in the pages of the Old Testament that far from conveying a restricted notion of God, or denying his lordship over the whole creation, the Jerusalem temple, more than any other institution of Ancient Israel, was the centre of a faith which asserted that Yahweh, the God of Israel, was lord of the whole earth. To show how this came about, and the importance of the particular ideas and hopes which came to be associated with the temple on Mount Zion, is the aim of this inquiry. As a starting-point it is essential to glance briefly at the general Near Eastern background to the Old Testament, and especially at the religion of the Canaanite peoples, who were so closely associated with Israel in the period of their origins and early development. It is also important to consider the dominant hypotheses which have been advanced as reconstructions of the religion of the Hebrew patriarchs, and to note the particular ideas of the divine presence to which this religion has been thought to bear witness. All of these together provide an indispensable background to an understanding of the idea of the divine presence in Israel.

Israelite religion properly began with the events of the exodus and the conclusion of a covenant on Mount Sinai, in the accounts of both of which the figure of Moses is prominently presented. The close relationship between the worship of Yahweh and a religious assembly on Mount Sinai suggests to us the possibility that this mountain was already regarded as a divine abode before the arrival of the Israelites there. It seems to have continued to be regarded as such by the early Israelites, whilst at the same time Israel possessed two primary cult-objects, the ark and the tent of meeting, both of which were held

ix

in high regard as symbols of Yahweh's presence. They eventually influenced the Jerusalem temple cult in a number of ways. The pre-monarchic period of Israel's history holds a great many enigmas and unsolved problems, but perhaps none is more important for our study than that which concerns the Yahwistic temple in Shiloh. What were its origins, its significance, its cult and cult-furnishings? None of these questions can be readily answered with any degree of confidence, although certain plausible hypotheses are worthy of serious attention. Its importance was very probably greater than many historians of Israel's religion have conceded, and a number of far-reaching innovations may well have been adopted by the Israelite tribes during the brief period in which this sanctuary flourished. After its destruction by the Philistines it left a legacy of cultic ideology which gained a new significance when taken up in the worship of the temple of Jerusalem.

This temple, which Solomon built, came to play a prominent part in the growth of Israel's religion, and it exercised a controlling influence on the maintenance of the Yahwistic tradition. In order to understand how it came to enjoy this unique and privileged position in Israel a thorough re-examination is called for of its meaning and interpretation. This must commence with a study of the circumstances of David's reign, in which the worship of Yahweh was first introduced into Jerusalem. A number of factors, some historical and some derived from Canaanite religious ideas, led to the decision to erect a temple for Yahweh on Mount Zion. For important reasons this decision was not put into effect until Solomon's reign, when a temple was built on the pattern provided by Canaanite-Syrian religious architecture. A most important aspect of this building was its close association with the Davidic court, and its wide-ranging claims of a political and national character. It belonged inseparably to the ideals and aims of the Davidic-Solomonic state. A momentous event in the history of this temple took place in Josiah's reign (621 B.C.), with a cult-reform and the centralization of the entire Yahweh cult at Jerusalem. The Jerusalem cult tradition became virtually synonymous with the Israelite religious faith.

The disruption and continual weakening of the Israelite state, and its eventual dissolution with the exile of 586 B.C., inevitably affected the temple, which was itself destroyed by the Babylonians. With this disaster, and the eclipse of the Davidic dynasty, Israel's political and religious aspirations were ruined, and a great crisis of faith engendered. Yet among the exiles the desire to return and to rebuild the temple was eventually rewarded by the opportunity to do so, and after many setbacks a new building was erected in Jerusalem. In this rebuilt temple much of the earlier cult tradition was re-interpreted and given a new significance in the light of the historical judgments which had been experienced. It is plain that not all of the hoped-for blessings were granted to this small company of devoted Jews who restored the temple. Their hopes and ambitions, which derived in large part from the earlier ideology of the temple, became a part of the eschatological expectation of Judaism. Jerusalem and its temple came more and more to be regarded as symbols, and the belief in Yahweh's presence with his people, to which the temple had witnessed, became increasingly the subject of a future hope. As such Jerusalem and Mount Zion have passed over into Christian tradition as figures of heaven, where God and his people are at one. At the same time the actual temple continued as the centre of a very vigorous and productive religious activity. The Old Testament, as we have it, is a product of the collecting and editorial activity of Jerusalem scribes during the post-exilic era, and the knowledge which this literature gives to us of the Israelite-Jewish religion has passed through the selecting and interpreting activity of the temple community. During the Hellenistic age, even amongst the dispersion, an allegiance to the Jerusalem temple was virtually a badge of orthodoxy and of religious integrity, and, until its destruction in A.D. 70, the temple continued to have a most profound influence upon the Jewish religion. Once this sanctuary ceased to be the focus of Jewish religious life, that religion was forced to change very markedly, and to shift its centre of gravity from the temple to the sacred writings which the temple community had preserved. It is apparent from the pages of the New Testament, as well as from the writings from Qumran, that the significance and claims of the Jerusalem temple were subjects of the most far-reaching controversies, which deeply affected the development of the early Christian Church. In the New Testament the interpretation of the promises of Yahweh's presence with Israel was a matter which profoundly influenced its Christology, and for Jesus himself his attitude to the temple was perhaps the greatest offence that he offered to his fellow Jews. Such at least is suggested by the accusation raised at his trial. In every way, both for Jews and Christians, the fact of the Jerusalem temple was of inescapable importance.

CHAPTER I

SACRED MOUNTAINS, TEMPLES AND THE PRESENCE OF GOD

THE question of the divine presence was not patent of an obvious solution in early times, and, in the Ancient Near East various ways were adopted by men in an effort to make the presence of the gods accessible. Unless the presence of a god could be found, and its locality made known, then no possibility existed of establishing a fruitful communion between him and his worshippers. Yet even in the simplest religious experience an element of mystery and of supernatural 'otherness' surrounded the manifestations of a god. He was free to reveal himself wherever and whenever he willed, but he was not subject to the commands of men. It was, therefore, the urgent need of his worshippers to know where to find him in the hour of their need, and to secure his blessing for themselves, and for all who were dependent on them. It could not suffice to worship an unknown god whose presence remained a mystery, for such a god had to be found and approached. Men needed to come before his face and to know that their prayers were heard. Thus it was important not only to know the name of a god, but also to be informed of his dwelling-place so that he could be visited. In the developed religions of Mesopotamia the question of the divine dwelling-places assumed an important place, and each deity was assigned his or her abode. This was an essential element in the maintenance of order within the pantheon. Even where religion was less sophisticated, and where no such prominence was given to temples as in Mesopotamia, the question of knowing the place where the god's presence could be found was of vital interest. Gods could be expected to reveal their presence in the future where they had done so in the past, so that certain localities could be identified as the dwelling-places of gods, and appropriate altars erected, where a theophany had occurred. In such cases an important part of the tradition of the sanctuary was its foundation-legend, which told how first the place had been recognized as the abode of the god who was worshipped there. When the gods were regarded as the great lords of the earth and of the sky, whose rule was believed to extend throughout vast areas of the

I

universe, their presence could not be conceived as confined to one place on earth. Nevertheless such an earthly sanctuary could be made to symbolize, or represent, the cosmic divine abode. As a result one god could have more than one sanctuary or temple, which did not mean that he possessed more than one dwelling-place, but only that there were several copies of his one true dwelling-place which remained remote from the world of men.

The religions of the Ancient Near East do not seem to have been strongly mystical in tone, where the divine presence could be sought in an inward searching of the soul, nor yet did they possess a rational philosophy, with its concepts of deism or pantheism. Instead the most widespread attitude adopted towards the problem of the divine presence was to seek a solution in some form of symbolism, where a relationship was believed to be established between the natural and the supernatural worlds. Thus either by means of their form, or some inner mysterious quality, earthly objects were thought to be capable of becoming charged with supernatural power, and so of establishing a link with the persons and abodes of the gods. This kind of reasoning undoubtedly lies at the basis of the use of images, which could, on account of their shape or substance, become one with the god himself.[1] In a similar way the abode of a god could not be precisely defined and isolated, but it could be symbolized, and, as a result, the god could be effectively approached by men.

The great attachment in the ancient world to sacred mountains, regarded as divine abodes, is probably to be explained in this way.[2] The universe itself was thought of as a gigantic world-mountain, stretching from the entrance of the subterranean abyss to the highest point of heaven, and embracing all the inhabited world. A real mountain was therefore a fitting symbol for such a god, and expressed the belief that his power extended across all the territory where men dwelt. A certain elasticity was present even in the idea of 'land' itself, which could be interpreted both as a particular local region, and as the entire cosmos.[3] This elasticity of meaning provided a way of making a conscious identification between an inhabited locality and the whole universe, so that the god who was worshipped in a particular area as

---

[1] K. H. Bernhardt, *Gott und Bild*, Berlin, 1956, pp. 28ff.

[2] Cf. H. Frankfort, *The Birth of Civilization in the Near East*, London, 1951, p. 54; *The Art and Architecture of the Ancient Orient*, London, 1954, p. 6. Cf. also M. Eliade, 'Centre du monde, temple, maison', *Le symbolisme cosmique des monuments religieux*, Rome, 1957, p. 64, and *Images and Symbols*, London, 1961, pp. 41ff.

[3] Cf. S. Mowinckel, *Religion und Kultus*, Göttingen, 1953, pp. 75f., and *The Psalms in Israel's Worship*, Oxford, 1962, I, pp. 19, 134; II, p. 236. Such a width of meaning is found in the Hebrew 'ereṣ = 'land, world'.

the lord and giver of its life, was venerated at the same time as the creator of the universe. No hard and fast distinction, therefore, can necessarily be made between the local gods and the great high-gods who were worshipped in the Ancient Near East. The local gods were frequently identified as particular forms of the great universal gods. This is important when we come to consider the ideas of immanence and transcendence evidenced in Ancient Near Eastern religion. It becomes clear that no rigid classification can be made between those gods who were regarded as immanent in creation, producing fertility in its fields and flocks, and those who were transcendent, ruling the heavens and creating the universe. The gods were both transcendent and immanent, revealing themselves in the world of men, and yet remaining superior to it, and being unconfined by its spatial and temporal boundaries. The local sacred mountain was therefore the symbol, or representation, of the cosmos which formed the true abode of the deity whom men worshipped. It was thus the part which represented the whole.

If this interpretation of the attachment to sacred mountains may be regarded as valid, it must certainly also be applied to the great Ziggurats, or stage-towers, of Sumeria. These were an attempt on the part of men to build artificial mountains which could then serve as divine dwelling-places.[1] They formed a transition stage between the veneration of real mountains as divine abodes, and the building of man-made temples. The great temple of Marduk in Babylon was an example of this kind of stage-tower construction,[2] and shows how the Babylonian culture had inherited much from the earlier Sumerians.

Not every sanctuary, however, had its Ziggurat, and especially in Canaanite-Phoenician territory, a local mountain or hill was associated with the shrine. This seems to have been the case in Jerusalem, where the temple of Yahweh was closely related to Mount Zion, whilst in ancient Ugarit the temple of Baal was associated with Mount Zaphon, which lay several miles farther north in Syria.

So far as the religion and culture of Ancient Israel is concerned, which is the immediate subject of our study, it is becoming more and more apparent from comparative studies that the major channel through which the wider Near Eastern culture reached Israel was via the Canaanites. Such contacts between Israel and Mesopotamia

---

[1] Cf. H. Frankfort, *The Art and Architecture of the Ancient Orient*, p. 6; K. Möhlenbrink, *Der Tempel Salomos* (BWANT IV, 7), Stuttgart, 1932, pp. 43ff.; L. H. Vincent, 'De la tour de Babel au temple', *RB* 53, 1946, pp. 403ff.

[2] H. Gressmann, *The Tower of Babel*, New York, 1928, p. 15; A. Parrot, *The Tower of Babel* (Studies in Biblical Archaeology, No. 2), London, 1955, pp. 57ff.

which took place during the course of Israel's development were primarily mediated through the Canaanite city states, which were already established when Israel appeared in Palestine. In order, therefore, to obtain an understanding of the immediate background of Israel's religion, with its ideas of the divine presence, it is instructive to examine closely the ideas of the divine dwelling-places which were current in Canaanite mythology. We are fortunate in this regard in being able to draw upon the considerable body of mythological texts unearthed at Ras Shamra. These come from the ancient city of Ugarit, on the Syrian coast, and were redacted about 1400 B.C., although the material and ideas which they contain may go very much further back. They deal in particular with the activities of the gods of the Canaanite pantheon, of which El and Baal are the most prominent.[1]

Baal-Hadad appears as the most active of the Canaanite gods in Ugaritic mythology, and he it is who appears prominently as a god of the Canaanites in the Old Testament, although he was not in fact the head of the pantheon, since this title belonged to El. He was the young warrior god, the lord of the storms and thunder, who was responsible for the rains which gave fertility to the soil. Thus he was responsible for the welfare of the growing crops, and was honoured as the king of the gods.[2] There was ultimately one single Baal, so that when we read in the Old Testament of many Baals, it appears that a process of development and splintering has occurred, and that out of one high-god a multiplicity of local gods was developed.[3] This process is explicable when we note that many local sanctuaries for Baal were established and became his dwelling-places, each of which was a copy, or symbol, of his true dwelling-place. It is intelligible that the mythology which explained this symbolism was not always sufficiently grasped in popular thought to prevent the notion arising that there were many Baals, each with his own abode. In origin it is clear that all Baals were forms of the one god.

Baal's dwelling-place was on Mount Zaphon,[4] the mysterious

---

[1] On the ideas regarding the dwelling-places of the gods of Ugarit see O. Eissfeldt, 'Die Wohnsitze der Götter von Ras Schamra', *Kleine Schriften*, II, Tübingen, 1963, pp. 502–506.
[2] Cf. W. Schmidt, *Königtum Gottes in Ugarit und Israel* (BZAW 80), Berlin, 1961, pp. 21ff.
[3] O. Eissfeldt, 'Baalšamēm und Jahwe', *Kleine Schriften*, II, Tübingen, 1963, pp. 184ff.
[4] B'l ṣpn = 'Baal of Zaphon', *UM* 1, 10; 9, 14; 107, 10 (?); 125, 6–7, 107.
B'l mrym ṣpn = 'Baal of the summit of Zaphon', *UM* 51, V, 85; 67, I, 10–11; 'nt IV, 81–82.
B'l ṣrrt ṣpn = 'Baal of the heights of Zaphon', *UM* 49, VI, 12–13.

mountain of the north, which is known to us from the Old Testament as associated with a divine abode. No other deity is said to have dwelt there in the Ugaritic myths.[1]

Otto Eissfeldt first showed that Mount Zaphon was to be identified with the Jebel-el-Aqra, the highest mountain in Syria, lying 25–30 miles north-north-east of Ras Shamra, which was known in Greek and Roman times as Mons Casius.[2] Because of its prominence as a geographical feature the word Zaphon (Heb. *ṣāpôn*) came to be used to indicate a northerly direction among the Israelites, and presumably also the Canaanites.[3] However, behind this importance in Canaanite mythology of Mount Zaphon as the dwelling-place of Baal, we must recognize the very ancient belief that mountains were divine abodes. It is very probable that some connection with the north was already evident in the Mesopotamian background to the belief.[4]

The significance of Baal's dwelling upon Mount Zaphon must be understood in the light of the great reverence for sacred mountains throughout the Ancient Near East which we have already noted. In the Ugaritic mythological texts, in spite of the frequent repetition of the fact that Baal dwells on Mount Zaphon, and that it is his mountain and inheritance, we are not told very much that would enable us

---

[1] T. H. Gaster, *Thespis*, New York, 1950, pp. 138, 447 argues that El's mountain is also on Zaphon, and that this is also the Mount of Assembly, but this cannot be maintained.

[2] O. Eissfeldt, *Baal Zaphon, Zeus Kasios und der Durchzug der Israeliten durchs Meer*, Halle, 1932, pp. 5ff.

[3] Cf. *negeḇ* for 'south' and *yām* for 'west'. That the use of *ṣāpôn* to describe a geographical direction derives from its application to the Jebel-el-Aqra finds support in the fact that it only does so in the language of the Israelites and Phoenicians, and does not do so among the Babylonians or South Arabians. The noun is derived from a root meaning 'to look out'.

[4] Cf. H. Gressmann, *The Tower of Babel*, pp. 15ff.; B. Alfrink, 'Der Versammlungsberg im äussersten Norden', *Biblica* 14, 1933, pp. 41–67. Alfrink derives this idea from Babylonian astronomical speculation in which cosmic space is regarded as a great mountain with its peak in the north, at the Pole Star, where the realm of Anu lies. See also T. H. Gaster, *Thespis*, pp. 169–171 note, who claims that similar ideas existed in Egypt and even farther afield.

J. Morgenstern, 'Psalm 48', *HUCA* 16, 1941, p. 78 note, argues that the original Zaphon of north Semitic mythology, stemming from a very much earlier period than the Ras Shamra texts, must be sought farther north than Mons Casius in the Caucasus mountains in the region of the Black Sea. More recently W. F. Albright, 'Baal Zephon', *Bertholet Festschrift*, Tübingen, 1950, pp. 1ff., has argued that Baal's attachment to Mount Casius was simply a terrestrial reflection of the idea of the holy mountain in the northern heavens.

---

il ṣpn = 'God of Zaphon', *UM* 17, 13; 'nt III, 26, IV, 63.
ḥlb ṣpn = 'Hill of Zaphon', *UM* 113, 50.
ṣrrt ṣpn = 'Heights of Zaphon', *UM* 49, I, 29, 34; VI, 12–13; 51, V, 117; 'nt I, 21–22.
ṣrrt ṣp(')n = 'Heights of Zaphon', *UM* 62, 16.
ṣpn = 'Zaphon', *UM* 3, 34, 42; 9, 4, 7; 51, VII, 6; 76, III, 31; 'nt (pl. x) V, 5.

to discover why this mountain should have been regarded as the home
of a god. The fact that it was the highest peak in Syria would add
weight to the contention that Baal was the chief of the deities; the
exalted dwelling corresponding to the exalted position of Baal
among the gods.[1] Thus he was in some respects superior to El, although because the latter god was the titular head of the pantheon,
Baal needed his permission to build a palace for himself.

For an interpretation of the religious significance of Mount
Zaphon we must therefore fall back upon our general understanding
of the symbolism of sacred mountains in the Ancient Near East.
Baal was the god of the storms and rains, which brought fertility
to the earth. He was also, as his name implies, the owner and lord
of the land where his worshippers dwelt. It seems very probable,
therefore, that Baal's Mount Zaphon symbolized the land which
Baal owned, and where his power was operative. Ultimately this was
thought to be cosmic in extent, and embraced the entire universe,
but in practice it was referred to the land where his worshippers dwelt.
Thus certain cosmic traits are featured in the honour due to Mount
Zaphon as Baal's dwelling-place, which is in fact what we should
expect from our knowledge of the nature of Baal.[2] Although, in the
texts themselves, this meaning of Mount Zaphon is not clearly brought
out, as we can hardly expect that it should, it has left many traces in
later literature. There are certain striking passages in the Old Testament which bring a great deal of additional light to the subject.

In Isa. xiv. 4–21 we have a taunt-song uttered against the king of
Babylon, which, as has long been recognized, uses an old myth of the
fall of a divine being, the Morning Star, from the height of heaven
to the depths of Sheol. The most important verses for our purpose
are 12–15:

> 'How you are fallen from heaven,
>   O Day Star, Son of Dawn.
> You are cut down to the ground,
>   Who laid the nations low.
> You said in your heart,
>   "I will ascend to heaven;
> Above the stars of El,

---

[1] We may note in this regard that no ordinary god could fill Baal's throne on
Mount Zaphon. When Baal lay dead in the realm of Mot, Aṭṭar attempted to do so,
and was speedily rejected. *UM* 49, I, 25–37.

[2] The cosmic scope of the divine dwelling-places is suggested in the texts by the
immense distance which separates them. Anat makes a journey of 'a thousand
leagues, ten thousand furlongs' to reach Baal's abode on Zaphon from El's dwelling.
UM 51, V, 85–86, 118–119; 'nt IV, 82.

I will set up my throne;
I will dwell on the Mount of Assembly
In the recesses of Zaphon;
I will ascend above the heights of the clouds,
I will make myself like unto 'Elyon."
But you are brought down to Sheol,
To the depths of the Pit.'
(Isa. xiv. 12–15).

At the back of the myth we can discern a description of the Morning Star, the planet Venus, appearing in the heavens, only to disappear again in the face of the rising sun. From the section of the myth preserved in Isa. xiv we learn several features regarding Mount Zaphon. It was the abode of 'Elyon, who was a deity worshipped in pre-Israelite Jerusalem, and mentioned elsewhere as a Canaanite god. We learn also that Zaphon was the Mount of Assembly, where the court of the gods was held, and which is referred to in the Ugaritic myths, where it is a mountain distinct from Zaphon, and the abode of El.[1] Isa. xiv clearly gives us a later tradition of Canaanite mythology where there are a number of changes from the ideas evidenced in the Ras Shamra texts. A point of special significance in Isa. xiv. 13–14 is that Zaphon's height is said to reach above the stars of El, and to stretch above the clouds, so that it was considered to be of cosmic proportions.

We must set alongside this poem from the book of Isaiah a passage in Ezek. xxviii, where we have certain allusions to the same group of mythological ideas, which derive from the beliefs surrounding Mount Zaphon. Although the mountain is not specifically named, but is simply called 'the holy mountain of God', the similarities are so close to the ideas of Mount Zaphon that we cannot deny that we are here faced with the same basic stock of mythological imagery.[2] The section in Ezek. xxviii. 12–19 is a lament for the king of Tyre, and part of this may be quoted:

'You were the signet of perfection,
Full of wisdom and perfect in beauty.

[1] *UM* 137, 14, 17, 20, 31. It is also called the 'Mountain of Ll', which T. H. Gaster, *Thespis*, pp. 138, 447, emends to 'Mountain of El'. This is quite unjustified, and in the Ugaritic texts the evidence points to the view that Zaphon, the Mount of Assembly and the abode of El were three distinct mountains. So O. Kaiser, *Die mythische Bedeutung des Meeres in Ägypten, Ugarit und Israel*, (BZAW 78), Berlin, 1959, pp. 53ff.; cf. also W. Schmidt, *Königtum Gottes in Ugarit und Israel*, p. 24.
[2] On this lament and its mythological imagery, see H. G. May, 'The King in the Garden of Eden: a Study of Ezekiel 28: 12–19', *Israel's Prophetic Heritage*, ed. B. W. Anderson and W. Harrelson, London, 1962, pp. 166–176; J. L. McKenzie, 'Mythological Allusions in Ezekiel 28: 12–18', *JBL* 75, 1956, pp. 322–327.

You were in Eden, the garden of God;
  Every precious stone was your covering,
Carnelian, topaz and jasper,
  Chrysolite, beryl and onyx,
Sapphire, carbuncle and emerald;
  Your settings were worked in gold,
  And your engravings.
On the day when you were created,
  They were prepared.
With an anointed guardian cherub I placed you;
  You were on the holy mountain of god;
You walked in the midst of fiery stones.
  You were perfect in your ways
  From the day of your creation,
  Until iniquity was found in you.
In the abundance of your trade
  You were filled with violence, and you sinned;
So I expelled you from the mount of god,
  And the guardian cherub drove you out
  From the midst of the fiery stones.'
              (Ezek. xxviii. 12–16)

The stones of fire mentioned in verses 14 and 16, as well as the jewels of verse 12, may perhaps be identified with stars,[1] thus demonstrating that the mount of god reaches above the stars as in Isa. xiv. 13. Another possibility is to regard them as the 'thunder-stones', which the god used as flints to make lightning.[2] Of particular interest in this poem, based on an old Canaanite myth, is the identification of the mount of god with Eden, the garden of god.[3]

From these references we find corroboration of the idea that Mount Zaphon was believed to be a world-mountain, reaching up to the height of heaven, so that Baal's domain was really cosmic in extent. We must ask then how this belief was related to the cult that was celebrated in Baal's honour. We know that a temple for Baal existed in Ugarit, and there is also evidence of a place called Baal Zephon, or Zaphon, lying north-east of the Nile delta.[4] From Psalm xlviii. 3 (EVV. 2) we also learn that Mount Zion could be called

---

[1] So H. G. May, 'The King in the Garden of Eden', p. 170.

[2] J. L. McKenzie, op. cit., p. 322. In this case they may compare with the *abn brq*, which some interpreters find mentioned in the Ugaritic myths. See F. C. Fensham, 'Thunder-stones in Ugaritic', *JNES* 18, 1959, pp. 273–274.

[3] Further evidence from the Old Testament for the belief in Mount Zaphon as the home of a deity is to be found in Job xxxvii. 22. Cf. also Ezek. i. 4. Outside the Old Testament we may also compare 1 Enoch xvii. 2–8; xviii. 2, 6–10; xxiv. 2–xxv. 5; lxxvii. 4.

[4] Exod. xiv. 2, 9 (P); Num. xxxiii. 7 (P).

Mount Zaphon. We find, therefore, that other places could be identified with Mount Zaphon and partake of its holiness. Probably in all these cases we have evidence of derivative cults of the Baal-Hadad, whose dwelling was on Mount Zaphon. The importance of such sanctuaries, or sacred mountains, was that at these the divine presence could be manifested, and the connection between the cult-site and the mythological abode of Baal was provided by the symbolism of temple or mountain. As Baal was the owner of the land, the establishment of correct worship of him was important for the maintenance of the right to continue as his tenants. The sacred area symbolized the dedication of all the land to him, its rightful owner, just as the offering of tithes symbolized the dedication of all the crops to the divine giver. In the worship of Baal, therefore, the problem of locating the divine presence was overcome by the symbolism of the cult, and so Baal's presence could be made real to his people for the blessing of their crops, as well as the receipt of their homage and offerings.[1] The presence of Baal was, therefore, very much associated with definite sites and sanctuaries.

The other Canaanite deity about whom we possess a good deal of information is El, who was a kind of Canaanite Zeus, and is described as the 'Father of mankind'.[2] His symbol was the bull, as may be inferred from the title that he is accorded, 'the bull El'.[3] He, like Baal, is spoken of as king, although we have not a sufficient account of El's activities to know how he obtained his kingship.[4] El was the head and father of the Canaanite pantheon[5], and had the highest honour amongst the gods. His counsel was sought in important matters concerning the relations between the gods, and his permission and blessing was desirable for the success of any new venture, such as the building of a temple for Baal. In many ways we find that El's headship of the pantheon was a very nominal matter. Baal is shown as

[1] An important section of the Baal epic concerns the building of a temple for him in which an argument arises whether the finished temple is to have a window. This ought most probably to be connected with the 'windows of heaven' (cf. Gen. vii. 11; viii. 2, etc.), through which rain was believed to be poured out upon the earth. Thus the fitting of a window to Baal's temple was related in mythopoeic fashion to the possibility of rain upon the earth.

[2] Ug. 'ab adm' = 'Father of mankind.' *UM* Krt 37, 43, 136, 151, 297.

[3] Ug. 'tr il' = 'Bull El.' *UM* 49, IV, 34, VI, 26–27; 51, I, 4 (?), II, 10; III, 31, IV, 1, 38–39, 47; 126, IV, 3; 129, 16, 17, 19, 21; 137, 16, 33, 36; 2 Aqht 1, 24; 'nt (pl. vi) IV, 7, (pl. vi) V, 18, 21 (?), 43, (pl. ix) III, 26; (pl. x) IV, 12, V, 22; Krt 41, 59, 76–77, 169.

[4] W. Schmidt, *Königtum Gottes in Ugarit und Israel*, pp. 18ff.

[5] O. Eissfeldt saw among a section of the population of Ugarit, *c.* 1400 B.C. evidence of a tendency to give El a monarchical position among the gods and to regard the other gods as mere emanations of the divine power. Thus there was a kind of incipient monotheism. *El im Ugaritischen Pantheon*, Berlin, 1951, pp. 59f.

much more active among the gods, and El is subjected to insults and indignities from other members of the pantheon. Whatever the reason may have been, El was on the way out and Baal was on the ascendant as the chief god. Possibly these relations among the gods reflect the relations of social groups among the Ugaritians.

The abode of El is said to be upon *ḫršn* which may be translated as 'world-mountain'.[1] This is said to be situated 'at the source of the rivers, in the midst of the channels of the two oceans'.[2] It contains 'seven rooms, eight openings.'[3] These two rivers are a reflection of the belief that at the horizon of the earth there is a region where heaven and earth meet, and where the underground ocean, which fills the seas and springs, meets the upper ocean, from whence the rains are poured out.[4] The abode of El, therefore, was believed to be situated at a remote distance, at the very edge of the earth, where sky, land and underworld were united by the mighty world-mountain of El. It was not a subterranean dwelling-place,[5] but a mountain which held earth, sky and underworld together.[6] Thus it formed a link between the sky and the land, the realm of the gods and the dwelling-place of men. It appears, therefore, that in Ugaritic mythology the ideas about El's abode bear a resemblance to those regarding Baal's dwelling on Mount Zaphon. Both were concerned with mountains which, in their mythological ideology, were believed to encompass

[1] *UM* 'nt (pl. ix) II, 23, III, 22. This word is to be connected with the Akkadian *ḫuršānu*, meaning 'mountain of trial after death, ordeal'. So G. R. Driver, *Canaanite Myths and Legends* (Old Testament Studies 3), Edinburgh, 1956, p. 139.

[2] *UM* 49, I, 5–6; 51, IV, 21–22; 129, 4; 2 Aqht VI, 47–48; 'nt (pl. vi) V, 14–15.

[3] *UM* 51, V, 85–86, 118, 119; 51, VII, 25–26; 'nt (pl. vi) V, 19, 34–35. A thorough examination of the evidence in the Ras Shamra texts regarding El's abode is made by M. H. Pope, *El in the Ugaritic Texts* (SVT II), Leiden, 1955, pp. 61ff.; cf. also O. Kaiser, *Die mythische Bedeutung des Meeres in Ägypten, Ugarit und Israel*, pp. 47ff.

[4] Cf. W. F. Albright, 'The Mouth of the Rivers', *AJSL* 35, 1918/9, pp. 190ff.; J. Gray, *The Legacy of Canaan* (SVT V), Leiden, 1957, p. 80 note; W. Schmidt, *Königtum Gottes in Ugarit und Israel*, p. 6.

[5] M. H. Pope, *El in the Ugaritic Texts*, pp. 61ff., argues that the dwelling-place of El was thought to be under the earth in a subterranean watery fastness, basing his arguments upon O.T. parallels (Job xxxviii. 16–17; 2 Sam. xxii. 16; cf. Job xxvi. 5; xxviii. 11), which speak of a subterranean origin of the seas and springs. Cf. also O. Kaiser, op. cit., pp. 49ff. Pope then builds upon this view a contrast between El's subterranean watery abode and his dwelling on a mountain, and concludes that El had been banished from his mountain height into the lower depths of the world. El, argues Pope, is the prototype of the fallen deity, who appears in the mythology of Isa. xiv. and Ezek. xxviii.

[6] M. H. Pope, *El in the Ugaritic Texts*, pp. 72ff., seeks to find a definite location for El's abode at Khirbet Afqa, 23 miles north-east of Beirut, midway between Byblos and Baalbek. On one side of the hill is a lake, and on the other an underground stream which is connected to the lake, and which fills it at certain seasons of the year. It is possible that such a definite geographical location was identified with the world-mountain of mythology, but it does not affect the issue of our study, for the real nature of El's dwelling must be sought in myth and not geography.

the entire universe. In consequence we may conclude that the ideas about the manner and effect of El's presence were very similar to those of Baal. El too was a god of the land, and the primary need of his worshippers was the blessing and continued tenure of their land. Their sanctuaries and temples, dedicated to El, were symbolic of the world-mountain where El ruled, and by this symbolism the divine presence was thought to be revealed among his worshippers, which procured the blessing of El in the land.

Anat, the principal goddess of the Canaanites, is said to have had her dwelling-place on a mountain called *Inbb*,[1] but there is no evidence which would enable us to define this any further.

The belief in these mythological abodes of the gods in Canaanite religion is expressive of a pronounced tendency to identify the respective deities as gods of the land. Such gods were to be worshipped at special places, where shrines were established, and which were identified with their cosmic dwelling-places. By the aid of mythology, and the symbolism of the cult, the presence of the god was thought to be manifested in his sanctuary. Because the gods were the owners of the land a special part of the land needed to be set apart for them, both as an acknowledgment of the divine ownership, and as the means by which the divine blessing could flow out through all the land.

In consequence, the people of Canaan among whom the Israelites settled and established their own distinctive Yahweh worship, had a developed and flourishing religion, which was firmly adapted to the belief in the divine blessing of the soil. They possessed many sanctuaries, at several of which quite imposing temples had been built, and where elaborate myths and legends related the conditions of life and worship to the world and activities of the gods.

The religion of Canaan undoubtedly formed a strong and persistent influence upon the Israelite tribes, and its sanctuaries provided an environment of vigorous religious activity which the Israelites could hardly ignore. Yet in the earliest period it is apparent that Israel not only distinguished its own heritage of Mosaic Yahwism from the religion of the Canaanites, but also regarded both of these as distinct from the religion of its ancestors.[2] We must ask, therefore, what this religion was, and what ideas of the presence of god it possessed.

The narratives of Genesis present the patriarchs as a semi-nomadic people, dwelling in tents, who expressed their faith by the setting

---

[1] *UM* 'nt (pl. ix) II, 14.
[2] Joshua xxiv. 2, 14, 15.

up of altars to mark the sites of divine theophanies. Only the simple rock altars marked any fixed and enduring attachment to these holy places, and the gods who appeared at them are given various names. Abraham is said to have built an altar to Yahweh at Shechem,[1] where later Jacob is said to have set up an altar to El-Elohe-Israel.[2] Abraham is also said to have built an altar on a mountain east of Bethel, between Bethel and Ai,[3] and at Hebron-Mamre.[4] At Salem (Jerusalem) he is said to have been blessed by Melchizedek, the priest of El-'Elyon.[5] Hagar is said to have received a revelation from a deity called El-Roi, at a place called Beer-Lahai-Roi.[6] The Priestly writer consistently represents the deity who appeared to Abraham as El-Shaddai, although no specific locality is linked with this name.[7] Abraham is also said to have planted a tamarisk tree at Beersheba, and to have called upon the name of El-'Olam there.[8] This appears to represent a secondary carrying-over to Abraham from the Isaac traditions, since in Gen. xxvi. 25, 33 (J) it is Isaac who is said to have built an altar to Yahweh at Beersheba, and the traditions of Isaac show that this is the locality where he was remembered.[9] The name of the god of the sanctuary at Beersheba in pre-Israelite times, however, must have been El-'Olam.

The original setting of the Abraham traditions seems to have been in the vicinity of Hebron-Mamre,[10] so that they were handed on in a southern milieu, becoming the property of the tribe of Judah, and eventually given prominence in the age of David. By this time they had become associated with the worship of Yahweh, so that the Yahwist historian, probably writing in Solomon's reign, could present Yahweh as the god invoked by Abraham. This was in accordance with the theory that the name Yahweh had been in use from primeval times.[11] This is at variance with the evidence which we have elsewhere, that the name of Yahweh was introduced to the Israelites

---

[1] Gen. xii. 7 (J).
[2] Gen. xxxiii. 20 (E).
[3] Gen. xii. 8 (J); xiii. 3–4 (J).
[4] Gen. xiii. 18 (J); xviii. 1ff. (J).
[5] Gen. xiv. 17–24.
[6] Gen. xvi. 13–14 (J).
[7] This name also appears in the ancient poem preserved by the Yahwist, known as the Blessing of Jacob (Gen. xlix. 25), so there is no doubt that it was the genuine name of an old pre-Israelite god of Canaan. Cf. W. F. Albright, 'The Names Shaddai and Abram', *JBL* 54, 1935, pp. 173–204.
[8] Gen. xxi. 33 (J).
[9] A. Jepsen, 'Zur Überlieferungsgeschichte der Vätergestalten', *WZ* Leipzig, 1953/4, p. 269b. Cf. A. Weiser, 'Isaak', *RGG*³, III, cols. 902f.
[10] A. Jepsen, op. cit., p. 270a; A. Weiser, 'Abram', *RGG*³, I, cols. 68–71.
[11] Gen. iv. 26 (J).

by Moses.[1] On every count this seems to represent the historical fact, so that references to Abraham's having invoked the name of Yahweh must be anachronistic. A later age has read back its own religious allegiance into the earlier period.

Jacob is said to have founded sanctuaries at Mahanaim, where he received a vision of the divine host,[2] and at Peniel, where he wrestled with an angel.[3] The most famous of the Jacob traditions tells how he set up a stone pillar at Bethel, after he had received a dream-vision of a stairway, or ramp, stretching from earth to heaven.[4] Jacob is reported to have called the place Bethel, or El-Bethel, which must be connected with the name of the god Bethel who was worshipped there.[5] An interesting aspect of this vision is that it provides an explanation of the symbolism of the shrine of Bethel. The sacred stone was not worshipped because the god was thought to be inside it, but because it was related to a mysterious stairway connecting to the divine dwelling in heaven. The stone was therefore the symbol, and the sanctuary tradition preserved the myth, which explained its origin and meaning.

After due allowance has been made for the Yahwist's anachronistic use of the name Yahweh, and the theoretical presentation of the Priestly writer that the patriarchs worshipped El-Shaddai, we are left with a number of references in which the patriarchs are associated with forms of the god El. It is not surprising, therefore, that some scholars have argued that the patriarchs venerated El as their god.[6]

---

[1] Exod. iii. 13ff. (E); vi. 3 (P); Joshua xxiv. 2.

[2] Gen. xxxii. 2 (E); cf. Gen. xxxii. 7–8 (J).

[3] Gen. xxxii. 30 (E). For the priority of this location of the Jacob traditions east of Jordan see A. Jepsen, op. cit., p. 270, and A. Weiser, 'Jakob', *RGG*[3], III, cols. 517–520.

[4] Gen. xxviii. 10–22 (JE), xxxv. 7 (E).

[5] Gen. xxxi. 13 (E); xxxv. 7 (E). A. Jirku, 'Neues keilinschriftliches Materiel zum Alten Testament', *ZAW* 31, 1921, pp. 158f., suggested that El-Bethel was here the name of the god, but W. W. Graf Baudissin ('El Bet-el', *Vom Alten Testament. Karl Marti Festschrift* (BZAW 41), 1925, pp. 1ff.), whilst admitting the existence of a god Bethel in Old Testament times, argued that the meaning in these two texts can only be 'the god of Bethel'. The surest evidence in the Old Testament for the existence of the god Bethel is to be found in Jer. xlviii. 13, but O. Eissfeldt ('Der Gott Bethel', *Kleine Schriften*, I, Tübingen, 1962, pp. 206–233) also finds evidence of him in Amos iii. 14b; v. 4, 6; Hos. x. 15; xii. 5 (EVV 4). Eissfeldt rejects von Baudissin's arguments as inconclusive, and finds in these references in Genesis (xxxi. 13 and xxxv. 7) evidence that a god Bethel was worshipped in pre-Israelite times in the city Bethel. He regards the name as primarily given to the stone through which the presence of the god was manifested (Gen. xxviii. 18), and which was related in some way to the god El. For the god Bethel see also A. Vincent, *La religion des Judéo-Araméens d'Éléphantine*, Paris, 1937, pp. 562ff., and J. P. Hyatt, 'The Deity Bethel and the Old Testament', *JAOS* 59, 1939, pp. 81–98.

[6] H. Gressmann, *Mose und seine Zeit*, (FRLANT 18), Göttingen, 1913, pp. 53ff., 210f., 426ff., 433; R. Dussaud, *Les découvertes de Ras Shamra (Ugarit) et l'Ancien*

However, all we can say is that at one stage the clans descended from the patriarchs, or some groups of them, were connected with the worship of the Canaanite god El. Yet this can hardly have been the original religion of the patriarchs, which the Old Testament regards as distinct from that of the Canaanites.[1] All the references to the veneration of El by the patriarchs present this as occurring on Canaanite soil, and usually at specific cult-places which are named. There is no doubt that at one time a god El-'Elyon was worshipped at Jerusalem, an El-'Olam at Beersheba, and an El-Bethel at Bethel, but it was not the patriarchs who founded such shrines, and introduced the worship of such gods. Rather these gods and their sanctuaries were established by the Canaanite inhabitants, and these stories must be interpreted as the result of attempts by the Hebrew clans and tribes who settled in their vicinity to take over the sanctuaries, or at least to participate in their worship. In doing so they sought to make such a cult legitimate for themselves by telling how their ancestors had initiated the worship in these places.[2]

The most significant and widely accepted of the hypotheses that have been put forward regarding the original religion of the patriarchs and their clans, before their settlement in Canaan, is that of A. Alt.[3] In following up the clue suggested by the Elohist's account of Yahweh's revelation to Moses,[4] Alt explained the patriarchal religion as a worship of gods associated with particular persons. These gods were closely linked with the ancestors of the Israelite clans, so that the god took his name from the person to whom he had first revealed himself. Thus the god of Abraham was believed to have appeared first to Abraham, and was thereafter known from this original manifestation, and continued to be worshipped in those circles which traced their ancestry to this patriarch. Similarly the god of

[1] Joshua xxiv. 2, 14, 15.
[2] A. Alt, 'Der Gott der Väter', *KSGVI*, I, München, 1953, p. 7; cf. O. Eissfeldt, 'El and Yahweh', pp. 32ff., and 'Jahwe, der Gott der Väter', *ThLZ* 88, 1963, cols. 485ff.; H. G. May, 'The Patriarchal Idea of God', *JBL* 60, 1941, pp. 113–128.
[3] A. Alt, 'Der Gott der Väter', *passim*; cf. also L. Rost, 'Die Gottesverehrung der Patriarchen im Lichte der Pentateuchquelle,' *Oxford Congress Volume*, (SVT VII), Leiden, 1960, pp. 346ff.; O. Eissfeldt, 'El and Yahweh', p. 32; V. Maag, 'Der Hirte Israels. Eine Skizze von Wesen und Bedeutung der Väterreligion', *Schweizerische theologische Umschau* 28, pp. 2–28.
[4] Exod. iii. 1ff.

Testament[2], Paris, 1941, pp. 168f. Cf. J. Barr, 'The Problem of Israelite Monotheism', *TGUOS* 17, 1959, p. 60.

At times the name El was used in a purely appellative sense, meaning simply 'god', and this became common in the later period. Thus the name of the god El could be interpreted in a harmless way in Israel, by regarding it simply as a generic description of Yahweh. Cf. O. Eissfeldt, *El im ugaritischen Pantheon*, pp. 29, 53; M. H. Pope, *El in the Ugaritic Texts*, pp. 5ff.

Isaac had first appeared to the head of the Isaac clans, whilst the god of Jacob was venerated in the clans which looked to Jacob as their ancestor. If this thesis is followed then there were at least three gods of the patriarchs, and not one.

Such a religion was well fitted to the way of life of a semi-nomadic people, since it was concerned with clan groups, rather than with holy places. When such people settled down, then very frequently these gods of the ancestors would be identified with the high-gods of the established sanctuaries. In this way we can conceive that the descendants of the patriarchs brought their religion into the Canaanite sanctuaries, and related it to the cult that was practised there. The result, as we have seen, was that the patriarchs came to be linked with the Canaanite god El.

It seems probable that such gods were not wholly anonymous, but were called by distinctive names: the Shield of Abraham,[1] the Fear (more probably Kinsman) of Isaac,[2] and the Strong One of Jacob.[3] The important feature of this religion for our study is that the gods were not thought to be connected with specific places, as was general for the Els and Baals of the Canaanites, but to certain groups of people. Thus it offered a distinct contrast to the religion of Canaan. M. Buber[4] elaborates upon this and argues that the gods of the patriarchs were 'leader-gods' who were in a personal relationship to their worshippers. They were entirely distinct from those of the Canaanite religion with its basis in nature, and its emphasis upon fertility, in which the deities had a close and continuing relationship to the soil and to particular places. For the patriarchs their gods were not associated with the soil, nor with special holy places, but were bound together with their worshippers and were believed to accompany them on their wanderings. In accordance with the semi-nomadic life of the ancestors of the Israelites, so their gods also were believed to move from place to place as the leaders of their adherents. The importance of such a conception must be particularly seen in the personal relationships which this involved between the god and his worshippers, and to the fruitful possibilities which this possessed for religion. Thus the gods of Abraham, Isaac and Jacob were markedly different from the gods of Canaan, and a particular feature of this distinctiveness lay in the manner and nature of the divine presence.

[1] Gen. xv. 1 (JE). Cf. E. A. Leslie, *Old Testament Religion*, New York, 1936, pp. 67f.
[2] Gen. xxxi. 42, 53 (E). Cf. W. F. Albright, *From the Stone Age to Christianity*,[2] New York, 1957, pp. 188f., 321 note.
[3] Gen. xlix. 24 (J).
[4] M. Buber, *The Prophetic Faith*, New York, 1949, pp. 31–42.

We might sum up the contrast by saying that the religion of the patriarchs represents a religious personalism, whereas that of Canaan a religious materialism. In the one the presence of the gods was linked with certain definite persons, and in the other with certain definite places. The religion of the patriarchs shows a real personal communion between men and the deity who acted as their leader. The primary needs of the proto-Israelite clans were not directed towards the soil, but towards their own family and clan relationship. Kinship was the basis of their social order and the continuance of life, with protection from enemies, was dependent upon the maintenance of the proper ties of kinship. The common worship of the clan god served as a binding force which held the clan together, and his protecting presence was believed to accompany them wherever they moved. Thus the activity of the god could be found within the family, not tied to this or that place, but manifested in the corporate worship of those who shared a family bond. If we accept the views of Alt, therefore, as to the original nature of the patriarchal religion, we can discern within it a very important conception of the nature of the divine presence. This was not, as in the Canaanite religion, bound to local cult-sites, but associated with family and clan groups. From the nature of the case this is what we should expect a religion of unsettled semi-nomadic groups to have been, and features of such a faith are still preserved in the stories of Genesis. Even if not every aspect of Alt's reconstruction is assured, or acceptable, the ideas of the gods as linked to clan-groups must surely have characterized the religion of the proto-Israelite settlers in Canaan.[1]

When the semi-nomadic life began to be forsaken, and more settled ways adopted, with this too came the temptation to adopt the religion of the Canaanite neighbours, with its promise of blessing in the land. Amongst some Hebrew clans this temptation was no doubt resisted, and the older gods continued to be revered until Yahwism triumphed in the post-Mosaic age. When this occurred then the ideals of family and clan loyalty, and of the significance of individual persons, was a rich and fruitful legacy that the old patriarchal religion offered.

---

[1] The most important criticism of Alt's reconstruction, and the most credible alternative to it, is that based upon the arguments of H. G. May, who viewed the patriarchal religion as a worship of the 'God of my father'. See H. G. May, 'The Patriarchal Idea of God', pp. 123ff., and 'The God of My Father—a Study of Patriarchal Religion', *Journal of Bible and Religion* 9, 1941, pp. 155–158, 199–200; cf. also J. P. Hyatt, 'Yahweh as the God of My Father', *VT* 5, 1955, pp. 130–136; K. T. Andersen, 'Der Gott meines Vaters', *St.Th.* 16, 1962, pp. 170–188. On this view the ancestral deity had no specific name, and was not first denoted by his relation to a named person, but was connected with the worshipper's immediate ancestor.

CHAPTER II

YAHWEH AND MOUNT SINAI

THE examination of the general background of religion and culture in which Israel found itself when it was established as the people of Yahweh in Palestine *c.* 1200 B.C., shows that a prominent feature of Canaanite religion was its belief in the function of sanctuaries as divine abodes. This influence from Canaan came to play an important part in the development of Israel, and eventually affected the building of a temple for Yahweh in Jerusalem. Yet Israel distinguished sharply between its own Yahwistic tradition and both the religion of its Canaanite neighbours and that of the patriarchs. The devotion to Yahweh as the God of the covenant, which bound together the twelve tribes constituting Israel, was the primary unitary factor in the life of the federation.[1] The very existence of Israel was held to be dependent on the grace of Yahweh.

The maintenance of this common faith was served by the establishing of a central sanctuary to which all the member tribes of the federation sent delegates for an annual, or septenniel, celebration of the making of the covenant. In the early days of Israel's existence in Canaan this covenant sanctuary was probably at Shechem, but it is possible that in course of time other shrines were used for this purpose. Eventually the sanctuary at Shiloh fulfilled this function, until its destruction by the Philistines. These recurring covenant celebrations undoubtedly contained some form of public recital of the events which had brought Israel into being, and which had constituted it as the people of Yahweh. The covenant ceremony was, in effect, a reliving of the past in order to enter once again into its meaning and significance. This confessional account of the origin of the covenant centred most especially upon the two major events: a deliverance out of Egypt, and an encounter with Yahweh, the God who had wrought this deliverance, upon Mount Sinai. It is unlikely that all the twelve member tribes of Israel had been involved together in these events, but only some of them. Nevertheless those who had done so had made their experience the dominant feature in the community's

---

[1] Cf. M. Noth, *Das System der Zwölf Stämme Israels* (BWANT IV, 1), Stuttgart, 1930, pp. 56ff.

confession of faith.[1] Out of the whole federation it is the Joseph tribes, Ephraim and Manasseh, which seem those most likely to have been involved. This proto-Israelite community was first brought together as the covenant people of Yahweh at Kadesh, a sanctuary in the desert region south of Palestine.[2] The fact that their traditions located a number of incidents involving Yahweh and the people in the vicinity of this shrine, points to its importance as the first home of the covenant people of Yahweh.

It was in the region of Kadesh that Moses officiated as priest and leader of the community, and only subsequently, after his death, did this company of Yahweh-worshippers cross the Jordan and establish itself west of that river. At this time it was expanded by the incorporation of other tribes, and came to bear the name Israel.[3]

There is no doubt that the origins of Israel as Yahweh's covenant community were believed to lie in historical events that had taken place before the community had crossed the Jordan, and there is no reason for believing that this tradition was fundamentally false. Israel placed all the emphasis in explanation of its existence upon the mighty acts of Yahweh. Out of sheer grace he had seen the plight of a group of helpless Hebrew slaves, had made them into his people, and had brought them into the land of Canaan. Our present concern is to discover how this people thought of the presence of Yahweh, and in what manner they conceived his appearing among them. In this regard the most important of the traditions that have been handed down to us concerns a description of a theophany upon Mount Sinai.[4] The Israelite tradition asserted that, after a period of wandering in the wilderness, those who had been delivered out of Egypt journeyed to Mount Sinai and experienced there a theophany of

[1] Cf. M. Noth, *Das System der Zwölf Stämme Israels*, pp. 70ff.

[2] Cf. W. Beyerlin, *Herkunft und Geschichte der ältesten Sinaitraditionen*, Tübingen, 1961, pp. 165ff.; M. L. Newman, *The People of the Covenant. A Study of Israel from Moses to the Monarchy*, New York-Nashville, 1962, pp. 72ff.

[3] Many factors seem to point to the conclusion that some federation of tribes, probably six in number, was already established in Canaan, with its centre at Shechem, before being converted to Yahwism under Joshua. Cf. M. Noth, *Das System der Zwölf Stämme Israels*, pp. 79f., 91. It is probable that they already bore the name Israel before adopting Yahwism, which would explain the fact that the name is compounded with that of the Canaanite god El. Perhaps he was the El-Elohe-Israel, whose altar was said to have been set up by Jacob (Gen. xxxiii. 20 (E)). He may even be connected with the El-Berith, or Baal-Berith, worshipped in Shechem (Judges viii. 33; ix. 4, 46). Cf. R. Smend, *Die Bundesformel* (Theologische Studien 68), Zürich, 1963, pp. 14f., 36. For the importance of the assembly at Shechem under Joshua see M. Noth, *Das System der Zwölf Stämme Israels*, pp. 65ff.; *Das Buch Josua*², Tübingen, 1953, pp. 135ff., and *A History of Israel*², E.T., London, 1960, pp. 92ff. Cf. also H. J. Kraus, *Gottesdienst in Israel*², Neukirchen, 1962, pp. 161ff.

[4] Called Sinai in J and P, Horeb in E and D.

Yahweh. The reason for this visit to Sinai is traced back to a previous appearance of Yahweh on the mountain to Moses, and to his command that Moses should assemble the people there.[1] When the people had prepared themselves to meet Yahweh, then, in terrifying splendour, he descended upon the mountain and established a covenant between them and himself. By the hand of Moses the decalogue was delivered to the people as the terms of the covenant, and the whole event was concluded by the eating of a sacrificial meal in which seventy elders acted as representatives for the community.

The fact that Yahweh is very closely associated with Mount Sinai has provoked the suggestion that he was in a special sense the god of this mountain, which formed his dwelling-place, where he could normally be expected to appear.[2] In this case the reverence for the mountain as a holy place, and more especially as the place where a god could be found, must antedate the rise of Yahweh worship in Israel. The Israelite records never explicitly describe Mount Sinai as the dwelling-place of Yahweh, with only one possible exception. This is to be found in the Blessing of Moses, where it is possible to translate one verse as:

'From the abundance of the earth and its fullness,
And the favour of the one who tented on Sinai.'
(Deut. xxxiii. 16)[3]

[1] Exod. iii. 12 (E).

[2] G. Westphal, *Jahwes Wohnstätten* (BZAW 15), Giessen, 1908, pp. 8, 11, claimed that the designation of the place as the 'mountain of God' (Exod. iii. 1 (E)), implied that Yahweh dwelt on the mountain. Westphal believed that Yahweh was a storm god who could be said to be bound to the mountain in some way. A. Alt ('Der Gott der Väter', pp. 5–6 note) regarded Mount Sinai as an ancient holy place on which Yahweh had been venerated as the local numen. Cf. also J. Gray, 'The Desert Sojourn of the Hebrews and the Sinai-Horeb Tradition', *VT* 4, 1954, pp. 148ff.; M. Noth (*Exodus*, E.T., London, 1962, pp. 159f.) regards the E stratum of Exod. xix as witnessing to the belief that Yahweh dwelt permanently on the mountain. Cf. also H. Wildberger, *Jahwes Eigentumsvolk*, (ATANT 37), Zürich, 1960, p. 10. The attempt of H. Gressmann, *Mose und seine Zeit*, pp. 29, 112f., 192f., 416ff., to locate Mount Sinai in a volcanic region in north-west Arabia, on the eastern side of the Gulf of Akaba, cannot now be considered as probable. Gressmann was followed by W. J. Phythian-Adams, *The Call of Israel*, Oxford, 1934, pp. 141ff., 166ff. The distance between such a region and Egypt or Kadesh is too great to make it the likely destination of slaves escaping from Egypt. This volcanic region was certainly occupied by the Midianites at a later period, but such a nomadic people could well have been encountered by Israel far removed from that district.

Whether the name Yahweh already belonged to the god of Mount Sinai, or whether it was previously used by the Hebrews either as a name or an invocation, must remain an uncertainty. J. Barr, 'The Problem of Israelite Monotheism', p. 61, has argued that 'Yahweh' was used in pre-Israelite times, not as a name, but as a phrase expressing the divine presence and action. Cf. also W. F. Albright, *From the Stone Age to Christianity*,[2] pp. 16, 260; D. N. Freedman, 'The Name of the God of Moses', *JBL* 79, 1960, p. 152.

[3] The translation is from F. M. Cross and D. N. Freedman, 'The Blessing of Moses', *JBL* 67, 1948, pp. 194, 206. It presupposes the emendation of *sînay* for *s^enê*

In spite of this lack of direct concrete evidence on the part of the Old Testament records, our knowledge of ancient religion in general, and especially of the persistent attachment to holy places, makes it probable that already for a long time Mount Sinai had been regarded as the place where a god would manifest himself. Probably the name Yahweh had been given to him by others, for the Israelites were certainly not the first to use it. This fact, however, is of very little consequence for our study of Israel's faith. It was not the outward features, either of names or cult, that distinguished Israel, but the fact that such names and practices had been filled with an entirely new content. Whatever Israel borrowed in its allegiance to the god of Mount Sinai was of no real importance beside the fact that they worshipped him as the God, who, out of sheer grace, had delivered them out of slavery and called them to be his people.

This gave birth to what was essentially a wholly new religion, although, as the Old Testament itself freely concedes, and as every analogy from comparative religion corroborates, there was woven into this many features of earlier belief and cult. It is perfectly credible that these borrowed features included the acceptance by the proto-Israelites of a belief in Mount Sinai as a divine abode, and its connection with their own understanding of Yahweh as the God of the exodus and the Mosaic covenant.[1] Mount Sinai was itself, therefore, very probably already the subject of a sacred tradition concerning a theophany when it became central for the Israelite covenant faith. Old ideas of a divine self-revelation took on a new meaning because of the distinctive context of faith with which they were now associated. The theophany itself became a central act of the covenant. As ensuing generations of Israelites recalled the founding of the covenant, they inevitably associated it with a manifestation of Yahweh as the God of Sinai. Further than this, however, it is abundantly clear from numerous passages of the Old Testament, especially in the Psalter, that the Israelite cultic festival which recalled and re-affirmed the making of the covenant on Mount Sinai pointed to a re-enactment of Yahweh's theophany. Yahweh appeared again in Israel's midst, as he had appeared to their ancestors in the days of Moses, when the covenant had first been made.[2] Since all of our written sources giving an account

---

[1] The possible connection of the God of Mount Sinai with the religion of the Kenites, and so its place in the so-called 'Kenite hypothesis', is beyond the scope of the present study. It is not possible to proceed beyond conjectures in the face of the paucity of certain evidence.

[2] The cultic setting of the Sinai narrative was argued by S. Mowinckel, *Le Décalogue*, Paris, 1927, pp. 114ff. Mowinckel argued that the entire pericope

of the making of the covenant derive from an age long after the original event had occurred, it is not possible for us to elicit exact details of what originally took place, because the later traditions and cult-practices of Israel have influenced the record of the event.[1]

The oldest Sinai-narrative[2] which the Old Testament gives to us, therefore, is not a first-hand reporting of the event by an eye-witness, but is the literary deposit of a cultic tradition which originally formed the festival legend of Israel's covenant renewal celebration. The central act of this festival was Yahweh's self-revelation to Israel, which re-asserted his grace towards them, as well as his claim upon them.[3] At first this covenant ceremony took place in the vicinity of Kadesh, and it is possible that from there regular pilgrimages were undertaken to Mount Sinai.[4] With the migration to Canaan, and the appearance of Israel there, all attempt at regular pilgrimages must have been dropped.[5] Instead, in the sanctuaries of Canaan Yahweh appeared to the Israelite tribes from his traditional home in the south, and revealed his presence among them as the God of the covenant. The idea of his presence, therefore, was both cultic in its expression

---

[1] That a 'theophany-tradition' existed in Israel, which was closely associated with the revelation on Mount Sinai is argued by A. Weiser. See his *The Psalms*, London, 1962, pp. 29ff., etc., and 'Zur Frage nach den Beziehungen der Psalmen zum Kult; Die Darstellung der Theophanie in den Psalmen und in Festkult', *Glaube und Geschichte im A.T.*, Göttingen, 1961, pp. 303–321. Cf. also W. Beyerlin, *Die Kulttraditionen Israels in der Verkündigung des Propheten Micha* (FRLANT 72), Göttingen, 1959, pp. 30ff., and H.-P. Müller, 'Die kultische Darstellung der Theophanie', *VT* 14, 1964, pp. 183–191. A criticism of Weiser's theory of such a 'theophany-tradition' is made by H. Bückers, 'Zur Verwertung der Sinaitraditionen in den Psalmen', *Biblica* 32, 1951, pp. 401–422.

[2] Exod. xix. 2b–xxiv. 14 (JE).

[3] That the tradition of a covenant on Mount Sinai was inseparably related in Israel to the belief in Yahweh as the God of the exodus seems by far the most probable explanation of the intertwining of grace and law in the idea of the covenant. The covenant of Sinai was rooted in the divine grace shown at the exodus. Cf. A. Weiser, *Introduction to the O.T.*, London, 1961, pp. 83ff., W. Beyerlin, *Herkunft und Geschichte der ältesten Sinaitraditionen*, esp. pp. 190ff.

[4] Cf. Deut. i. 2.

[5] Perhaps 1 Kings xix. 7–18 is evidence that pilgrimages to Sinai-Horeb were still not unknown in Elijah's time.

---

reflected the cultic background of the autumnal Enthronement Festival as it was celebrated in Jerusalem. Cf. also G. von Rad, 'Das formgeschichtliche Problem des Hexateuch', *Ges. Stud. zum A.T.*, München, 1958, pp. 15ff., who traced it back to the pre-monarchic period, finding its basis in the celebration of the Feast of Tabernacles in Shechem. See also his *Old Testament Theology*, I, Edinburgh, 1962, pp. 187ff. M. Noth, in his traditio-historical studies, has also argued strongly for the independent origin of the Sinai narrative, separating it from the exodus and conquest themes. See his *Überlieferungsgeschichte des Pentateuch*, rep. Stuttgart, 1960, pp. 63ff. That the account of what took place on Mount Sinai has undergone a long period of preservation in the cult before being written down in its present form is also basic to the important studies of W. Beyerlin and M. L. Newman referred to above.

C

as well as rooted in a historical tradition of the founding of the covenant. The record of a historical encounter was woven into the legend
of the cult as an explanation of its meaning and purpose. Yahweh's
revelation in the past became the pattern and promise of his revelation in the present, so that his presence with Israel was an inseparable feature of the covenant faith. Yahweh was the God of Mount
Sinai, but he was also the Holy One in the midst of Israel.

The account of Yahweh's revelation to Israel on Mount Sinai,
therefore, is not a simple record of a unique historical event, but a
literary account of a theophany of Yahweh which continued to be
repeated in Israel's cultic life. Undoubtedly it goes back to a unique
event when the covenant was inaugurated, but it also betrays evidence
of the cultic re-presentation of that original event. This is of value in
our quest for an understanding of the manner in which Yahweh's
presence was conceived to come to Israel at the sanctuaries in Canaan,
because the most distinctive, and in some sense the normative, idea
of that presence was determined by the story of the appearance
of Yahweh on Mount Sinai. In this process of tradition-history it
appears that features of divine epiphanies, drawn from several different sources, have been introduced into the account. Thus storm
imagery, volcanic phenomena,[1] and general ideas of theophanies
already current in Near Eastern religion,[2] have all affected the presentation. Features of cultic realities and acts have become part of the
historical account which they were intended to symbolize.[3] Whilst
we cannot elucidate clearly, therefore, from the Sinai narrative what
actually took place on Mount Sinai, we can find within it evidence of
the great importance of the idea of a theophany for the understanding
of the covenant in Israel. The covenant pointed to Yahweh's active
presence in Israel for salvation and judgment.

The tradition of the theophany on Mount Sinai is further elaborated
for us by a number of early poetic descriptions of Yahweh's self-
revelation to Israel in the land of Canaan. These, with one exception,

---

[1] The E strand of the Sinai pericope presents Yahweh's appearance as accompanied by storm phenomena, whilst the J strand describes it in terms which suggest
a volcano in eruption.

[2] The idea of a cultic theophany was certainly not unique to Israel, and undoubtedly other (Canaanite) ideas of theophanies influenced Israel's cult and faith.

[3] Cf. the trumpet-blast (Exod. xix. 13, 16), and the regard for Mount Sinai as a
sacred *temenos* (Exod. xix. 12f.). The cultic background is probably also the
explanation of the cloud as a symbol of Yahweh's presence (Exod. xix. 9, 16, 18),
which derives from the cloud over the incense altar. Cf. Lev. xvi. 2, 13, and see S.
Mowinckel, *Psalmenstudien II*, rep. Amsterdam, 1961, p. 152. The cloud became a
regular symbol of Yahweh's presence (Exod. xiii. 21, 22; xiv. 19, 20, 24; xx. 21;
xxxiii. 9, 10; Num. xi. 25; xii. 5; xiv. 14 (all JE); Isa. vi. 4; 1 Kings viii. 10), and
was subsequently elaborated into the doctrine of Yahweh's glory.

may be dated in the tenth century B.C., or earlier, and provide evidence for the close relation which was at one time thought to exist between Yahweh and Mount Sinai. Each of these poems tells of the appearance of Yahweh in a theophany, coming to bless his people in Canaan. There is a close similarity between the ideas of the different poems, and in some instances also the similarity of language is very marked. This strongly supports our claim that there was a traditional description of a divine epiphany from the region of Sinai, and that this has been drawn upon in these poems. The fact that the covenant ceremonies of Israel recalled the original theophany of Sinai makes it probable that it was in the context of Israel's worship that such a 'theophany-tradition' was maintained.

The first of the passages that describe this appearance of Yahweh is contained in the Blessing of Moses (Deut. xxxiii.):[1]

> 'Yahweh came from Sinai;
> And dawned from Seir upon us;[2]
> He shone forth from Mount Paran.
> He came from the ten thousands of holy ones,[3]
> With flaming fire at his right hand.'[4]
> (Deut. xxxiii. 2)

How Yahweh was believed to come is described in verse 26:

> 'There is none like God, O Jeshurun,
> Who rides through the heavens to help you,
> And in his majesty through the skies.'
> (Deut. xxxiii. 26)

The second passage describing Yahweh's theophany from the south is contained in the Song of Deborah (Judges v.), which dates from the twelfth century B.C.:[5]

> 'Yahweh, when thou didst go forth from Seir,
> When thou didst march from the fields of Edom;
> The earth shook,
> And the heavens poured;
> Yea, the clouds poured water.

[1] Dated by G. E. Wright in the latter period of the Judges, sometime in the eleventh century B.C. 'The Book of Deuteronomy', *Interpreter's Bible*, II, 1953, p. 527. S. Mowinckel places it in the ninth century B.C. *Der achtundsechzigste Psalm*, Oslo, 1953, p. 76.
[2] Reading *lānû* instead of *lāmô* with LXX, Syr. and Vulg.
[3] Or perhaps 'from Meribath Kadesh'. Cf. LXX.
[4] Reading *'ēš dôleqet* instead of *'ešdāt lāmô*.
[5] A. Weiser, 'Das Deboralied', *ZAW* 71, 1959, pp. 67–97, argues that this is not a victory poem but a liturgical composition prepared for the Israelite covenant festival after the defeat of Sisera. Thus the cultic tradition of Yahweh's theophany is presented in it.

The mountains trembled before Yahweh, Lord of Sinai,[1]
Before Yahweh, Israel's God.'

(Judges v. 4–5)

Verses 20–21 of the same poem suggest that Yahweh's appearance was related to the storm which caused an unexpected swelling of the river Kishon which materially aided the Israelite victory.

In Psalm lxviii. 8–9 (EVV. 7–8) we have a passage which compares very closely with the verses cited above from Judges v. This psalm is from the Jerusalem temple, as is shown by verses 16–17, 30 (EVV. 15–16, 29). It must be dated sometime in the tenth century B.C.[2] Yahweh is the 'rider of the heavens' (verse 34 (EVV. 33)), who came riding through the deserts as the leader of his people.[3] The section that is important for our study reads:

'O God, when thou didst go forth before thy people,
　When thou didst march through the desert;
The earth quaked, yea the heavens poured,
　Before Yahweh, Lord of Sinai;
　Before Yahweh, Israel's God.
Abundant rain, O God, thou dost shed,
　Over thy inheritance, when it is exhausted.
Thou hast founded it,
Thy family inhabits it.
　In thy goodness, thou dost provide for the needy.'

(Ps. lxviii. 8–11 (EVV. 7–10))

This passage shows how Yahweh's coming is connected with the giving of the rainfall that was so necessary for the fertility of the land and the life of Israel. The description of Yahweh's coming to Jerusalem from his home on Mount Sinai is more explicit still in verse 18 (EVV. 17):

'Yahweh came from Sinai in holy power.'[4]

---

[1] This interpretation of *zê sînay* is contested. It is defended by W. F. Albright, 'The Names Shaddai and Abram', p. 204, and also in 'The Song of Deborah in the Light of Archaeology', *BASOR* 62, 1936, p. 30. H. Birkeland ('Hebrew *Zāe* and Arabic *Ḏū*', *St. Th.* 2, 1948, pp. 201–202) rejects such an interpretation, on the grounds that *zê* cannot bear this meaning in Hebrew. Birkeland's claim, however, is rejected by J. M. Allegro, 'Uses of the Semitic Demonstrative Element Z in Hebrew', *VT* 5, 1955, pp. 309–312. S. Mowinckel follows Birkeland's arguments, and rejects the words as a gloss, both in Judges v. 5 and Ps. lxviii. 8 (EVV. 7). (*Der achtundsechzigste Psalm*, pp. 31f.).

[2] S. Mowinckel, op. cit., pp. 54f., 68.

[3] Hebrew *rôḵēḇ bā'ᵃrāḇôṯ* = 'riding through the deserts' is usually emended to read *rôḵēḇ be'āḇôṯ* = 'rider of the clouds'. So A. Weiser, *The Psalms*, pp. 477, 484. A. R. Johnson, *Sacral Kingship in Ancient Israel*, Cardiff, 1955, p. 70, retains the Massoretic text.

[4] Reading *bā' missînay* instead of *bām sînay*. For the rendering cf. S. Mowinckel, op. cit., pp. 41, 46.

The final passage in which Yahweh's arrival from what is apparently his home in the south is described in the psalm which concludes the prophecy of Habbakuk:[1]

> 'God came from Teman,
>   And the Holy One from Mount Paran.
> His glory covered the heavens,
>   And the earth was full of his praise.
> His brightness[2] was like the light,
>   Rays flashed from his hand;
> And he made[3] his power a covering.'
>
> (Hab. iii. 3–4)

Although this psalm is probably to be dated as a unit to the late seventh century B.C., as Mowinckel maintains, it contains features which go back to very early ideas of Yahweh's epiphany. Verses 9–11, describing a rainstorm, show that this theophany is drawn from ideas of Yahweh's appearance in a thunderstorm, as W. F. Albright asserts.[4]

In three of these passages (Judges v., Ps. lxviii, Hab. iii) the description of the theophany is strongly suggestive of storm phenomena, for there is mention of the accompanying rainfall. It may also be true for the fourth passage (Deut. xxxiii). In this case the belief in some relationship between Yahweh and the southern thunderstorms may have helped to form the tradition. All of these passages, with the exception of Hab. iii, where old traditions have been woven into a later composition, antedate our earliest connected histories relating the conclusion of the covenant on Mount Sinai. They point to a belief that Yahweh was the God of Sinai, but that his presence was in no way bound there.[5] As he had once appeared in the past to his people on the sacred mountain, so in the hour of his people's need, and in their worship, he came to them. The actual

---

[1] This psalm ought probably to be detached from the prophecy of Habbakuk as a separate composition, as it is not included in the Qumran commentary on Habbakuk. Both W. F. Albright ('The Psalm of Habbakuk', *Studies in O.T. Prophecy*, ed. H. H. Rowley, Edinburgh, 1950, pp. 1–18) and S. Mowinckel ('Zum Psalm des Habakuk', *ThZ* 9, 1953, pp. 1–23) defend the place of the psalm in Habbakuk's prophecy. Mowinckel dates the psalm between 625–601 B.C., regarding Habbakuk as a temple prophet. Albright contends that the psalm is composed of four separate units of very much earlier origin which the prophet has rearranged and reworded.

[2] Reading *wᵉnoghô* with LXX and Syr.

[3] Reading *wᵉśām* for *wᵉśām*.

[4] W. F. Albright, 'The Psalm of Habbakuk', p. 8. S. Mowinckel, 'Zum Psalm des Habakuk', pp. 16, 23, relates the psalm to the Enthronement Festival.

[5] W. F. Albright, *From the Stone Age to Christianity*,[2] pp. 262–263, argues against the idea that Mount Sinai was thought of as Yahweh's abode. But in 'A Catalogue of Early Hebrew Lyric Poems (Psalm 68)', *HUCA* 23, Part I, 1950/51, p. 24, he concedes that in earliest Israel Yahweh was thought to have a preferred home in the southern mountains.

descriptions of the theophany began to assume a traditional form, so that the language and ideas employed took on a fairly fixed form, and there can be no doubt that this took place in the cult-liturgy of Israel. Most especially such a preservation and fixation of tradition occurred in the hymns of the covenant festival, which relived and renewed the events which had inaugurated the covenant on Mount Sinai. From a very early period, therefore, and almost certainly from the time when Israel was first established as the people of Yahweh west of the Jordan, there was a very distinctive doctrine of Yahweh's presence. Israel was not bound either to the symbol of a visible image of God, nor to one particular place for its own worship. The covenant festival, in which Israel confessed anew its faith in Yahweh who had brought them out of Egypt, was an occasion when Yahweh's very presence was revealed in their midst. This did not preclude the belief in Yahweh's presence at other times, and in less dramatic ways, but it pointed unequivocally to a particular situation in which their God appeared to them. The basis of Israel was not to be found merely in a record of past history, but in a continued experience of the divine presence to which that history bore testimony. The God of Israel was not far off on a distant pilgrimage site, but present in the united worship of his people. Each celebration of the covenant festival testified that 'Yahweh came from Sinai in holy power'.[1]

That Yahweh himself had promised to come to his people in this way was certainly the belief in early Israel. This is clearly shown by an important passage in which Yahweh declares to Moses his intention of accompanying the Israelites on their journeys into Canaan:

'Moses said to Yahweh, "See, thou sayest to me, bring up this people; but thou hast not made known to me whom thou wilt send with me. Yet you have said, I know you by name, and you have also found favour in my sight. Now then, if I have found favour in thy sight, make known to me thy ways that I may know thee and find favour in thy sight. See too that this nation is thy people." And he said, "My presence will go with you and I will give you rest." Then he said to him, "If thy presence will not go with me, do not carry us up from here. For how shall it be known that I have found favour in thy sight, I and thy people? Is it not in thy going with us, so that we are distinct, I and thy people, from every nation which is on the face of the earth?" Then Yahweh said to Moses, "This very thing that you have spoken I will do; for you have found favour in my sight, and I know you by name!"'

(Exod. xxxiii. 12–17 (J)).

[1] Ps. lxviii. 18 (EVV. 17). G. Henton Davies, 'Tabernacle' *IDB*, IV, p. 505a, argues that the belief in Yahweh's tabernacling presence was Moses' greatest contribution to Israel's faith.

Perhaps there were some in Israel who had thought of Yahweh as bound in some way to Sinai, so that the migration to Canaan was a departing from him. Consequently it was out of a certain religious tension and struggle that the belief gained a firm hold that Yahweh had given his word to Moses that his presence (Heb. *pānîm*) would be with his people. The way in which this word was fulfilled was given outward expression in the cult and worship of Israel.

In the light of this cultic tradition of Yahweh's presence we can discern an idea that became of vital importance in the whole development of Israel's worship. The patriarchal religion had thought of the divine presence in a personal and clan relationship, whilst the Canaanite sanctuaries strongly emphasized the belief in a divine attachment to certain places. Both of these traditions contributed something to Israel's religious growth, but neither was allowed to obscure the fact that primarily Yahweh was the god of the covenant, who revealed his presence to his people, as he had done on Mount Sinai. This both associated the divine presence with certain historical events, whilst at the same time imbuing the covenant with a sense of the active power and presence of Yahweh which marked him as the living God.

CHAPTER III

THE ARK, THE CHERUBIM AND THE TENT
OF MEETING

ONE of the strongest features of Israel's faith was its deep antipathy to any representation of the deity in image form. There is no valid evidence to prove that Israel ever did permit or value images of Yahweh, and so no reason exists for doubting that the prohibition of images of Yahweh goes back to the Mosaic origins of Yahwism. The divine presence in Israel was in no way linked to any kind of image, or symbolic representation of Yahweh. None the less we have seen that Israel possessed a cult in which the presence of Yahweh was vividly proclaimed and asserted, and it was inevitable that some kinds of cultic institutions and furnishings should have existed. The covenant itself, and the ceremonies at which it was renewed, were associated with certain holy objects which were thought to belong to Yahweh and to his cult. These were the ark and the tent of meeting, both of which were, in a vital way, connected with the presence of Yahweh. Both of them were portable and were carried about by the people in their journeys.

The whole question of the original significance of the ark and of its connection with the tent of meeting is still a matter of debate, but certain features have become clearer in recent discussion. Its name implies that it was a box,[1] but in the Old Testament it has become so intimately connected with Yahweh's presence that the view has gained wide acceptance that it came to be regarded as Yahweh's throne on which he was thought to be invisibly seated.[2] W. Reichel's original proposal of this suggestion was largely based on parallels from popular cults of pre-classical culture, but M. Dibelius made a careful

[1] Heb. *'ārôn*. Cf. Gen. l. 26 where the same word is used of Joseph's coffin, and 2 Kings xii. 10f. (EVV. 9f.) where it applies to a chest used to keep contributions towards the upkeep of the temple (also 2 Chron. xxiv. 8ff.). The Deuteronomists, in their reinterpretation of the ark, regard it simply as a container for the two tablets of the law.

[2] This view was proposed originally by Wolfgang Reichel, *Über die vorhellenischen Götterkulte*, Vienna, 1897, and *Theologische Arbeiten aus dem Rheinischen wissenschaftlichen Predigerverein*, N.F. V. The theory was most effectively elaborated and argued by M. Dibelius, *Die Lade Jahwes*, (FRLANT 7), Göttingen, 1906, to whom I am indebted for the references to Reichel's studies. Cf. also J. Meinhold, 'Die Lade Jahves: ein Nachtrag', *ThSK* 74, 1901, pp. 593–617.

examination of the evidence of the Old Testament. Firstly we have
to account for the fact that the ark is intimately bound up with the
presence of Yahweh. Where the ark is, Yahweh is.[1] Secondly the ark
is related to Yahweh's enthronement upon the cherubim.[2] A difficulty arises here, of which Dibelius was aware, but to which many of
his followers have not paid attention, in that Yahweh is said to be 'the
enthroned one of the cherubim'.[3] Dibelius, therefore, suggested that
there were cherubim carved upon the sides of the ark,[4] and was thus
forced to resort to an unsubstantiated hypothesis to support his
theory that the ark was a throne. Thirdly Dibelius argued for the throne
conception from the ancient rubric preserved for us in Num. x. 35–36:

'And whenever the ark set out, Moses said, "Arise, O Yahweh, and let
thine enemies be scattered; and let those who hate thee flee before thee."
And when it rested he said, "Return,[5] O Yahweh, to the ten thousand
thousands of Israel." '

(Num. x. 35–36 (JE)).[6]

In this passage Yahweh, on Dibelius' interpretation, is thought to
be present with the ark, by means of which he dwells with Israel.
The fourth, and most direct, piece of evidence for the throne-con-
ception of the ark is to be found in Jer. iii. 16–17:

'And when you shall multiply and increase in the land in those days,
says Yahweh, men will no more say, "The ark of Yahweh's covenant."
It shall not come to mind, nor will they remember it, nor shall it be
missed; it shall not be made again. At that time they will call Jerusalem
Yahweh's throne and all nations shall gather to it, for the name of
Yahweh in Jerusalem, and they will no more follow the stubbornness of
their evil heart.'

(Jer. iii. 16–17).

Here the parallelism of thought seems to require the meaning
that the ark, as Yahweh's throne, will be replaced by the whole of
Jerusalem which will fulfil this function.

[1] This is especially apparent in the History of the Ark, 1 Sam. iv. 1–vii. 2;
2 Sam. vi.
[2] 1 Sam. iv. 4; 2 Sam. vi. 2; 2 Kings xix. 15; 1 Chron. xiii. 6.
[3] The Hebrew is a participle and noun in construct.
[4] M. Dibelius, op. cit., pp. 23ff.
[5] M. Dibelius, op. cit., pp. 10f., reads $šᵉbâ$ = 'dwell, be seated' instead of
$šûbâ$ = 'return'.
[6] This rubric is of great significance for our understanding of the way in which
Yahweh was thought to manifest his presence with the ark, but it has been variously
interpreted. It belongs to the cult in which the ark played a prominent part (Ps.
lxviii. 2 (EVV. 1); cxxxii. 8). Instead of implying that Yahweh was permanently
present with the ark, it can better be understood as implying that Yahweh appeared
from his heavenly dwelling (or Sinai) to manifest his presence over the ark. Cf.
A. Weiser, *The Psalms*, p. 781; R. de Vaux, 'Arche d'alliance et tente de réunion',
A la rencontre de Dieu. Mémorial A. Gelin, Le Puy-Lyons-Paris, 1961, p. 66.

Following the study of Dibelius, and in general adherence to the reasons that have been outlined, the theory that the ark was regarded as the throne of the invisible Yahweh has gained a considerable measure of acceptance among scholars. This has not gone unchallenged, and several criticisms have been urged against such a view.[1] The greatest difficulty for the supporters of this conception is that of the name of the ark, and the fact that it is never once explicitly described as a throne. Why call it a box, if it were a throne? Dibelius felt this difficulty, and suggested that the box-like form of the ark gave rise to this usage.[2]

Against the theory that the ark was a throne on which Yahweh was thought to be invisibly seated, we may adduce the following arguments:

1. The name itself implies that it was a box and not a throne. There is no parallel to be found for assuming that thrones were box-like in form, or that a confusion could have arisen in the name. Neither is there any reason for assuming that a hidden motive lies behind the avoidance of the title 'throne'.

2. Yahweh's enthronement is related primarily to the cherubim, not to the ark. We shall see that the Old Testament evidence suggests that originally the cherubim and the ark were not related. Dibelius has no support for his argument that there were carved cherubim on the ark.

3. The position of the ark in the temple, located lengthwise, is incompatible with its use as a throne, unless we are prepared to accept that Yahweh was thought not to face the congregation in the temple, but to be seated sideways on. This is exceedingly improbable.

4. The evidence of Jer. iii. 16–17 does not prove that the ark was thought of as a throne, but only that it was associated with a throne. This, in any case, we know from the connection of the ark with the cherubim.

5. A further objection against the idea that the ark was in itself a throne may be adduced from the Priestly account of the ark.[3] Here the ark is to be manufactured as a box $2\frac{1}{2} \times 1\frac{1}{2} \times 1\frac{1}{2}$ cubits overlaid

---

[1] See especially K. Budde, 'Imageless Worship in Antiquity', *ET* 9, 1897/8, pp. 396–399; 'Die ursprüngliche Bedeutung der Lade Jahwes', *ZAW* 21, 1901, pp. 193–197, and 'War die Lade Jahwes ein leerer Thron?' *ThSK* 79, 1906, pp. 489–507. G. von Rad accepts that the ark was understood as Yahweh's throne, but argues that an earlier theology existed about the ark, and has been suppressed. *Old Testament Theology*, I, p. 237 note.

[2] M. Dibelius, op. cit., pp. 95ff.

[3] Exod. xxv. 10–22.

with gold. On to this is to be placed a *kappōreṯ* (mercy-seat), which seems to fulfil the purpose of a throne. It is above the *kappōreṯ* that the presence of God is located.[1] Yahweh's enthronement is therefore primarily related to the *kappōreṯ*, and the cherubim which flank it, rather than to the ark.[2] Although caution must be exercised lest we claim too much for the Priestly Document as a witness to the pre-exilic period, it is apparent that the Priestly writer did not regard the ark as a throne, but described the mercy-seat to fulfil this purpose.

6. The evidence of 1 Sam. iv. 1–vii. 2, the account of the wanderings of the ark, does witness to the presence of Yahweh with it, but this only means that the ark was a potent 'extension' of Yahweh's person.[3] Yahweh could be present with the ark, without necessitating that it be regarded as a throne.[4]

These considerations, taken together, raise serious objections against the theory that the ark was thought to be a throne on which Yahweh was invisibly seated, and this objection becomes still stronger when we examine the question of the nature and significance of the cherubim. This is vitally important for the meaning of the ark, and the question of the latter's significance cannot be solved without regard to it. The cherubim represent the cloud-chariot of Yahweh on which he rides through the skies.[5] They are heavenly creatures of the storm-clouds in which the divine presence is discerned. Thus the cherubim are heavenly beings, the servants of Yahweh, who inhabit paradise, or heaven.[6] Solomon's temple was decorated with them,[7] and we may also note that Ezekiel's vision of the temple describes it as decorated with cherubim as fitting symbols for a divine

---

[1] Exod. xxv. 22 etc.
[2] Cf. M. Haran, 'The Ark and the Cherubim: Their Symbolic Significance in Biblical Ritual', *IEJ* 9, 1959, pp. 32ff. Haran argues that the cherubim form a distinct symbol from the ark, and that in the Priestly Document the ark is the footstool of the throne. Cf. also H. Schmidt, 'Kerubenthron und Lade', *Eucharisterion. H. Gunkel Festschrift*, ed. H. Schmidt, 1923, I, pp. 131ff., and 143ff. The interpretation of the ark as a footstool is suggested by 1 Chron. xxviii. 2.
[3] Cf. A. R. Johnson, *The One and the Many in the Israelite Conception of God²*, Cardiff, 1961, pp. 23ff.
[4] Cf. K. H. Bernhardt, *Gott und Bild*, pp. 28ff.
[5] 1 Chron. xxviii. 18; Deut. xxxiii. 26; Pss. xviii. 11 (EVV. 10); lxviii. 5, 34 (EVV. 4, 33) xcix. 1; Hab. iii. 8.
[6] Gen. iii. 24; Ezek. xxviii. 16. For the origin of the name of the cherubim in Babylonian intercessory deities see E. Dhorme, 'Le nom des chérubins', *Recueil Édouard Dhorme*, Paris, 1951, pp. 671–683. This, however, says nothing about whence Israel derived the idea of these creatures, and how they were conceived and interpreted. A. S. Kapelrud ('The Gates of Hell and the Guardian Angels of Paradise', *JAOS* 70, 1950, pp. 151–156), seeks to trace back a belief in the cherubim, as the guardians of the divine throne, to Sumerian door-divinities.
[7] 1 Kings vi. 29.

dwelling-place.[1] Ezekiel, in his inaugural vision, saw Yahweh seated upon his firmament-throne, which a later editor has interpreted as that of the cherubim.[2] We cannot be in any doubt, therefore, that the cherubim were related to Yahweh, because he was the God of the skies, who came to his people from heaven, and that the cherubim were thought to draw, or even to form, his chariot. The fullest and most convincing examination of the question of the cherubim in the light of Ancient Near Eastern iconography, together with a detailed study of the Old Testament references, is by R. de Vaux, who concludes that they were a form of the winged sphinx.[3] Their origin goes back to Ancient Egypt, but they became popular throughout the Near East, and in Syria two basic conceptions appeared; the sphinxes which guarded the sacred tree, and the sphinxes of judgment, associated with a throne.[4] From the evidence of many countries it appears that the representation of a throne, supported by sphinxes on each side, was a Phoenician creation.[5]

M. Dibelius sought to establish a chronological separation of the two distinct functions of the cherubim, one as Yahweh's throne-bearers, and the other as protective spirits.[6] From the iconographic evidence, however, it is apparent that the creatures were associated with both functions from an early period.[7]

The wide popularity of the idea of the cherubim in the Near East, especially in Phoenician-Syrian circles, in the form of winged sphinxes supporting a throne, make it virtually certain that it was from a Canaanite source that they were adopted into the religious symbolism of Israel.[8]

Thus we are led on to the conclusion that the ark came to be associated with Yahweh's throne because of the connection that came

[1] Ezek. xli. 18ff.

[2] Ezek. i. 4ff.; ix. 3ff.; x. 1ff., esp. x. 20. Most recent commentators regard the identification of the cherubim of chapter x with the creatures of the inaugural vision as secondary. See W. Eichrodt, *Der Prophet Hesekiel* 1–18, (ATD 22/1), Göttingen, 1959, pp. 52f.

[3] R. de Vaux, 'Les chérubins et l'arche d'alliance. Les sphinx gardiens et les trônes divins dans l'ancien Orient', *MUSJ* 37, 1961, pp. 93–124. Cf. M. Haran, 'The Bas-reliefs on the Sarcophagus of Ahiram King of Byblos in the Light of Archaeological and Literary Parallels from the Ancient Near East', *IEJ* 8, 1958, pp. 15–25.

[4] R. de Vaux, 'Les chérubins et l'arche d'alliance', p. 101.

[5] R. de Vaux, 'Les chérubins et l'arche d'alliance', p. 113.

[6] M. Dibelius, op. cit., pp. 33, 72ff. Dibelius claimed that the conception of the cherubim changed when the conception of the ark changed to being a box containing the law-tablets. Cf. also H. Gressmann, *Die Lade Jahwes und das Allerheiligste des salomonischen Tempels*, (BWANT II, 1), Stuttgart, 1920, pp. 6ff.

[7] R. de Vaux, 'Les chérubins et l'arche d'alliance', p. 101. Cf. M. Haran, 'The Ark and the Cherubim', pp. 37f.

[8] R. de Vaux, 'Les chérubins et l'arche d'alliance', p. 113.

to exist between the ark and the cherubim. This then raises the important question; was the ark always related to the cherubim, and if not can we point to any occasion when this came about? An important text in this regard is to be found in 2 Sam. vi. 2, which reads:

'And David rose up and went with all the people who were with him from Baale-Judah, to bring up from there the ark of God, which is called by the name of Yahweh of Hosts who sits enthroned on the cherubim.'

(2 Sam. vi. 2)

Here the ark is simply called 'the ark of God', whilst the cherubim-throne is related to the specifically Israelite name of 'Yahweh of Hosts'. Moreover the formula used, 'which is called by the name of . . .', has been thought to suggest that here the ark of another god, perhaps from Shiloh, has been secondarily attached to the conception of Yahweh, who is enthroned on the cherubim.[1] K. Galling claims that such a phrase is an old legal formula for the exchange of property in which the name of the new owner was publicly proclaimed over the property he had acquired.[2] Thus Galling argues that the ark was originally the property of some other god than Yahweh, and an echo of its transfer to him is to be found in the above text.

Against this we must offer the objection, following W. Beyerlin,[3] that the proclamation of the divine name held an ancient and important place in worship, so that we cannot define the usage here as an exchange of property; rather it refers to the ritual use of the name of Yahweh.[4] We cannot then draw any conclusions from 2 Sam. vi. 2 as to how, or when, the ark was introduced as the major cult-object in Israel. It does, however, support the contention that the cherubim-throne conception was not originally invested in the ark, but came to be so because at some stage in Israel's religious development Yahweh came to be thought of as enthroned on cherubim.[5] We are still left with the question of discerning when this came about. The first certain knowledge that we possess of the existence of carved cherubim in Israel

---

[1] K. Galling, 'Die Ausrufung des Namens als Rechtsakt in Israel', *ThLZ* 81, 1956, cols. 65–70. Cf. also E. Kutsch, 'Lade Jahwes', *RGG*³, IV, cols. 197–199.
[2] Cf. Deut. xxviii. 10; Amos ix. 12; Isa. iv. 1; Jer. xiv. 9; xv. 16; xxv. 29; Ps. xlix. 12. (EVV. 11).
[3] W. Beyerlin, *Herkunft und Geschichte der ältesten Sinaitraditionen*, p. 157. Cf. also W. Zimmerli, 'Ich bin Jahwe', *Gottes Offenbarung. Gesammelte Aufsätze*, München, 1963, pp. 11–40. Zimmerli particularly points to the use of the divine name in the cultic theophany.
[4] Cf. Num. vi. 22–27; Exod. xx. 7, 24.
[5] O. Eissfeldt, 'Jahwe Zebaoth,' *Miscellanea Academica Berolinensia*, Berlin, 1950, pp. 139ff.; R. de Vaux, 'Les chérubins et l'arche d'alliance', pp. 123f.; H. J. Kraus, *Gottesdienst in Israel*², pp. 150, 207f.

is from the account of Solomon's temple, when we learn that two
cherubim stood in the inner shrine,[1] and that the walls were decorated
with cherubim in relief.[2] Some scholars have concluded that any
reference to Yahweh as enthroned upon cherubim before the construction of the temple must therefore be anachronistic.[3] The two
references which fall into this category are 1 Sam. iv. 4, when the ark
was at Shiloh, and 2 Sam. vi. 2, with which we have already dealt,
and which refers to the fetching of the ark out of obscurity in David's
reign. If these texts can be relied upon they carry back the existence
of the idea of the cherubim-throne in Israel at least to the time when
Shiloh was the central shrine of the amphictyony. It has been suggested consequently, by O. Eissfeldt, with a good measure of probability, that there existed some representation of cherubim in the
sanctuary of Yahweh in Shiloh which furnished the prototypes for
the great carved cherubim which were placed in the temple built by
Solomon.[4] This is only a conjecture, since we have no direct mention
of such, but the fact that at Shiloh the ark was placed in a temple,[5]
and that such a temple must, in its architecture, have been modelled
on Canaanite prototypes, makes such a hypothesis quite credible.
Whether such cherubim were carved images, or merely represented
in a less dramatic way, we do not know. In every way the period when
the ark was at Shiloh seems the most likely time when the idea of
Yahweh's cherubim-throne became attached to it.[6] What its function
was before this time we do not certainly know, but it may well have
been used as a container for the covenant law of the Israelite amphictyony,[7] and may even have been invested with significance as the

---

[1] 1 Kings vi. 23–28.

[2] 1 Kings vi. 29.

[3] H. Schmidt, 'Kerubenthron und Lade', p. 143; K. Galling, 'Die Ausrufung des
Namens als Rechtsakt in Israel', col. 69.

[4] O. Eissfeldt, 'Jahwe Zebaoth', pp. 144ff.; 'Silo und Jerusalem', *Strasbourg
Congress Volume* (SVT IV), Leiden, 1957, p. 146. Cf. R. de Vaux, 'Les chérubins et
l'arche d'alliance', pp. 119, 123f. The argument of E. Nielsen ('Reflections on the
History of the Ark', *Oxford Congress Volume* (SVT VII), pp. 61–74) that the ark
was a Benjaminite cult-object set in the shrine of El-'Elyon at Shiloh is unacceptable. The ark was a cult-object belonging to a number of tribes, and it is improbable
that El-'Elyon was associated with Shiloh. Rather the deity worshipped here in
Canaanite times was more likely an El-Sebaoth. Cf. R. de Vaux, 'Les chérubins et
l'arche d'alliance', p. 123; O. Eissfeldt, 'Jahwe Zebaoth', pp. 139, 146f.

[5] 1 Sam. i. 9, 24; iii. 3, 15.

[6] It is at the same time that the title Yahweh Sebaoth came to be attached to
Yahweh (O. Eissfeldt, 'Jahwe Zebaoth', pp. 139ff.), and very probably the idea of
his divine kingship was also adopted into Israel at this time. Thus the cherubim
formed his royal chariot-throne. Cf. W. Schmidt, *Königtum Gottes in Ugarit und
Israel*, p. 78.

[7] Cf. W. Beyerlin, *Herkunft und Geschichte der ältesten Sinaitraditionen*, pp. 157
note, 168.

pedestal on which the invisible Yahweh stood.[1] Such a double function is not to be precluded. In any case the probability is that it was
an old-established cult-object, coming from the unsettled stage of
Israel's existence.[2] That it was a container for the law-tablets was
certainly the view of the later Deuteronomists, at the time of the
end of the monarchy, and this may well rest on a genuine recollection.

We are therefore able to come to the following conclusions regarding the ark:

1. It was not a throne, but sometime, probably when it was at
Shiloh (i.e. before 1050 B.C.), it came to be associated with the cherubim-throne.

2. The cherubim were mythological creatures in Canaanite religion whence the Israelites adopted them and associated them with
their own ideas of the presence of Yahweh, and of the theophany
in which he revealed himself. The old rubric of Num. x. 35–36
belongs to this conception of the deity who rides on the storm-
clouds which are characterized as cherubim, in order to come to the
help of his people. A Sinai-theophany tradition was already well
established in Israel, and so the cherubim idea was simply an em-
bellishment of what was already a fixed feature of Israelite worship.

3. The original significance of the ark was probably that of a container, in which were kept the law-tablets of the covenant. As such
a container it is not impossible that it was thought to serve as a pedestal for the invisible deity who guarded the covenant-law at his feet.

4. The ark was kept at the central sanctuary of the Israelite federation, because of its primary function in the covenant rites, but when and
where it was first adopted by Israel is unknown. It must go back at
least to the time when the federation had its centre at Shechem, and
most probably to the period when the ancestors of Israel were at
Kadesh.

A further important institution which is closely related to the
presence of God in the Old Testament is to be found in the tent of
meeting which is traced back to the wilderness. The earliest account
of this tent[3] was later elaborated by the Priestly Writing into the

---

[1] Cf. R. de Vaux, 'Les chérubins et l'arche d'alliance', pp. 119, 122; 'Arche
d'alliance et tente de réunion', p. 68.

[2] Cf. O. Eissfeldt, 'Lade und Stierbild', *Kleine Schriften*, II, pp. 290f.; R. de
Vaux, 'Arche d'alliance et tente de réunion', pp. 58f.; G. Henton Davies, 'Ark of the
Covenant', *IDB*, I, p. 225a.

[3] Exod. xxxiii. 7–11 (E); cf. Num. xi. 16–17, 24, 26; xii. 5, 10 (all JE), Deut. xxxi.
14–15 (E).

tabernacle, of which the account is given in Exod. xxv–xxx, xxxv–xl. Although this Priestly account is built upon the earlier tradition, it is so much the expression of the Priestly viewpoint that we must defer consideration of it until we examine the whole belief of the Priestly writers concerning the presence of God. The Elohistic account cannot be dated precisely, but it is certainly early and must contain a genuine tradition from the pre-monarchic period of Israel's history.

The introductory section to the mention of the tent is found in Exod. xxxiii. 1–6 (JE) and narrates how the Israelites, when setting out from Mount Sinai took off their ornaments as a sign of repentance and mourning.[1] Then follows the account of the tent of meeting:

'Now Moses would take the tent and pitch it outside the camp, a long way off, and he called it the tent of meeting. And every one who inquired of Yahweh would go out to the tent of meeting, which was outside the camp. And it would be that whenever Moses went out to the tent, then all the people got up and stood, each one at his tent door, and they watched Moses until he had entered the tent. When Moses entered the tent the pillar of cloud would descend and stand still at the door of the tent and would speak with Moses. And when all the people saw the pillar of cloud standing at the door of the tent, then they would all rise up and worship, every one at his tent door. And Yahweh would speak to Moses, face to face, as a man speaks to his friend. And when Moses returned to the camp, then his servant, Joshua-ben-Nun, a young man, did not leave the tent.'

(Exod. xxxiii. 7–11)

This tent was therefore a shrine for the receiving of oracles and the divine presence was not thought to be permanently resident there but to appear whenever Moses entered the tent to inquire of God. The fact that Joshua is said to have remained in the tent may

---

[1] Many scholars have claimed that the real significance of this action must have been that the ornaments were used for the manufacture of a sacred object, the ark, the description of which has fallen out after verse 6. This was regarded as a deliberate omission on the part of the Priestly editors who no longer wished to include a separate account of the making of the ark, beside their own. The ark, which the missing section introduced, was then supposed to have been placed in the tent of meeting mentioned in verses 7–11. See S. R. Driver, *Introduction to the Literature of the O.T.*[9], Edinburgh, 1913, p. 38. There seems, however, no reason to doubt that the removal of the ornaments was an act of mourning, as the narrative states, so that it offers no evidence that the tent of meeting did contain the ark. Cf. M. Noth, *Exodus*, pp. 254ff.

indicate that a priest officiated in it in order to receive such revelations as Yahweh might give. There is no mention of the ark in this tent, and in fact the earliest sources, whilst mentioning both institutions, do not connect them with each other. The tent is mentioned in Exod. xxxiii. 7–11 (E), and the ark in Num. x. 33–36 (JE), xiv. 44 (JE), but they are not said to have been related to each other. That the ark was separated at one time from the tent of meeting has been argued by several scholars.[1] It has been particularly stressed by G. von Rad, who sees two entirely different conceptions of Yahweh's presence represented by the two; the ark which, he claims, pointed to a permanent presence of Yahweh, and the tent of meeting, which indicated only a temporary presence in a theophany.[2]

This rigid distinction between a theology of Yahweh's dwelling and a theology of his epiphany cannot be conceded, as we have already shown that the presence of Yahweh over the ark was understood in terms of a theophany in which he came and appeared to his people, as the rubric of Num. x. 35–36 shows.[3] There is, therefore, no compelling reason why the ark should not from the first have been placed in the tent of meeting.[4] Some scholars have sought to find positive proof of the presence of the ark in the tent from Exod. xxxiii. 7, where the text reads, 'and pitched for it (or him)', (Heb. $w^e n\bar{a}\dot{t}\hat{a}$ $l\hat{o}$). It is reasonable to regard the pronoun here as referring to an antecedent mention of the ark, which has fallen out.[5] The argument is weighty, but not absolutely compelling. If the ark were in fact present in the tent, it is strange that the cloud appears at the door of the tent, and not over the ark. This does not amount to proof that the two institutions were at one time unrelated to each other, for we have little information as to how, or where, Yahweh was thought in early

[1] R. Hartmann, 'Zelt und Lade', *ZAW* 37, 1917/18, esp. pp. 213ff.; G. von Rad, 'Zelt und Lade', *Ges. Stud. zum A.T.*, pp. 120ff. Cf. also his *Old Testament Theology*, I, pp. 234ff.; M. Haran, 'The Nature of the "Ohel Mo'edh" in Pentateuchal Sources', *JSS* 5, 1960, pp. 50ff.; M. Noth, *Exodus*, pp. 254ff.; M. L. Newman, *The People of the Covenant*, pp. 55ff. Newman claims that the ark was the cult-symbol of the northern tribes, whilst the tent belonged to the south. This is in accordance with his thesis that from the days when the covenant community was at Kadesh there were two covenant traditions in Israel, one northern and one southern.
[2] G. von Rad, 'Zelt und Lade', pp. 122ff.; *Old Testament Theology*, I, p. 236.
[3] Cf. Ps. lxviii. 2 (EVV. 1). lxxx. 2 (EVV. 1); cxxxii. 8. That the ark pointed to a theophany as the manner and sign of Yahweh's presence is convincingly argued by W. Beyerlin, *Herkunft und Geschichte der ältesten Sinaitraditionen*, pp. 134ff. Cf. also R. de Vaux, 'Arche d'alliance et tente de réunion', pp. 66ff.
[4] So E. Sellin, 'Das Zelt Jahwes', *R. Kittel Festschrift*, (BWAT 13), Stuttgart, 1913, pp. 168–192; W. Beyerlin, *Herkunft und Geschichte der ältesten Sinaitraditionen*, pp. 134ff.; R. de Vaux, *Ancient Israel*, London, 1961, pp. 301f., and, in greater detail, 'Arche d'alliance et tente de réunion', p. 70.
[5] So E. Sellin and R. de Vaux.

D

times to appear by the ark. The later Priestly authors certainly regarded the cloud of the divine glory as appearing immediately above the ark,[1] but this may be only their interpretation.

The whole question of the original relationship between the ark and the tent is a very vexed one, in which absolute conclusions are not possible. In any case by the time Shiloh became the central sanctuary of Israel, and when, as we have seen, important developments in Israel's cultic symbolism took place, the two were united.[2] Whether they were already united before this time it is not possible to say with certainty, and in any case it is not of any very great moment for our study.[3] They both clearly witnessed to a very similar view of the divine presence, manifested in a cloud theophany, and were important in Israel's worship for the receiving of oracles. Together they formed the foremost sanctuary of Yahweh, in which Israel believed that his presence appeared to their chosen representatives, and revealed his will and purpose to guide their conduct and shape their destiny. At Shiloh the title 'tent of meeting' seems to have been applied to a more permanent and substantial structure than a tent, which could also be called a temple.[4] All in all this sanctuary witnessed developments of decisive importance taking place in Israel's worship and understanding of Yahweh. Owing to the very fragmentary nature of our sources for this period we are left to infer what these developments were, without being able to rely on any very positive statement. There is no doubt, however, that in its day Shiloh had a very great significance for Israel, and no study of the development of Israel's worship and religious thinking can afford to ignore its importance.[5] Later generations, looking back, came to regard Shiloh as the place which Yahweh had first chosen as his dwelling-place in Canaan.[6] The source from which Israel drew these innovations must assuredly have been from the neighbouring Canaanites, and it is most intelligible to regard these developments as proceeding under a strong influence from an older Canaanite sanctuary at Shiloh itself. Of this we know virtually nothing at all, but a reasonable

[1] Exod. xxv. 22; xxx. 6; Lev. xvi. 2, 13.
[2] 1 Sam. ii. 22.
[3] G. von Rad, *Studies in Deuteronomy* (SBT 9), London, 1953, p. 43, suggests that the tent belonged to a southern group of six tribes centred at Hebron, whilst the ark belonged to a northern group around Shechem. Cf. also M. L. Newman, *The People of the Covenant*, pp. 55ff. Such a hypothesis is attractive, but cannot be considered as more than a possibility.
[4] 1 Sam. i. 9; iii. 3.
[5] O. Eissfeldt, 'Silo und Jerusalem', pp. 138ff., argues that Shiloh had the same meaning for Israel that afterwards attached to Jerusalem, but this goes too far.
[6] Ps. lxxviii. 60; cf. Jer. vii. 12.

hypothesis is that it was dedicated to an El-Sebaoth, who was regarded as the divine king, enthroned upon cherubim.

At Shiloh Israel's cult assumed a more elaborate form, in which
several religious symbols and ideas, in part of diverse origin, were
welded together into a unity. Cult-objects and cultic traditions, each
related in its own way to the belief in the presence of the deity,
were united together, and given a positive expression and place in
Israel's worship. The primary Israelite conception of the presence
of Yahweh as coming to them from Mount Sinai, came to possess
its own distinctive cult-furniture with which this theophany was
regularly associated. The importance of these permanent institutions,
and the building in Shiloh of a permanent sanctuary, must not be
overlooked, for they strengthened the tendency to associate Yahweh's
presence with one particular shrine, and so to enhance its prestige
among all the altars and sanctuaries that Israel used. The prominence given to Shiloh in this regard was cut short by the destruction
of the place, and the capture of the ark by the Philistines *c.* 1050 B.C.

CHAPTER IV

THE CONQUEST OF JERUSALEM AND THE BUILDING OF THE TEMPLE

BOTH the ark and the tent of meeting played a prominent part in the religious development of early Israel. Together they possessed a significance which exceeded that of any other cult-object or shrine, and the sanctuary where they were located became inevitably the foremost sanctuary of Yahweh, and the centre of the Israelite federation. At Shiloh we have seen that Israel possessed a central sanctuary, equipped with the ark, where the Mosaic tradition of worship was implanted, in which Israel recalled the events of the exodus and the theophany on Mount Sinai. Yet already the ties which bound Yahweh to this southern mountain home were beginning to loosen, and features drawn from the Canaanite cult, with its interest in the blessing of the soil and the divine sovereignty over creation, came to figure more noticeably in Israel's religion. It seems likely that part of this development took place in Shiloh, where aspects of the cult of a Canaanite deity, probably El-Sebaoth, were adopted by Israel. Yet Canaan was a land full of sanctuaries and altars, at each of which a divine presence was believed to be manifested. Undoubtedly Israel must have used many of these altars, and claimed them as legitimate shrines for the worship of Yahweh. Thus the ancient law of the altar in the Book of the Covenant assures Israel that Yahweh will appear to it at every altar which he has appointed.[1]

When the sanctuary of Shiloh was destroyed by the Philistines, therefore, and the ark of Yahweh captured,[2] the cult of Yahweh did not cease, although it had suffered a severe setback. Eventually under Saul's leadership some breathing-space was gained from the Philistine pressure, until the battle of Mount Gilboa once again brought Israel to the brink of disaster, with the defeat of Israel and the death of Saul. With David's swift rise to power, first in Judah, and then over all Israel, the Philistines were defeated, and Israel had freedom to assert itself. There could not now be a return to the earlier conditions in which Israelites and Canaanites had lived side by side in a measure of tolerance

---

[1] Exod. xx. 24, 'In every place, where I cause my name to be remembered I will come to you and bless you'. On this law see J. J. Stamm, 'Zum Altargesetz im Bundesbuch', *ThZ* 1, 1945, pp. 304–306.

[2] 1 Sam. iv. 22.

and independence. David, partly led by circumstance and partly by desire, was bent on the unifying of Israel, and the strengthening of its resources to enable it to counter any repetition of the Philistine menace. No longer could Israel continue as a loose federation of tribes, and the movement towards an Israelite state, already initiated by the institution of the monarchy under Saul, was carried forward extensively. Eventually it reached its culmination and goal under Solomon.[1] A prominent feature of David's reign, therefore, was the subjugation of the neighbouring states, and their incorporation into an Israelite empire. With this went the assimilation of the population of Canaan into one national entity. Israelite and Canaanite could no longer continue as members of separate religious and national groups. They had to be welded into one whole, under an Israelite head, to form an Israelite state. Wherever the Canaanites resisted the will of David they were defeated by force of arms, and compelled to accept the new order of things. Thus the capture of Jerusalem, a Jebusite city-fortress, by David's captain Joab, served two purposes at once. It removed a pocket of resistance, and it provided an excellent site for the capital city of the new state. As such it was to be the religious and political centre for all Israel. Prior to David's time it had had no association with any one of the tribes so that no occasion for jealousy or rivalry would be given. To mark its unique relationship to David it was called the 'city of David', and seems to have been claimed as a personal holding of the king.[2] David himself commenced building operations to extend the city, and to strengthen its fortifications. It does not appear that the Jebusite population were expelled or repressed in any way; rather the new king's policy on capturing the city appears to have been one of conciliation, and of the integration of the Jebusite population into the Israelite state. Already Jerusalem was a substantial city with a flourishing life of its own when David captured it, so that although the city had no previous significance for Israel, it was certainly not without its own shrines, with their priests, and long-established cultic traditions.

As a part of the new order in Israel David brought up the ark, which seems to have been left in relative obscurity since the Philistines had captured it, and set it in Jerusalem.[3] By this act David

---

[1] For the Davidic state see A. Alt, 'Die Staatenbildung der Israeliten in Palästina', *KSGVI*, II, pp. 33ff.; R. de Vaux, *Ancient Israel*, pp. 94ff.

[2] A. Alt, 'Jerusalems Aufstieg', *KSGVI*, III, pp. 253ff., emphasizes the importance of the role of David in the rise of Jerusalem. He attributes the prominence of the city to its unique association with the founder of Judah's royal dynasty.

[3] 2 Sam. vi. M. Noth, 'Jerusalem und die israelitische Tradition', *Ges. Stud. zum A.T.*[2], München, 1960, pp. 172ff., emphasizes the great importance of this event in

brought over the old traditions of the amphictyony to his new capital, and established it beyond any question as the chief sanctuary of Yahweh.[1] The ark was placed in a tent-sanctuary, which was pitched for it, although H. H. Rowley[2] has conjectured that some time during his reign David took the ark out of its tent and placed it in the shrine, originally Jebusite, over which Zadok officiated as priest. This is in accordance with the theory, accepted by Rowley, that Zadok, who suddenly appears in the Israelite records of this period, was originally a priest of the Jebusites, who was confirmed in office by David.[3] This is a possibility which must be reckoned with, although there is insufficient evidence to build any certain reconstructions of the history of Israel's priesthood and cult upon it.[4] In any case such evidence as we have of the age of David makes it certain that there was a good deal of borrowing by Israel from the religious traditions of the vanquished gods of Canaan. Especially was this true in regard to the idea of Yahweh as creator and sustainer of the world of nature. This was a very natural tendency in the circumstances, and in no way reflects on the sincerity of David's faith in Yahweh. The very aggressiveness and buoyancy of Yahwism led to the adoption of many of the features of Canaanite religion, which possessed a much more elaborate cult and liturgy than did Israel. Israel did not feel that its faith was threatened by what it borrowed, nor that Yahweh was rivalled by the old gods of Canaan. Such a persistence of earlier rites and customs, when a sanctuary was taken over by the devotees of a new god, was commonplace in Ancient Israel, as it has been throughout the history of religion in general.

Certainly the Davidic era marks a great upheaval in Israel's life and faith, so that it is particularly valuable to examine what evidence we have of the pre-Israelite cult in Jerusalem, and to seek to discover what gods were worshipped there before Yahweh supplanted them all.

---

[1] The Chronicler claims that during the reigns of David and Solomon the tent of meeting stood on the high-place of Gibeon (1 Chron. xvi. 39; xxi. 29; 2 Chron. i. 3–6), but no historical credence can be attached to this.

[2] H. H. Rowley, 'Zadok and Nehushtan', *JBL* 58, 1939, p. 127.

[3] Cf. A. Bentzen, 'Zur Geschichte der Sadokiden', *ZAW* 51, 1933, pp. 173ff. Bentzen was following S. Mowinckel, *Esra den Skriftlärde*, Oslo, 1916 (unavailable to me). See also H. H. Rowley, 'Zadok and Nehushtan', pp. 113ff., and 'Melchizedek and Zadok (Gen. 14 and Psalm 110)', *Bertholet Festschrift*, Tübingen, 1950, pp. 461–472; C. E. Hauer, 'Who Was Zadok?', *JBL* 82, 1963, pp. 89–94.

[4] R. de Vaux, *Ancient Israel*, pp. 114, 374, is very sceptical of such a theory of Zadok's origin. Cf. also G. von Rad, *Old Testament Theology*, I, p. 249 note.

---

establishing the pre-eminence of Jerusalem among Israel's sanctuaries. So also T. C. Vriezen, *Jahwe en zijn Stad*. Amsterdam, 1962, p. 4.

We should not expect to find only one deity but probably several forming a pantheon of gods worshipped by the Jebusites. The name of the city itself suggests the Semitic deity Shalem-Shulman.[1] That he was still revered there may find an echo in the name of two of David's sons, Absalom and Solomon. However, we must note that Absalom was born to David in Hebron,[2] and Solomon's name was apparently originally Jedidiah,[3] and Solomon was the name adopted by him at his accession to the throne.[4] This may well, therefore, have some particular connection with Jerusalem, although the worship of Shalem was quite widespread, and was in no way confined to one sanctuary.

Another deity whom we should connect with Jerusalem is Zedek,[5] whose name is often associated with the city. In this regard we may note the names of Melchizedek, the king of Salem,[6] and of Adoni-zedek[7] and Zadok, the chief priest of the temple in Solomon's time.

The most important clue for the discovery of the nature of the worship of pre-Israelite Jerusalem, and of the god, or gods, venerated there, is to be found in Gen. xiv. 18–24. This is a narrative telling how Abraham, after defeating a coalition of kings from the lands of the Near East, offered tithes to Melchizedek, king of Salem. The patriarch is said to have been blessed by Melchizedek in the name of 'El-'Elyon, lord of sky and land'.[8] In Gen. xiv. 22 this El-'Elyon is identified with Yahweh, and as Salem is Jerusalem it is clear that the present form of the story comes from after David's conquest of the city, when the worship of Yahweh was introduced there. It is in fact in every way probable that the story itself is an adaptation of traditional material used to explain and legitimize certain developments in David's reign.[9] There is no doubt, however, that El-'Elyon

---

[1] Cf. J. Lewy, 'The Šulmān Temple in Jerusalem', *JBL* 59, 1940, pp. 519–522; N. W. Porteous, 'Shalem-Shalom', *TGUOS* 10, 1943, pp. 1–7.

[2] 2 Sam. iii. 2.

[3] 2 Sam. xii. 25.

[4] Cf. A. M. Honeyman, 'The Evidence for Regnal Names among the Hebrews', *JBL* 67, 1948, pp. 22f.

[5] Cf. A. R. Johnson, *Sacral Kingship in Ancient Israel*, pp. 31f.; G. Widengren, *Psalm 110 och det sakrala kungadömet i Israel*, (*UUÅ* 1941, 7, 1), Uppsala, 1941, p. 5. Widengren identifies *ṣedeḳ* in Ps. 89, 15 (EVV. 14) as a divine hypostasis.

[6] Gen. xiv. 18; Ps. cx. 4.

[7] This is the original form of Adonibezek (Judges i. 5–7).

[8] Gen. xiv. 19, 22.

[9] The exact significance of the story is debated. It establishes the right of El-'Elyon, now identified with Yahweh, to receive tithes and homage from Israel, which is represented by the ancestor Abraham. Thus it also affirms David's right, as heir and successor of the Jebusite kings 'after the order of Melchizedek' to receive tithes and homage from Israel. That David accepted the city-kingship of Jerusalem is confirmed by Ps. cx. 4. Cf. H. J. Kraus, *Psalmen* (BKAT), Neukirchen,

was the chief god of pre-Israelite Jerusalem, and that his name and authority were taken over by the conquering Israelites and vested in Yahweh, who had vanquished the old deity and usurped his throne.[1] It is therefore of great importance for us to find out more about El-'Elyon, and to discover how he fits into the Canaanite pantheon as we have come to know it. The connection of El-'Elyon with Jerusalem, as also certain literary references which connect him with other divine titles, has led certain scholars to conclude that Shalem and Zedek were all identical with El-'Elyon.[2] There is some plausibility in this, as the Canaanite pantheon presents us with a variety of deities who were sometimes identified with each other, or with others of the west-Semitic pantheon. We need to remember, however, that in Israel the titles of many gods were claimed for Yahweh, so that the particular developments in Israel cannot be taken as general for the Ancient Near East. In fact the local pantheons betray such differences that we cannot claim that Canaanite religion was always, everywhere, the same.

It has been suggested that El-'Elyon is a combination of the titles of two originally separate gods, so that El-'Elyon arose out of the

[1] Cf. A. R. Johnson, 'The Rôle of the King in the Jerusalem Cultus', *The Labyrinth*, ed. S. H. Hooke, London, 1935, pp. 81ff., 89, 92, 96, 101f., 111; *Sacral Kingship in Ancient Israel*, esp. pp. 42ff.; J. Schreiner, *Sion-Jerusalem. Jahwes Königsitz*, (SANT 7), München, 1963, pp. 19f.; H. Schmid, 'Jahwe und die Kulttraditionen von Jerusalem', *ZAW* 67, 1955, pp. 168–197.

[2] H. S. Nyberg, op. cit., p. 356, claims that 'Al, El-'Elyon, El-Shaddai, Shalem and Zedek were all titles of the same god. Nyberg's identification of 'Al with El (op. cit., p. 335), however, certainly cannot be maintained. G. Widengren, *Sakrales Königtum im Alten Testament und im Judentum*, Tübingen, 1953, p. 47, identifies El-'Elyon with Shalem; cf. also his *Psalm 110 och det sakrala kungadömet i Israel*, p. 5 note. H. Schmid, op. cit., p. 177, suggests that Zedek was another name for 'Elyon, and E. Voegelin (*Order and History*, Vol. I, *Israel and Revelation*, Louisiana, 1956, p. 277) suggests that both Shalem and Zedek were hypostases of 'Elyon. S. Mowinckel, *The Psalms in Israel's Worship*, I, pp. 132f, suggests that Melek, Zedek and Shalem were probably conceived as manifestations of El-'Elyon.

1960, II, pp. 879ff. H. S. Nyberg, 'Studien zum Religionskampf im Alten Testament', *ARW* 35, 1938, pp. 329–387, goes further and sees Gen. xiv as presenting Israel's claim to Canaanite land through recognition and homage to El-'Elyon, as the owner of the land. H. H. Rowley, who accepts that Zadok was the priest-king of Jerusalem who was confirmed in office by David, interprets Ps. cx. 4 as referring to Zadok, and sees Gen. xiv. as affirming the legitimacy of Zadok's priesthood for Israel ('Melchizedek and Zadok (Gen. 14 and Ps. 110)', pp. 461ff., and 'Zadok and Nehushtan', pp. 113ff.). Even if Zadok were originally a Jebusite priest, it seems very improbable that it was Zadok and not David who was installed in Melchizedek's office. Ps. cx. 4 more naturally refers to the royal figure addressed in the remainder of the psalm, and Melchizedek was certainly a king as well as priest (Gen. xiv. 18). Certainly also the Judean royal ritual was borrowed from a Canaanite source, which must have taken place in Jerusalem. Cf. G. von Rad, 'Das judäische Königsritual', *Ges. Stud. zum A.T.*, p. 206.

fusion of two distinct deities.[1] G. Levi Della Vida, who argued for this view, thought that this duality was reflected in the ascription 'Lord of sky and land', so that El was originally the god of the land, and 'Elyon the god of the sky. This view must now be decisively rejected.[2] The unity of sky and land as the sphere of a single god's activity is perfectly intelligible, especially where the fertility aspect is prominent. The rain from the sky produces fertility in the fields so that a vital relationship between sky and land is a simple deduction from an observation of nature. Another important point is that ''Elyon' is not in itself an independent name, but an epithet meaning 'high, exalted' (EVV. Most High), which serves to qualify the generic title El.[3] Consequently it was not only a suitably honorific ascription for a deity, but is best understood as implying that such a god was the head of the pantheon.[4] Further the formation of such a divine name is closely paralleled by such others as El-Roi, El-Shaddai and El-'Olam, who were all manifestations of the one god El. Every likelihood points, therefore, to the same being true of El-'Elyon.[5] There are, however, two sources of evidence which have led to some doubt about this identification of El-'Elyon with El. In the first instance certain extra-biblical references seem to refer to El as a deity distinct from 'Elyon. These are notably the Sujin inscription,[6] and the Phoenician genealogy of gods found in Philo Byblius.[7] Secondly there are two references in the Old Testament itself which seem to carry the implication that 'Elyon was in some way identified with Baal. The first is in Isa. xiv. 13–14 where the Babylonian

---

[1] G. Levi Della Vida, 'El Elyon in Genesis 14: 18–20', *JBL* 63, 1944, pp. 3, 8. Cf. also Millar Burrows, *An Outline of Biblical Theology*, Philadelphia, 1946, p. 55; A. R. Johnson, *Sacral Kingship in Ancient Israel*, p. 44; R. Dussaud, *Les découvertes de Ras Shamra (Ugarit) et l'Ancien Testament*, pp. 112f., 155f.

[2] H. S. Nyberg, 'Studien zum Religionskampf', p. 352; O. Eissfeldt, 'El and Yahweh', p. 28 note; L. Fisher, 'Abraham and His Priest King', *JBL* 81, 1962, p. 266 note.

[3] O. Eissfeldt, 'El and Yahweh', p. 28 note; R. Lack, 'Miscellanea Biblica: les origines de Elyon, le Tres-Haut, dans la tradition cultuelle d'Israel', *CBQ* 24, 1962, pp. 57f. Lack accepts that properly such a title belonged to El, who was the great high-god of the Semites.

[4] Cf. Ps. lxxxii. 6, where the lesser gods are termed 'sons of 'Elyon'. It is synonymous with the title 'Al = 'exalted', which also appears in the Old Testament as a divine title. See H. S. Nyberg, *Studien zum Hoseabuch*, (*UUÅ* 6) Uppsala, 1935, pp. 58ff.; 'Studien zum Religionskampf', pp. 329ff.; cf. G. R. Driver, 'Hebrew 'Al ('High One') as a Divine Title', *ET* 50, 1938/9, pp. 92–93.

[5] Cf. O. Eissfeldt, 'El and Yahweh', p. 28 note; W. Schmidt, *Königtum Gottes in Ugarit und Israel*, pp. 78f. note; R. Lack, 'Les origines de Elyon', pp. 49, 59ff.

[6] Cf. *Ancient Near Eastern Texts Relating to the O.T.*[2], ed. J. B. Pritchard, Princeton, 1955, pp. 503f.; G. Levi Della Vida, 'El Elyon in Genesis 14. 18–20', pp. 1ff.

[7] Cf. C. Clemen, *Die phönikische Religion nach Philo von Byblos* (*MVAG* 42, 3), Leipzig, 1939, p.24.

king is mockingly said to have boasted that he would ascend above
the stars of El, sit on the Mount of Assembly in the remote fastnesses
of Zaphon, and become like 'Elyon. This implies that 'Elyon dwells
on Mount Zaphon, and that this is situated above the stars of El. In
the Ugaritic myths we learn quite categorically that Zaphon is the
abode of Baal-Hadad. Further Psalm xlviii. 3 (EVV. 2) identifies
Mount Zion with Mount Zaphon, and it is most likely that this
identification arose from the cult of El-'Elyon. There is some evidence,
therefore, that El-'Elyon bore some relationship to Baal, and in fact
a number of scholars have sought to identify the two gods.[1] M. H.
Pope has sought to discern in 'Elyon a deity who was quite separate
from either El or Baal, and suggests that he might have been the
grandfather of El.[2]

It appears, therefore, that when taken as a whole the evidence
regarding the nature of El-'Elyon is conflicting. The form of the
name suggests a connection with El, whilst his dwelling-place was
that of Baal, and some references distinguish him from El. Nevertheless, in spite of all these considerations, the probability remains
that El-'Elyon was originally a form of the great Semitic high-god
El, whom we encounter as the head of the pantheon at Ugarit. The
weight of the extra-biblical evidence which distinguishes him from
El is not strong when examined critically. Philo Byblius does not
offer a reliable account of the early Phoenician pantheon, since many
late Hellenistic features have been introduced into it.[3] It is plain
also that the gods of the north-west Semites were not ordered in a
fixed and unchangeable pantheon, but at different times, and in the
various local sanctuaries, there were a great many variations and
distinctions. There was not one fixed, unchangeable pantheon, but
only a multiplicity of deities arranged in different degrees of pre-
eminence and variously identified at each local shrine. No absolute
uniformity was attained, and the changing political scene, as well as
regional differences were not without influence.[4] This probably

---

[1] A. Vincent, *La religion des Judéo-Araméens d'Éléphantine*, p. 127; G. von Rad,
Genesis, London, 1961, p. 174; J. A. Montgomery, 'The Highest, Heaven, Aeon,
Time, etc. in Semitic Religion', *HTR* 31, 1938, p. 145. We might also point out that
in the Ugaritic myths Baal is described by the adjective 'exalted' (Ug. *'ly*), which is
cognate with the Hebrew *'elyôn*. See *UM* 126, III, 6–7, 8–9.

[2] M. H. Pope, *El in the Ugaritic Texts*, p. 58.

[3] O. Eissfeldt, 'El and Yahweh', p. 28 note; R. Lack, 'Les origines de Elyon', pp.
57f.

[4] R. Lack, 'Les origines de Elyon', pp. 48f., accepts that properly the title
'Elyon' belongs to El, who was the great high-god of the Semites, but he finds a
southern (Arabian) tradition, which used the epithet of El, and a north-western
(Phoenician) tradition which used it of Baal.

explains the distinction between 'Elyon and El in the Sujin inscription, where the epithet 'exalted' has been applied to another god, who was most likely Baal.[1] In consequence of this Canaanite tendency to identify gods with each other, and to merge their various attributes with those of other gods, it is quite possible that in Jebusite Jerusalem El-'Elyon, who was a form of the god El, had borrowed some features from the cult of Baal. These most especially concerned the idea of his dwelling-place on Mount Zaphon. In the same way the identification of this mountain with the Mount of Assembly represents a development from the mythology found at Ugarit.[2] We conclude, therefore, that El-'Elyon was a manifestation of the god El, and that his particular cult celebrated in ancient Jerusalem had associated with him some aspects of the mythology of Baal.

The fact that El-'Elyon was thought to have Mount Zaphon for his abode makes it probable that it was through this cult that Mount Zion came to be identified with Mount Zaphon, and so came to be regarded as the dwelling-place of a god. The hill, like Mount Zaphon itself, was thought to be symbolic of the cosmos where the god reigned. Thus a distinctive Canaanite doctrine of the divine presence was well known in Jerusalem before the Israelites established the worship of Yahweh there. This lies behind the very description of El-'Elyon as 'Lord of sky and land'.[3] El-'Elyon was the lord and owner of the land, and ultimately this lordship extended throughout the entire world, in accordance with the mythological basis of the idea. In practice, however, it was predominantly relevant to that part of Canaan which had some kind of feudal allegiance to Jerusalem.[4] By rendering tithes of the produce of the land, the inhabitants sought to secure for themselves the privilege of using El-'Elyon's land, and of receiving his favour and blessing. When Gen. xiv. 22 identifies El-'Elyon with Yahweh it becomes clear that the Israelites, when they came to assert that Mount Zion was Yahweh's dwelling-place, did so under the influence of this ancient Jebusite belief. It was a

---

[1] R. de Vaux, *Ancient Israel*, p. 310, seeks to avoid the difficulty posed by the Sujin inscription by regarding the conjunction as used explicatively, 'El who is 'Elyon'. This is unacceptable in view of the parallel references to other gods.

[2] See above p. 7.

[3] Gen. xiv. 19, 22. For the meaning of the verb *qānâ*, the participle of which is here rendered as 'lord', see P. Humbert, 'Qânâ en Hébreu biblique', *Bertholet Festschrift*, pp. 259–266. Humbert stresses that basically the verb means to possess', and notes the mythological colouring of the occurrences where it is connected with 'creating'. Cf. also G. Levi Della Vida, 'El Elyon in Genesis 14. 18–20', p. 1 note.

[4] On this significance of the word 'land' see above p. 2.

religious tradition inherited from the Jebusites, which was adopted and re-interpreted by the conquering Israelites, when they replaced El-'Elyon by Yahweh. Alongside of this borrowing from Canaan must be added the fact that David had brought the ark, the traditional Israelite symbol of the divine presence, into the city. Thus both factors combined to give a unique status to Jerusalem among all the shrines of Israel, and to associate Yahweh's presence with Jerusalem in a very special way. The result of these new influences in the Israelite cult was a new emphasis upon the power of Yahweh over creation, and a new interest in the relationship between the cult and the bless-ing of the land. Israel's hold over the land of Canaan was divinely sanc-tioned by Yahweh's replacement of El-'Elyon, and his adoption of the latter's titles and property.[1]

Although the worship of Jerusalem was truly Israelite in character and intent, we may discern a very real tension between the ideas associated with the ark, and its tradition of Yahweh's mighty acts in history, and the fundamentally mythological character of the belief in Mount Zion as a divine dwelling-place. The one held to a belief in Yahweh's presence as manifested to Israel in his coming from Mount Sinai, whilst the other proclaimed a permanent relation-ship between Yahweh and his earthly abode.[2] From very early times Israel's conception of God possessed features which were distinctly 'unmythological', and it is clear throughout the pages of the Old Testament, that there was in Israel a progressive breaking away from myth in favour of a more concrete and historical understanding of God and his activity.[3] It would be wrong, however, and contrary to the evidence, to neglect the strong influence of myth on the cult of Yahweh in Jerusalem, and to overlook the inheritance from the worship of El-'Elyon in pre-Israelite times.[4] It is significant that Yahweh's dwelling in Jerusalem came to be expressed in terms of his 'election' of Mount Zion[5], so that history rather than myth was looked to as the justification of his abode there, even though it was essentially

---

[1] Cf. especially Ps. cxv. 15; cxxi. 2; cxxiv. 8; cxxxiv. 3; cxlvi. 6.

[2] Cf. T. C. Vriezen, *Jahwe en zijn stad*, p. 13.

[3] See especially G. E. Wright, *The Old Testament Against Its Environment*, (SBT 2), London, 1950, and also *God Who Acts* (SBT 8), London, 1952; B. S. Childs, *Myth and Reality in the Old Testament* (SBT 27), London, 1960.

[4] T. C. Vriezen, *Jahwe en zijn stad*, pp. 3f., claims that the mythological features of the Jerusalem cult have been overstressed. Cf. also R. de Vaux, *Ancient Israel*, pp. 310f., who is very cautious about Israel's borrowing from the El-'Elyon cult. The mythological character of the tradition of the election of Mount Zion, as basically a borrowing from the pre-Israelite worship of El-'Elyon, is set out by E. Rohland, *Die Bedeutung der Erwählungstraditionen Israels für die Eschatologie der alttestamentlichen Propheten*, Diss. Heidelberg, 1956, pp. 119ff.

[5] Ps. lxxviii. 68; cxxxii. 13.

a mythological idea that was so expressed.[1] This election of Mount Zion was indissolubly connected with the divine election of David and his dynasty to be rulers of Israel.[2] This is well brought out in Ps. cxxxii:

> 'Yahweh swore to David a sure promise
> Which he will not repudiate:
> "One of the sons from your body
> I will set on your throne.
> If your sons keep my covenant
> And my testimonies which I shall teach them,
> Their sons also forever
> Shall sit upon your throne."
> For Yahweh has chosen Zion,
> He has desired it for his habitation;
> "This is my resting-place forever.
> Here I will dwell for I have desired it." '
> (Ps. cxxxii. 11–14)

The origin of this twofold doctrine of Yahweh's election of David and of Mount Zion cannot be precisely dated, but it must certainly be early, and most probably it dates back to the Davidic-Solomonic

[1] H. J. Kraus, *Gottesdienst in Israel*[2], p. 237 note, insists that the mythological tradition inherited from the Jebusites was completely reminted in Israel, and that the election of Mount Zion had nothing essentially to do with myth, but referred to the setting of the ark in Jerusalem. Cf. also *Psalmen*, I, p. 345. Whilst it would be wrong to overstress this mythological inheritance from the Jebusites, it is also wrong to neglect it. For the following reasons it seems more probable that the doctrine of Yahweh's election of Mount Zion was the Israelite expression of a belief which was ultimately mythological in its origins:
(*a*). It is Mount Zion that Yahweh has chosen, not Jerusalem; i.e. the fact of the 'holy mountain' is of primary importance and cannot be dissociated from the general Ancient Near Eastern attachment to sacred mountains.
(*b*). Mount Zion was identified with Mount Zaphon, Ps. xlviii. 3 (EVV. 2), a mountain celebrated in Canaanite mythology.
(*c*). There are features in the O.T. which invest Mount Zion with a cosmic significance. This is only explicable on the basis of a mythological association.
(*d*). The Psalter venerates Mount Zion as a source of blessing for Israel (e.g. Ps. xiv. 7; xx. 3 (EVV. 2); liii. 7 (EVV. 6); cxxviii. 5; cxxxii. 13–15; cxxxiii. 3; cxxxiv. 3). Whilst this could be simply a consequence of the belief in Yahweh's presence there, it is more natural to regard it as a result of the belief in Yahweh's presence, mediated through his sacred mountain; i.e. there are features of 'myth' which cannot be overlooked.
[2] Cf. esp. Ps. ii. 6; lxxviii. 67ff.; 1 King viii. 25f. The close relationship between the divine election of Mount Zion and the promises to David and his dynasty is argued by J. Schreiner, *Sion-Jerusalem*, pp. 77, 103ff., 135. It is impossible to accept the claim of E. Rohland, op. cit., pp. 122ff., 247, that the tradition of the election of Mount Zion was originally separate from that of the election of David, and was only combined with it quite late (in the exilic age?). For the covenant between Yahweh and David see 2 Sam. xxiii. 5; 2 Chron. vi. 14f; xiii. 5; Isa. lv. 3; Jer. xxxiii. 21; Ezek. xxxiv. 23; Ps. lxxxix. 4ff. (EVV. 3ff.).

age. It is inseparably bound up with the oracle of Nathan, the promises of which, in nucleus, must have originated in David's own
days. Such a doctrine of Yahweh's election of an individual, and of
a cult-site, therefore, antedates the appearance of Deuteronomy,
which introduced a very distinctive usage of the terminology of election in Israel.[1]

The declaration of Yahweh's choice of the Davidic dynasty was,
beyond question, a piece of political theology intended to secure the
royal throne in Jerusalem, and to serve as a divine authorization for
its occupants. The same is true of the allied doctrine of Yahweh's
election of Mount Zion, which sanctioned the installation of the
ark in the new cult-centre of Israel, and at the same time upheld the
adoption by Israel of features borrowed from the cult of El-'Elyon.
The introduction of a Yahweh sanctuary in Jerusalem was closely
related, therefore, to the Davidic royal house, and its foundation was
claimed to have been established by a unique revelation of the divine
will and purpose. It was Yahweh's chosen sanctuary.

In the light of what we know of the significance of sacred mountains in Canaan, and throughout the Ancient Near East in general,
we can see that this choice of Mount Zion was not only intended to
authorize the retention of the ark in Jerusalem, but signified Yahweh's
right of possession of the land of Canaan.[2] Thus it had far-reaching
political consequences, since it was connected with Israel's claim
to dominion over land that had once belonged to the Canaanites.
How far such a claim extended we do not know, and we must particularly think of the boundaries of the Jebusite city-state of Jerusalem.
Nevertheless, as the royal sanctuary of the Israelite state, it was
capable of being interpreted as a claim, in the name of Yahweh, to
lordship over a much wider area. It is not too much to argue, therefore, that the doctrine of the joint election of David and Mount
Zion was nothing short of a divine authorization and sanction for the
whole Davidic state. Yahweh had chosen Mount Zion, which, in its

---

[1] Cf. G. E. Mendenhall, 'Election' *IDB*, II, pp. 78a, 80a; K. Koch, 'Zur Geschichte der Erwählungsvorstellung in Israel', *ZAW* 67, 1955, pp. 205ff.; S.
Amsler, *David, roi et messie* (Cahiers théologiques 49), Neuchâtel, 1963, pp. 37ff.
H. J. Kraus, *Psalmen*, I, p. 547, argues that Ps. lxxviii and cxxxii have been
influenced by Deuteronomic usage, but this is not so, since the distinctiveness of
Deuteronomy lies in its application of the idea of election to Israel, not in the coining
of a new expression.

[2] H. J. Kraus, *Psalmen*, I, p. 547, interprets both Ps. lxxviii. 54 and Exod. xv. 17
in the light of the symbolism that the elect mountain represents the holy land. Cf.
also K. Galling, *Die Erwählungstraditionen Israels*, (BZAW 48), Giessen, 1928, p. 4,
who suggests that the election of Mount Zion was (pars pro toto) a religio-political
election of Israel. Cf. also my article 'Temple and Land: a Significant Aspect of
Israel's Worship', *TGUOS* 19, 1963, pp. 16–28.

religio-political meaning, entitled Israel to possession of the land of Canaan, and he had chosen David to rule over it. These two assertions comprise the whole religious basis of the state that David established, and which flourished so pretentiously under Solomon.

It is instructive, therefore, to recall that the Yahwist's history (J), which probably dates from early in Solomon's reign, has as its great theme the promise of the land to the patriarchs, leading up to the fulfilment in the conquest under Joshua.[1] A similar presentation of Israel's origins as a divinely guided pilgrimage of Israel leading to the possession of the land of Canaan is the theme of two early Israelite psalms; Ps. lxxviii and Exod. xv. 1–18, the Song of Miriam. Both follow a similar pattern in which the climax is found in the establishing of Mount Zion as Yahweh's abode, and Israel's possession of the land of Canaan. In both of these psalms the land of Canaan is closely identi-fied with Yahweh's holy mountain. The presupposition of both poems is to be found in the existence of the Davidic-Solomonic empire, with Yahweh's claim to Mount Zion as his abode, and Israel's possession of Canaanite territory. Every probability points to this age as the period when such psalms were composed.[2] Psalm lxxviii. combines Israel's possession of the land with Yahweh's choice of David as ruler of his people[3] It describes Israel's conquest of Canaan in the following way:

'And he struck down all the first-born in Egypt,
    The first fruits of their strength in the tents of Ham.
Then he led out his people like sheep,
    And guided them in the wilderness like a flock.
He led them safely, so that they were not afraid;
    But the sea overwhelmed their enemies.
And he brought them to his holy land,
    To the mountain which his right hand had acquired.
He drove out nations before them;

---

[1] Cf. G. von Rad, 'Verheissenes Land und Jahwes Land im Hexateuch', *Ges. Stud. zum A.T.*, pp. 89ff.; 'Das formgeschichtliche Problem des Hexateuch', pp. 67ff.

[2] Psalm lxxviii has often been dated in the later period of the monarchy, and has been thought to reflect Deuteronomic influence. However no decisive objection can be raised against the claim that it was composed in the age when it concludes its own *heilsgeschichte*; i.e. in the age of the empire of David and Solomon. Cf. O. Eissfeldt, *Das Lied Moses, Deuteronomium 32, 1–43, und das Lehrgedicht Asaphs, Psalm 78 samt einer Analyse der Umgebung des Mose-Liedes*, (BSAW 104), Leipzig, 1958, pp. 41ff.; A. Weiser, *The Psalms*, p. 540; B. D. Eerdmans, *The Hebrew Book of Psalms* (OTS IV), Leiden, 1947, pp. 379ff.

[3] Ps. lxxviii. 70–72.

He divided the inheritance by lot,
And settled the tribes of Israel in their tents.'

(Ps. lxxviii. 51–55)

In this passage verse 54, in its parallelism, relates Yahweh's mountain to the holy land, which is divided among Israel's tribes as their inheritance (Heb. *naḥelâ*).[1]

The Song of Miriam describes the same situation:

'Thou hast led in thy kindness the people whom thou hast redeemed,
Thou hast guided them by thy power to thy holy abode.
The peoples have heard, they tremble;
Writhing has seized the inhabitants of Philistia.
Now are the chiefs of Edom troubled;
The leaders of Moab, trembling seizes them.
All the inhabitants of Canaan have melted away.
Terror and dread fall upon them;
Because of the greatness of thy arm,
They are as still as a stone.
Till thy people, O Yahweh, pass by,
Till the people pass by whom thou hast acquired.
Thou wilt bring them in and plant them on the mountain of thy inheritance,
The place for thy dwelling which thou hast made, O Yahweh;
The sanctuary, O Lord, which thy hands have established.
Yahweh is king for ever and ever.'

(Exod. xv. 13–18)

It is significant that in these psalms Israel's possession of the land of Canaan is related to Yahweh's abode on Mount Zion. This corroborates the argument, based on the Canaanite and Ancient Near Eastern ideas of divine abodes, that Yahweh's choice of Mount Zion was expressive of the belief that the whole land of Canaan now belonged to him.[2] Thus the land was Yahweh's to give to his people

---

[1] R. Lack ('Les origines de Elyon', pp. 59ff.) argues that if Ps. lxxviii. 54 is referred to Mount Zion, it disturbs the movement of the psalm, which reaches its climax with the election of David and Mount Zion in verses 67ff. This objection is not weighty once we realize the symbolic nature of Yahweh's mountain as representing the land, so that it can in fact signify the land.

[2] J. Wellhausen, *Prolegomena to the History of Ancient Israel*, Meridian ed., New York, 1957, p. 22 note, referred the mention of Yahweh's 'holy abode' and 'sanctuary' to the whole land of Canaan which he believed was thought of as Yahweh's dwelling-place. So also M. Noth, *Exodus*, p. 125. For the idea of Canaan as Yahweh's abode see also E. Jacob, *Theology of the Old Testament*, London, 1957, p. 256. Yet nowhere in the Old Testament is the land of Palestine spoken of as Yahweh's dwelling-place, nor can it be described as his sanctuary. Quite consistently in the Old Testament Yahweh's holy mountain is Mount Zion (Pss. ii. 6; iii. 5 (EVV. 4); xv. 1; xliii. 3; xlviii. 2 (EVV. 1); xcix. 9), and this must be the reference here. So. S. Mowinckel, *Der achtundsechzigste Psalm*, p. 73; J. Pedersen, *Israel III–IV*, Copenhagen, 1940, pp. 407–408; H. Wildberger, *Jahwes Eigentumsvolk*, pp. 21f. note; J. Schreiner, *Sion-Jerusalem*, p. 209.

Israel. In Exod. xv. 17 we have mention of 'the mountain of thy inheritance', which has given rise to a good deal of discussion, in view of its mythological background. We are now in a position to understand the significance and associations of such a phrase.

First of all it needs to be noted that the designation of the dwelling-place of a god as 'the mountain, or land, of his inheritance' is found in the mythological texts of Ugarit.[1] It is therefore not to be disputed that such terminology was originally current in the mythology of Canaan. When we find it used in Exod. xv. 17 for Yahweh's dwelling-place, we are therefore justified in making the assumption that it has been borrowed by Israel from this Canaanite usage. This has been used by certain scholars as an argument that the Song of Miriam is of pre-monarchic date, and that Exod. xv. 13, 17 do not refer specifically to Mount Zion.[2] It is said to be a mythological phrase, borrowed from Canaan and used loosely by Israel of Yahweh's land. Before we can accede to this claim we must ask more precisely what significance the phrase had in Canaanite religion. The purport of such a description of the divine abodes was to designate the gods as owners of the land where their worshippers lived, and which formed the divine 'inheritance'. Thus the sanctuaries were symbolic of the divine ownership of the land. In the case of Mot, for whom no specific sanctuaries are likely to have existed, it is a reflection of the terminology used for the other gods. We cannot, therefore, interpret the myths without recognizing their background and setting in the cultic life of Ugarit. It would be wrong, therefore, to reckon on a purely literary dissemination of mythological ideas, instead of understanding them in the setting of the sanctuaries, where they originated and were preserved. The phrase 'mountain, or land, of his inheritance' is closely related to the divine throne, or city, in the Ugaritic myths, so that we have here a reflection of the belief, for

---

[1] *UM* 51, VII, 13–15, where Mot's dwelling under the earth is described by three terms in parallel as, 'his city', 'the throne where he sits' and 'the land of his inheritance'. These terms are repeated in a parallel passage *UM* 67, II, 15–17. In 'nt III, 26–27, Baal's dwelling-place is described as 'the rocks of El Zaphon' (or 'my mountain, El Zaphon'), 'the holy place' and 'the mountain of my inheritance'. There is a parallel passage to this in 'nt IV, 63–64. In 'nt VI, 14–16 the dwelling of the god *KTR* is described:
'Caphtor is the throne on which he sits,
Ḥkpt, the land of his inheritance.'
C. H. Gordon restores this phrase also in 'nt (pl. ix), III 1.

[2] W. F. Albright, *The Archaeology of Palestine* (rev. ed.), London, 1960, p. 233, dates the poem not later than the thirteenth century B.C. Cf. F. M. Cross and D. N. Freedman, 'The Song of Miriam', *JNES* 14, 1955, pp. 237–250. Cross and Freedman date the composition of the psalm in the twelfth to eleventh centuries and place its writing down in the tenth century B.C.

E

which we have already argued, that the local sanctuaries and 'sacred mountains' of the gods were intended to represent the land which the god possessed and ruled. The divine abode was explained through the medium of mythology and the local shrine was identified with the cosmic abode of the deity, the true 'mountain of his inheritance', which the local mountain merely symbolized. It is, therefore, very improbable indeed that the phrase was borrowed by Israel without reference to any specific sanctuary. Rather those scholars are right who see here a reference to Mount Zion, which had, since David's conquest of Jerusalem and the installation of the ark there, become the mountain of Yahweh's inheritance. It is therefore a confirmation of the belief that Mount Zion's significance as Yahweh's dwelling-place was that it represented the land of Canaan, and thus gave entitlement to Israel to dwell there. This is in accord with the progress of thought in the Song of Miriam which associates Yahweh's sanctuary with the planting of Israel in the land of the Canaanites, and describes the anxiety that this causes to the inhabitants of Moab, Philistia and Edom.[1]

Furthermore we can hardly fail to connect the term 'mountain of Yahweh's inheritance' with the description of the land of Palestine as Yahweh's inheritance, and as belonging to him.[2] Thus it is a key term in what von Rad has called the 'cultic' tradition of Israel's right to possess the land of Canaan.[3] This, as von Rad has pointed out,[4] really has its origin in Canaanite religion, and is paralleled by the more genuinely Israelite 'historical' tradition, in which the land became Israel's by right of conquest. Both ideas are equally ancient, and the 'cultic' tradition of the divine ownership of the land dominates many of the Pentateuchal laws. The two ideas were not unmixed, and, if the claim for the dating of Ps. lxxviii and Exod. xv. 1–18 in the Davidic-Solomonic age can be accepted, then we are presented here, at the beginning of the monarchic period, with a welding of the two ideas into one. Yahweh's choice of Mount Zion, signifying his ownership of the land of Canaan, is shown to have come about through

---

[1] J. Schreiner, *Sion-Jerusalem*, p. 210, points out that this psalm expresses the belief that the conquest of Canaan finds its proper goal in the building of a temple.

[2] Cf. Lev. xxv. 23. For the meaning of 'inheritance' (Heb. *naḥᵃlâ*), and its application to Israel's land see F. Dreyfus, 'Le thème de l'héritage dans l'Ancien Testament', *RSPT* 42, 1958, pp. 3–49; G. von Rad, 'Verheissenes Land und Jahwes Land im Hexateuch', pp. 92ff.; F. Horst, 'Zwei Begriffe für Eigentum (Besitz) *naḥᵃlâ* und *ᵃḥuzzâ*', *Verbannung und Heimkehr*, ed. A. Kuschke, Tübingen, 1961, pp. 135ff.

[3] G. von Rad, 'Verheissenes Land und Jahwes Land im Hexateuch', pp. 92ff. On the concern of the cult with the land see also H. Wildberger, 'Israel und sein Land', *Ev. Th.* 16, 1956, pp. 411ff.

[4] G. von Rad, 'Verheissenes Land und Jahwes Land im Hexateuch', p. 95.

the conquest of that land by the Israelites who were redeemed out of Egypt.[1]

From this study of the origins of Yahweh worship in Jerusalem, it is clear that from its very beginnings this sanctuary possessed a unique importance for Israel. This was occasioned by its possession of the ark, together with a unique association with David, the founder of Judah's dynasty. Alongside of this, however, we have also been able to trace the adoption by Israel of certain mythological ideas which had far-reaching importance for the religious and political changes which took place in the reigns of David and Solomon. Such a borrowing from a Canaanite sanctuary, after Israel's occupation of it, was certainly not unique to Jerusalem, but by dint of the political circumstances of David's time and the subsequent history of the city, it came to be of very great significance. Apart from two incidental references to Shiloh, Jerusalem is the only earthly shrine of Israel to be described in the Old Testament as Yahweh's dwelling-place. Very probably other shrines were once so described, but on account of its pre-eminence, made absolute by the Deuteronomic rejection in the seventh century of any other cult site for Yahweh, Jerusalem had an unrivalled position among Yahweh's sanctuaries.

If our presentation of the origin and significance of Mount Zion as Yahweh's dwelling-place is accepted, then it can no longer be maintained that it became Yahweh's abode because the temple was built there. Rather the reverse was the case and the temple was built there because Mount Zion had become Yahweh's abode. This places all the greater interest in the oracle of Nathan, preserved in 2 Sam. vii, which expressed a divine refusal of David's intention to build a temple for Yahweh, and which provided the basis for the belief in the divine authority of David's dynasty to rule over Israel. The circumstances of Nathan's prophecy are that David, living in a comfortable house when his kingdom is at peace, is desirous of building a

---

[1] The cultic significance of the term 'inheritance' is also found in Ps. xlvii. 5 (EVV. 4). This psalm bears every evidence of belonging to the pre-exilic Autumn Festival of Judah:

> 'He has chosen for us our inheritance,
> The splendour of Jacob which he loves.'
> (Ps. xlvii. 5 (EVV. 4)).

The 'splendour' (Heb. gā'ôn) of Jacob probably refers to the Jerusalem temple, thus connecting Yahweh's inheritance with Mount Zion and its temple. J. Schreiner, *Sion-Jerusalem*, p. 198, interprets 'splendour' here of the land of Canaan, but adds that it is especially applicable to Jerusalem and its temple. In Ps. lxxix. 1 the 'inheritance' is closely related to the temple, if it is not actually identified with it. Cf. also A. Caquot, 'Le psaume 47 et la royauté de Yahwé', *RHPR* 39, 1959, p. 318, who interprets 'inheritance' in Ps. xlvii. 5 as referring to the land of Canaan, and regards 'splendour' as a description of Jerusalem.

permanent resting-place for Yahweh (i.e. the ark). During the night Nathan is instructed to tell David that Yahweh does not want such a building, since he prefers a tent, but that Yahweh will build a house (i.e. dynasty) for David:

> 'Go and tell my servant David, "Thus says Yahweh; would you build me a house to dwell in? I have not dwelt in a house since the day I brought up the people of Israel from Egypt to this day, but I have been moving about in a tent and a tabernacle. In all the places that I went with all the people of Israel, did I speak a word with any of the judges[1] of Israel, whom I commanded to shepherd my people Israel, saying, why have you not built me a house of cedar?" '
>
> 'Moreover Yahweh declares to you that Yahweh will make you a house.'

(2 Sam. vii. 5-7, 11)

The meaning of the oracle[2] is quite clear, and its genuine historical basis is acknowledged by most scholars.[3] The real uncertainty exists, not as to whether or not Nathan actually did reject David's proposal for a temple, but as to why he did so. On what grounds was a temple incompatible with the worship of Yahweh, so that he preferred a tent? Such a rejection is especially difficult to understand in view of the fact that David's successor, Solomon, did build a most magnificent temple for Yahweh. That this was felt to be a problem is shown by the fact that an interpolator has introduced in verse 13a a promise that David's son will build a temple. This cannot belong to the original prophecy which rejects altogether the idea of a temple for Yahweh.[4] It is very improbable that any later editor would have introduced the idea that Nathan rejected the temple, if such were not present already in the historical tradition of David's reign. Although later

---

[1] Reading with the parallel in 1 Chron. xvii. 6. The Hebrew here has 'tribes'.

[2] Most scholars find the original form of Nathan's prophecy in verses 1-7, 11b, 16, 18-21, 25-29. Various additions have been added to this, notably that of verse 13a, which alters the whole import of the prophecy. So. L. Rost, *Die Überlieferung von der Thronnachfolge Davids* (BWANT II, 6), Stuttgart, 1926, pp. 47ff.; M. Noth, *Überlieferungsgeschichtliche Studien*, rep. Wiesbaden, 1957, pp. 64ff.; 'David und Israel in 2 Sam. 7', *Ges. Stud. zum A.T.*,[2] pp. 334-345, and E. Kutsch, 'Die Dynastie von Gottes Gnaden. Probleme der Nathanweissagung in 2 Sam. 7', *ZThK* 58, 1961, pp. 137-153. Rost finds a primary kernel of the oracle in verses 11b and 16, but Kutsch limits this to 11b only.

[3] So M. Noth, H. J. Kraus, J. Lindblom, J. Schreiner, M. Simon, R. de Vaux, S. Amsler.

[4] S. Mowinckel, 'Natanforjettelsen 2 Sam. kap. 7', *SEÅ* 12, 1948, pp. 204-213, finds in verse 13 the key to the whole prophecy. He regards it as an aetiological legend explaining why Solomon and not David built the temple. This is unconvincing and has not been generally accepted. Mowinckel rules out the possibility that opposition to the temple existed in early Israel, and regards the chapter as a late prose form of the acclaim of David's election in the cult-hymns (Pss. lxxviii, cxxxii).

ages did, in some voices at least, come to regard the temple in a critical light,[1] there was also a strong tendency, as the Chronicler makes plain, to heighten David's place as the cult-founder of Jerusalem. The Deuteronomists did not reject the temple outright, but simply re-interpreted it. It is more likely that we are here dealing with a contemporary viewpoint, than that of a later editor, who has expressed his conviction in a way that fitted ill with the historical facts. We cannot then resort to the supposition that a later hand has been at work, expanding Nathan's oracle to make it express a later theological viewpoint opposed to temples as such. The probability is that this prophecy presents a contemporary attitude, which did in fact influence David's decision regarding a temple.[2] Our concern is therefore to find out the background to such a rejection.

There are several grounds that give cause for careful consideration as to what underlies Nathan's opposition to the building of a temple. We have already seen that in fact a temple of some kind had existed at Shiloh, and unless its destruction by the Philistines came to be interpreted as a judgment for its erection, it is hard to see what objection could have arisen in David's time, which did not already exist then. In this regard Nathan's prophecy is not strictly true, since Yahweh had dwelt in a house in the period between the exodus and David's accession to the kingship. Further it is certain also that David himself secured the site on which the temple was built,[3] whilst the Chronicler, whose record is admittedly very idealized at this point, claims that David made all the preparations necessary for the building of a temple.[4] Solomon subsequently did build one, so that the opposition to such a building cannot have been so categorical that it was not quickly overruled. There has been no lack of suggestions as to the possible reasons that might have led to Nathan's prophetic rejection of David's proposal to build a temple.[5] Briefly they might be summarized under three main headings: (1) Israel's 'nomadic ideal' led to a disapproval of a permanent shrine for the ark.[6] (2) Reverence for the conditions of the old amphictyony, with its tent sanctuary, led to opposition for a building which was fundamentally

---

[1] Isa. lxvi. 1ff.; Acts vii. 48ff.
[2] S. Herrmann, 'Die Königsnovelle in Ägypten und in Israel. Ein Beitrag zur Gattungsgeschichte in den Geschichtsbüchern des A.T.', *WZ* Leipzig, 3, 1953/4, pp. 57ff., has sought to relate the form of the oracle to that of the Egyptian *Königsnovelle*, and defends an early date for the prophecy (p. 61).
[3] 2 Sam. xxiv. 15ff.
[4] 1 Chron. xxii. 1ff.
[5] Cf. the excellent summary in J. Schreiner, *Sion-Jerusalem*, pp. 8off.
[6] Cf. J. W. Flight, 'The Nomadic Idea and Ideal in the Old Testament', *JBL* 43, 1923, p. 212.

Canaanite in its origin and ideology.[1] (3) The political tensions within Jerusalem created opposition to David's control of the city cult.[2] These ideas are not all mutually exclusive, but objections can be raised against all of them. First the 'nomadic ideal' of early Israel has been greatly overstressed, and nomadism never provided Israel with its norm of orthodoxy.[3] Secondly attachment to the Israelite amphictyony did not preclude a temple for the ark at Shiloh. Thirdly we know very little about the motives for political dissension in David's time, but, aside from the personal rivalries within David's family, the main controversy was apparently between Judean–Jerusalem elements and the older Israelite traditions of Ephraim and the north.

J. Schreiner seeks a solution to the difficulty by suggesting that Nathan's oracle does not express an absolute rejection of a temple, but merely a qualitative rejection of a house 'to dwell in'.[4] Yahweh is free to manifest his presence where he wills, and cannot be made to dwell in an earthly building. Thus it is not a temple that is rejected but only the idea of Yahweh's dwelling in one. The oracle therefore explains how a temple should be understood. We may object against this, however, that in fact the oracle does reject a temple, on the grounds that Yahweh prefers a tent. If it were merely the idea of Yahweh's dwelling in a shrine that was opposed, then the tent ought also to have been rejected, since this was connected with Yahweh's dwelling in Israel. Nathan's oracle makes an explicit contrast between a tent and a house of cedar. Nevertheless it is valuable to realize that the oracle has been presented in such a way as to assert the divine sovereignty and freedom, by showing that, whilst David cannot do anything for Yahweh, Yahweh can build a house for David. The nega-

---

[1] Cf. R. de Vaux, *Ancient Israel*, pp. 329f.

[2] G. W. Ahlström, 'Der Prophet Nathan und der Tempelbau', *VT* 11, 1961, pp. 120ff., argues that Nathan was not a reactionary Yahwist, but a Jebusite, who opposed the erection of a temple which would have rivalled the older El-'Elyon temple of the Jebusites. Nathan was in support of Solomon's accession to the throne (1 Kings i. 8ff.), which represented a victory for the 'Jebusite' party. Thus in Solomon's time any necessity to oppose the building of a temple disappeared. Cf. also his *Psalm 89. Eine Liturgie aus dem Ritual des leidenden Königs*, Lund, 1959, pp. 184f.
    A Caquot, 'La prophétie de Nathan et ses échos lyriques', *Bonn Congress Volume* (SVT IX), Leiden 1963, p. 214, argues simply that David did not build the temple because the time was not ripe for it.

[3] The use of the word 'tent' (Heb. *miškān*) in 2 Sam. vii. 6 does not necessarily imply unsettled, desert conditions, since it was in common use in Canaanite society to describe a sanctuary. Cf. W. Schmidt, '*Miškān* als Ausdruck Jerusalemer Kultsprache', *ZAW* 75, 1963, pp. 91f.

[4] J. Schreiner, *Sion-Jerusalem*, pp. 90ff. Schreiner connects this reserve regarding Yahweh's 'dwelling', with a distinction between the use of the verbs *šākan* and *yāšaḇ*. This distinction, however, does not seem to arise before the appearance of the Deuteronomic literature.

tive response to David's proposal sets in greater contrast the positive aspect, which is the divine power to affirm and maintain the Davidic dynasty.

Whatever the motive behind Nathan's rejection of the temple may have been, it must surely have been a combination of religious and political considerations, in which the tent of the old amphictyony was contrasted with the proposed temple of the Davidic state. May a solution to the question not be found along these lines? Nathan's oracle provides the basis of the claim of the Davidic dynasty to rule Israel, and thus it amounts to a divine authorization for the form of a monarchic government which was established in the new Israelite empire. Israel changed from being a tribal federation to a state with firm territorial claims. We have already seen that, with the conquest of Jerusalem, and the effort to establish it as the capital of the Israelite state, Mount Zion had already come to be claimed as Yahweh's dwelling-place. This was of immense importance in claiming divine sanction for the new political situation, and was exemplified by the setting of the ark there, and by the adoption of a mythological understanding of Mount Zion as a divine abode. To have built a temple was quite naturally the next step, which would have affirmed beyond any question, the divine foundation of the state and the sacred authority of the Davidic dynasty.[1] King and temple belonged together as the pillars of state in Ancient Near Eastern society.[2] That this was also true of Israel is shown by the parallel mention of Yahweh's choice of David and Mount Zion in Psalms lxxviii and cxxxii.[3] Divine kingship and earthly kingship were not exclusive, but complementary, ideas in the Ancient Near East, and the earthly throne was linked to the divine throne from whence it derived its authority. It was the inevitable step that David should have sought to secure his throne by the erection of a temple to the God who was believed to have established his right to rule.[4] Such a divinely authorized state and monarchy represented a far-reaching change in Israel's religious and political thinking, for it was virtually a claim to a feudal structure for society, in which the king held an especially exalted place under Yahweh. It would have been most surprising if such a

---

[1] Cf. J. Schreiner, *Sion-Jerusalem*, p. 137, who states that the building of a temple was the inevitable consequence of David's claim to have founded an empire.
[2] Cf. K. Möhlenbrink, *Der Tempel Salomos*, pp. 48ff., 79.
[3] Cf. H. J. Kraus, *Die Königsherrschaft Gottes im Alten Testament*, Tübingen, 1951, p. 37; *Psalmen*, II, pp. 881ff.; *Gottesdienst in Israel²*, pp. 214ff.; K. Koch, 'Zur Geschichte der Erwählungsvorstellung in Israel', p. 211; J. Schreiner, *Sion-Jerusalem*, pp. 103ff.; A. Caquot, 'La prophétie de Nathan et ses échos lyriques', p. 215.
[4] Cf. Ps. ii. 6; 1 Kings, viii. 15ff.

great change had not called forth opposition and revolt. Nathan's oracle, therefore, may be interpreted as a check upon David's plan to build a temple, with its political as well as religious implications, in the name of the old Yahweh amphictyony, with its central focus in the sacred tent and the ark.

There are two objections which this view has to counter. (1) Why was no opposition raised to the placing of the ark in the temple in Shiloh? An answer may be found in the fact that the temple at Shiloh was never linked with a political claim to kingship, as was the case in Jerusalem, and was probably of more local significance. Further the temple at Shiloh continued to be called the 'tent of meeting',[1] which may well reflect a strong aversion to regarding it as a temple after the Canaanite pattern.[2] (2) David himself secured the site on which the temple was built, and Solomon carried out his father's intention. How is this consistent with David's acquiescence in Nathan's rejection of a temple for Yahweh? This must be understood in the light of the political situation then existing. Because of the political unrest of David's reign, especially from the northern tribes, with their older concept of Israel, David had to make some concessions. Not to build a temple was one of them. With the quelling of the revolts, however, David's position became very much more secure, and for the remainder of his reign and throughout that of Solomon, no formidable opposition could be raised.[3] In this situation no obstacle existed to the building of a temple. It is probable that a closely similar situation existed over the administration of Israel, for David's census,[4] undoubtedly for administrative and tax purposes, was regarded by the majority of the population as a sin against Yahweh, and its findings were therefore probably little used by the king. No effective opposition could be raised, however, against Solomon's using the census reports for his administrative reorganization of the state.

Nathan's oracle, therefore, explains why the founder of the dynasty did not also build the temple which honoured Yahweh's choice of David and Jerusalem. That this was considered a problem is shown by other texts, which have an aetiological colouring, and which explain the same situation.[5]

In spite of religious and political opposition, David was responsible for the securing of the site on which the temple was later built, as the

---

[1] 1 Sam. ii. 22; cf. Ps. lxxviii. 60.
[2] Cf. J. Schreiner, *Sion-Jerusalem*, p. 93 note.
[3] Cf. A. Alt, 'Das Königtum in den Reichen Israel und Juda', *KSGVI*, II, p. 121.
[4] 2 Sam. xxiv. 1ff.
[5] 1 Kings v. 17 (EVV. 3); 1 Chron. xxii. 7–10; xxviii. 2–7.

story of the purchase of the threshing-floor of Araunah, the Jebusite, explains how this site came to be acquired.[1] Whether David himself intended it to be the site of the temple, or merely of his altar, is uncertain.

The narrative of 2 Sam. xxiv is of composite literary form,[2] and it provides a divine authorization for David's altar set up in Jerusalem. The occasion is that of a plague, which struck Israel, and which was popularly associated with David's census of the people, being regarded as a punishment by Yahweh for this act. When the plague ceased David marked his contrition by building an altar to Yahweh. The historicity of this incident can hardly be doubted, presenting as it does so much of the contemporary religious outlook, and we may follow the Chronicler's interpretation that this was also the site of Solomon's temple. We can hardly avoid the suggestion, however, that before David's time the site had been set aside by the Jebusites as sacred. The probability is that this is in fact the reason for the introduction of Araunah into the story, and that the old Jebusite *hieros logos* of the site has been woven into the account of David's altar.[3] Araunah, on this interpretation, was not a contemporary of David's, but an earlier Jebusite, who had been responsible for making the place into a sacred site. This was through the appearance there of an angel, behind whom there probably lies a Canaanite god.[4] Thus Araunah could not have been an important figure in Jerusalem in David's time.[5] Araunah's threshing-floor, already a sacred site, was chosen and purchased by David for his altar. Threshing-floors as flat open spaces, were quite convenient for religious assemblies, especially during harvest time, when they may well have been the scenes of the thanksgiving and rejoicing. In particular we most naturally expect that the great rock, still revered in the Moslem shrine there, would have had some profound religious significance for the Jebusites. Most probably it was a primitive rock-altar, and continued to be used as such, but H. Schmidt[6] thought that it was a symbol of

---

[1] 2 Sam. xxiv. 15ff.; cf. 1 Chron. xxii. 1; 2 Chron. iii. 1.

[2] W. Fuss, '2 Sam. xxiv', *ZAW* 74, 1962, pp. 145ff.

[3] W. Fuss, op. cit., pp. 162ff.

[4] It is tempting to identify this deity as El-'Elyon (so H. Schmidt, *Der heiligen Felsen*, 1933, pp. 84, 86—quoted by Herbert Schmid, 'Jahwe und die Kulttraditionen von Jerusalem', p. 175), but there may have been other gods worshipped in Jerusalem in Jebusite times, so that no firm probability can be established.

[5] *Contra* S. Yeivin, 'Social, Religious and Cultural Trends in Jerusalem under the Davidic Dynasty', *VT* 3, 1953, pp. 149ff. Yeivin sees in Araunah the last Jebusite king. Cf. also G. W. Ahlström, 'Der Prophet Nathan und der Tempelbau', pp. 117f.

[6] H. Schmidt, 'Kerubenthron und Lade', p. 132 note. Schmidt considered the rock to have been the original footstool of Yahweh.

a divine presence and was eventually built into the inner sanctuary, the *d^ebîr*, of Solomon's temple. The Old Testament is strangely silent about this rock and its interpretation in Yahwism. It later came to be regarded in Jewish legend as the foundation stone of the world, and so, as the very first part of the world to be created, it was the navel or centre, of the earth, comparable to the Greek *omphalos*. [1]

The temple that Solomon built for Yahweh after David's death was constructed with the aid of Phoenician architects and craftsmen. As we have already shown, this was in line with the strong Canaanite influence that lay behind the project from the start. It would be utterly wrong, however, to regard it on this account as purely syncretistic and un-Israelite. It did in many ways serve to confirm in Israel ideas and practices that had been borrowed from Canaan, yet none the less it was and remained a thoroughly Israelite shrine. However much its outward furniture resembled that of its Canaanite–Phoenician prototypes, the God in whose honour all was built, and to whom alone worship might be rendered within its walls, was Yahweh, the God of Israel.

[1] For possible references to the significance of this rock in the Old Testament see H. W. Hertzberg, 'Der heilige Fels und das Alte Testament', *Beiträge zur Traditionsgeschichte und Theologie des A.T.*, Göttingen, 1962, pp. 45–53. For the Jewish legends surrounding the rock see R. Patai, *Man and Temple*, London, 1947, pp. 85ff.

CHAPTER V

THE PRESENCE OF GOD IN ISRAEL'S WORSHIP

WE recall that before the institution of the monarchy in Israel the main conception of Yahweh's presence with his people was of a re-enactment of his theophany, as it had once occurred at Sinai, so that Yahweh's coming to his people was his coming to them from this mountain. In accord with this the most important event in the worship of the tribes was their covenant celebration, which renewed and relived the events which had inaugurated the covenant on Mount Sinai. Thus the moment when Yahweh was most truly known to be in Israel's midst was the moment when the tribes pledged themselves to be loyal to him, and to one another. A permanent symbol of this divine theophany was the holy ark, which belonged to the sacred institutions of the covenant. When Yahweh came to be with his people he was believed to appear over the ark.[1] The use of this ark in military undertakings, connected with the Holy War, signified Yahweh's leadership of the armies of his people.[2] The tension that is apparent to us between the idea of a temporary presence in a theophany, and a permanent presence through a sacred cult-object, does not seem to have been felt in Israel.[3] Yahweh came to his people, and his presence was thought of in terms of a 'coming' to them in an epiphany, yet the symbols which were associated with this were filled with the divine power and holiness, so that they were a permanent witness to Yahweh's presence in Israel. The building of the temple seems not to have brought about any change in this feature of the cult. The temple was Yahweh's dwelling-place, yet it was so because in its worship he 'came' to manifest his presence there.[4] So, in effect, the

---

[1] Cf. the ancient rubric associated with the ark in Num. x. 35–36 (JE).
[2] Cf. 1 Sam. iv. 3–9.
[3] Cf. S. Mowinckel, *Psalmenstudien II*, p. 61; R. de Vaux, 'Arche d'alliance et tente de réunion', pp. 69f.
[4] The attempt of G. von Rad to distinguish between a 'dwelling-temple' and a 'theophany-temple' (*Old Testament Theology*, I, p. 237), following a suggestion of W. Andrae's (*Das Gotteshaus und die Urformen des Bauens im Alten Orient*, Berlin, 1930, pp. 14ff.—unavailable to me), and to conclude that the Solomonic temple was primarily a 'dwelling-temple' is unacceptable. K. Möhlenbrink points out that in the Ancient Near East all temples were both 'dwelling-temples' and 'theophany-temples', however illogical this may appear (K. Möhlenbrink, *Der Tempel Salomos*, pp. 134ff.). R. Hentschke, *Die Stellung der vorexilischen Schriftpropheten zum*

'permanent' dwelling of Yahweh in the temple was justified and explained on the basis of his appearing there in a theophany. In this way the tendency to regard Yahweh's presence in the temple as fixed and static can only be regarded as a loss of the true significance of the temple. In its manifestation in the cult, Yahweh's presence was always an active coming to his people, as he had come to rescue them out of Egypt to lead them into their own land. There is no doubt that many features of a divine epiphany were borrowed by Israel from the Canaanite cult, since here also the gods were thought to manifest themselves in this way,[1] but the Sinai-covenant tradition became an important interpretative factor.

The building of the temple by Solomon carried with it far-reaching changes in the nature and character of Israel's worship. It brought with it a new kind of ideology, and its magnificence made possible a much greater elaboration of the cultus and ritual. The temple served, more than anything else could possibly have done, to gain for the distinctive theology of Jerusalem and of the Davidic covenant a firm and enduring place in Israel's religion.

The temple itself was constructed in three major parts; the *'ûlām*, or porch; the *hêkāl*, or main hall, and the *d^ebîr*, or inner sanctuary. The *d^ebîr* is of most interest for our study for it was here that the deity was considered to dwell. In Assyrian and Phoenician temples it was here that the image, representing the earthly presence of the god, would be found. Israel possessed no image of Yahweh, and attempts to find traces of the existence of such images have failed to carry conviction because of the paucity of evidence.[2] We have no

---

[1] Cf. F. Schnutenhaus, 'Das Kommen und Erscheinen Gottes im Alten Testament', *ZAW* 76, 1964, p. 4.

[2] Cf. H. Th. Obbink, 'Jahwebilder', *ZAW* 47, 1929, pp. 264, 267ff.; K. H. Bernhardt, *Gott und Bild*, pp. 110ff., 154ff. For the opposite view see J. Morgenstern, *The Ark, the Ephod and 'the Tent of Meeting'*, Cincinnati, 1945, pp. 4 note and 107 note. Morgenstern thought of a golden image of Yahweh set up in the inner shrine of the temple until it was removed during the reform in the reign of Asa (899 B.C.). The reflection of the sun upon this image during the spring and autumn equinoxes, especially the latter (New Year's Day), was the glory of Yahweh. Morgenstern has subsequently modified this view, and argues now that only an empty throne stood in the *d^ebîr* of the temple. 'The King-God among the Western Semites and the Meaning of Epiphanes', *VT* 10, 1960, p. 185.

Kultus (BZAW 75), Berlin, 1957, pp. 47ff., argues that Israel's conception of Yahweh's 'coming' to his people in the cult contrasted with the idea of his permanent 'dwelling' at the sanctuary, which was essentially a Canaanite borrowing. This is too neat and modern a line of demarcation between cultic traditions of great complexity. It is clear that both in the Canaanite as well as the Israelite cult, ideas of the divine 'dwelling' and 'epiphany' were present.

certain reason to dispute the claim of the Old Testament that from Mosaic times Isreal's faith in Yahweh prohibited any material representation of him.

In the *d^ebîr* of the temple the ark was set, being overshadowed by the wings of the two carved cherubim.[1] These cherubim were fashioned on the basis of the symbolism that had been associated with Yahweh in the temple of Shiloh. Their theological relevance is that they point to the celestial power and mobility of Yahweh, so that there is no reason for thinking of him as though he were confined to the temple.

The furnishings of the temple were full of cosmic symbolism, as was in effect true also for the temple as a whole.[2] The very conception of such a building was founded on the belief that a correspondence existed between the earthly and the heavenly worlds.[3] Yahweh's house in Jerusalem was intended to be a copy, or symbol, of the cosmic 'house' where he had his abode. In this way the particular form of the Jerusalem cult emphasized the power of Yahweh over the natural order.

Various features of the temple furnishings have been singled out, and have been thought to show features of such a symbolism.[4] The great bronze sea[5] was symbolic of the Apsu, the vast primeval ocean. It has been suggested that the four groups of oxen which supported it were tokens of the four seasons of the year. The altar of burnt-offering seems to reflect Mesopotamian cosmic ideas.[6] The decoration of the temple with palm trees and cherubim, as well as the ornamental pomegranates on the masonry all suggest the fertility of the earth, or more exactly, of the paradise garden where Yahweh dwelt.

The meaning and function of the free standing pillars set up in the front of the porch has been a matter of debate. They have been claimed

---

[1] I Kings vi. 23–28.

[2] Cf. G. E. Wright, 'The Temple in Palestine-Syria', *BA* 7, 1944, p. 72, and *Biblical Archaeology*, London, 1957, p. 144. See also G. Westphal, *Jahwes Wohnstätten*, p. 208.

[3] Cf. G. B. Gray, *Sacrifice in the Old Testament*, Oxford, 1925, pp. 149ff. Gray sought to trace a distinction in the Old Testament between the idea of the temple as a copy of a temple in heaven, and as a copy of heaven itself.

[4] Cf. R. Patai, *Man and Temple*, pp. 105ff.; W. F. Albright, *Archaeology and the Religion of Israel*[3], Baltimore, 1953, pp. 148ff.; G. B. Gray, *Sacrifice in the O.T.*, p. 152; A. Parrot, *The Temple of Jerusalem* (Studies in Biblical Archaeology, No. 5), London, 1957, pp. 45ff.; E. L. Ehrlich, *Kultsymbolik im Alten Testament und im nachbiblischen Judentum*, Stuttgart, 1959, pp. 30f.; E. Burrows, 'Some Cosmological Patterns in Babylonian Religion', *The Labyrinth*, ed. S. H. Hooke, London, 1935, pp. 59ff.; J. Schreiner, *Sion-Jerusalem*, pp. 144ff.

[5] I Kings vii. 23–26.

[6] W. F. Albright, 'The Babylonian Temple-Tower and the Altar of Burnt-Offering', *JBL* 39, 1920, pp. 137–142.

as sacred pillars (Heb. *maṣṣēḇôṯ*)[1], or as symbols of the cosmic pillars which formed a gateway for the sun to pass through every morning,[2] or even as giant fire altars, perhaps related to solar imagery.[3] The inscriptions which they bore must certainly be connected with royal dynastic oracles,[4] and their primary symbolic purpose seems to have been related to the ideas of permanence and durability.[5]

The very shape of the temple has been thought to have a special significance,[6] as has also its orientation.[7] Several scholars have sought to relate the temple and its furnishings to solar imagery.[8] This has been thought to find support from the oracle which is said to have been given at the dedication of the temple:[9]

> 'Yahweh has set the sun in the heavens,[10]
> But has said that he would dwell in thick darkness.
> I have built thee an exalted house;
> A place for thee to dwell in forever.'
>
> (1 Kings viii. 12–13)

Further support may be found in the mention of the sun-chariots in 2 Kings xxiii. 11,[11] and of the idolatrous worship of the elders reported in Ezek. viii. 16–18. However, the oracle at the dedication of the temple does not identify Yahweh with the sun, but rather contrasts him with it.

---

[1] K. Möhlenbrink, *Der Tempel Salomos*, p. 114.

[2] J. Morgenstern, 'The King-God among the Western Semites', p. 149.

[3] W. F. Albright, *Archaeology and the Religion of Israel*[3], pp. 144ff.; cf. W. R. Smith, *The Religion of the Semites*[2], London, 1914, pp. 487ff.

[4] R. B. Y. Scott, 'The Pillars Jachin and Boaz', *JBL* 58, 1939, pp. 143–149; 'Jachin and Boaz', *IDB*, II, pp. 780a–781a.

[5] Cf. W. Kornfeld, 'Der Symbolismus der Tempelsäulen', *ZAW* 74, 1962, pp. 50–57, who compares the Egyptian Djed pillar.

[6] Cf. H. Gressmann, *The Tower of Babel*, p. 59, who thought the cuboid shape of the inner sanctuary was intended as a miniature representation of heaven. Cf. Rev. xxi. 10ff.

[7] K. Möhlenbrink, *Der Tempel Salomos*, pp. 79ff., regarded the temple as oriented towards the west, which was the direction from which the prevailing wind blew, and connected this with his claim that the cherubim were wind-spirits.

[8] F. J. Hollis, 'The Sun-Cult and the Temple at Jerusalem', *Myth and Ritual*, ed. S. H. Hooke, Oxford, 1933, pp. 87–110, and also in *The Archaeology of Herod's Temple*, London, 1934, pp. 132ff.; H. G. May, 'Some Aspects of Solar Worship in Jerusalem', *ZAW* 55, 1937, pp. 269–281; 'The Departure of the Glory of Yahweh', *JBL* 56, 1937, pp. 309–321; J. Morgenstern, 'The Gates of Righteousness', *HUCA* 6, 1929, pp. 17ff., 31ff., and also 'The King-God among the Western Semites', pp. 165f., 176ff. Cf. also the suggestion of A. R. Johnson, 'The Rôle of the King in the Jerusalem Cultus', pp. 83, 96, 100, that El-'Elyon was a solar deity.

[9] F. J. Hollis, 'The Sun-Cult and the Temple at Jerusalem', pp. 90ff., suggested that this oracle was occasioned by the eclipse of the sun in 948 B.C. This seems improbable.

[10] Following some LXX manuscripts.

[11] Cf. 2 Kings ii. 11.

Not all of these supposed symbolic references of features of the temple are convincing, but the essential claim that the temple and its furnishings did possess a cosmic, or naturalistic, symbolism must be upheld.[1] Such features were designed to stress the divine power over the created order, and to establish the temple as a source of blessing for the land and people of Israel. The underlying idea was that the temple was a microcosm of the macrocosm,[2] so that the building gave visual expression to the belief in Yahweh's dominion over the world and all natural forces. We need not suppose that every Israelite worshipper was conscious of this underlying mythological explanation of the sanctuary, but we do claim that those who worshipped there believed that the temple was a supernatural source of power, and that this power was very much concerned with the normal welfare of the people, with its herds and crops. From the temple the divine blessing and 'life' flowed out to Israel. The symbolism of the sanctuary was related to the meaning and function of the cult, so that the dramatic rituals through which Israel approached its God, had as their essential setting appropriate representations of the natural order. Primitive cult did not make a distinction between 'spiritual' and 'worldly', and the blessings that it was thought to bring were closely tied to the welfare and prosperity of men.[3] Thus the temple building, in which the cultic rites took place, signified the cosmic rule of the God who was worshipped there. This aspect of the temple-theology deserves particular attention when we are considering the ideas of Yahweh's presence to which the temple bears witness; far from conveying the belief that Yahweh was an earth-bound God, tied to his abode in Jerusalem, the whole outlook and purpose of the temple was to stress his creative and universal action. This is well attested in the psalms which were used in the temple, many of which derive from the pre-exilic period, and some of which may be placed quite early in the history of the Solomonic temple.

In the light of all that we have said about the meaning and purpose of the temple, it becomes clear that it is erroneous to regard it simply as a private royal chapel, attached to the Solomonic palace in

[1] R. de Vaux, *Ancient Israel*, pp. 328f., denies that the symbolism of the temple had any conscious significance for Israel, and argues that it was simply a consequence of the employment of Phoenician craftsmen and architects. This cannot be conceded, since such symbolism is closely related to the veneration of a sacred mountain (Zion), and even to the very existence of a temple at all. Nevertheless we must not ignore the uniqueness of Israel's worship, and its cultic traditions which had other aims than merely material prosperity.

[2] G. E. Wright, 'The Temple in Palestine-Syria', p. 72, and *Biblical Archaeology*, p. 144.

[3] S. Mowinckel, *Religion und Kultus*, Göttingen, 1953, pp. 6off.

Jerusalem, and without any significance for lay Israelites.[1] Although the ruling monarch played a considerable part in the rites of the temple, and the latter had a particular significance for the Davidic dynasty, Solomon's temple was throughout intended as a state sanctuary for all Israel. It was no private chapel of the king any more than the king himself could have been termed a private individual in Ancient Israel. Both king and temple belonged together as sources of divine life and blessing for the nation.

We find in the Psalter firm evidence that the belief in Yahweh's earthly dwelling-place on Mount Zion did not preclude the idea that he was a God of the skies, whose true dwelling was in the heavens, but rather it presupposed it. The earthly abode was a counterpart of the heavenly abode of Yahweh. Thus we read:

> 'Yahweh is in his holy temple;
> Yahweh's throne is in heaven.'
> (Ps. xi. 4)

The temple referred to here is probably that on Mount Zion, not the temple in heaven, but in either case the psalm presupposes that the two share a mysterious identity. The one is the symbol and the counterpart of the other. Quite frequently we discover that Yahweh's dwelling in heaven, and his presence on Mount Zion are mentioned in the same psalm, without any consciousness of contradiction between the two. There is in fact little attempt throughout the Psalter to rationalize, or 'theologize', the inherent tension between the earthly and the heavenly, the immanent deity on earth and the transcendent in heaven. Thus we find in Psalm xiv.:

> 'Yahweh looks down from heaven upon mankind.'
> (Ps. xiv. 2)

which continues just a few verses later:

> 'O that Israel's salvation would come out of Zion.'
> (Ps. xiv. 7)[2]

It is impossible to maintain that this uniting of Yahweh's dwelling in heaven and his abode on Zion is merely a consequence of a conflation of two traditions in the post-exilic period, for both ideas

---

[1] The conception of the temple as a private royal chapel is firmly and convincingly rejected by H. Vincent, 'Le caractère du Temple salomonien', *Mélanges bibliques rédigés en l'honneur de André Robert*, Paris, 1957, pp. 137–148. Cf. also R. de Vaux, *Ancient Israel*, p. 320; H. J. Kraus, *Gottesdienst in Israel*[2], pp. 214ff., and J. Schreiner, *Sion-Jerusalem*, p. 141.

[2] Cf. also: Ps. xx. 3 and 7 (EVV. 2 and 6); Ps. lxxvi. 3 and 9 (EVV. 2 and 8); Ps. lxxx. 2 and 15 (EVV. 1 and 14).

appear so frequently throughout the Psalms, and both can be found in psalms of undoubted pre-exilic origin.

In the Jerusalem temple the major festival of the religious calendar was the Feast of Tabernacles, celebrated in the autumn, when the new year began.[1] Some aspects of this feast undoubtedly had their origin in a borrowing from the Jebusite El-'Elyon cult, but in its essential features it became thoroughly Israelite in character, declaring the kingship of Yahweh, and his rule over creation. It continued, in a new form, and with a more elaborate cult, the older covenant celebration, which had bound the tribes together before the introduction of the monarchy. Thus it combined a recollection of the founding of the covenant on Mount Sinai with a declaration of Yahweh's primal triumph in the creation of the world. Ideas of the creation and of the sacred history, which brought Israel into being, were thus woven together in a remarkable way. Yahweh's power in creation, therefore, was particularly related to his purpose in and for Israel, with the result that the whole festival looked to the future, and contained an element of prophetic promise. It was directed not merely towards the blessing of a new year, but towards securing a new world order when the divine gifts of righteousness and peace would be fully realized on earth.[2] As a result the declaration of Yahweh's

---

[1] The literature on this important subject is extensive. See P. Volz, *Das Neujahrsfest Jahwes (Laubhüttenfest)*, Tübingen, 1912; S. Mowinckel, *Psalmenstudien II: das Thronbesteigungsfest Jahwäs und der Ursprung der Eschatologie*, rep. Amsterdam, 1961; *The Psalms in Israel's Worship*, I, pp. 106ff. Mowinckel claims that this was a Festival of the Enthronement of Yahweh, comparable to the Babylonian Akitu Festival, but his more recent work pays more attention to the distinctive Israelite elements that it contained. See especially *The Psalms in Israel's Worship*, I, pp. 118f., 130, 139. This brings the interpretation more into line with that of A. Weiser, *The Psalms*, pp. 26ff.; and 'Zur Frage nach den Beziehungen der Psalmen zum Kult', pp. 309ff. Weiser argues that this festival was the Jerusalem form of the older covenant renewal celebration of the amphictyony. He maintains that under the monarchy the ancient Sinai-theophany tradition was retained in the Jerusalem temple, thus preserving a fundamental aspect of Mosaic Yahwism.

H. J. Kraus denies that this feast celebrated and proclaimed Yahweh's enthronement, and argues that it was a Royal Zion Festival, which recalled the bringing of the ark into Jerusalem and the founding of the Davidic dynasty. The idea of Yahweh's enthronement, Kraus claims, is a development from the preaching of Deutero-Isaiah. See *Die Königsherrschaft Gottes im Alten Testament*, Tübingen, 1951; *Psalmen*, I, pp. 197–205, 342–345, II, pp. 879–883; *Gottesdienst in Israel*[2], pp. 210ff.

For the festival cf. also H. Schmidt, *Die Thronfahrt Jahwes am Fest der Jahreswende im alten Israel*, Tübingen, 1927; A. R. Johnson, *Sacral Kingship in Ancient Israel*; J. Schreiner, *Sion-Jerusalem*, pp. 191ff., 210ff.; H. Ringgren, *The Faith of the Psalmists*, London, 1963, pp. xiiff.; E. Lipinski, 'Les psaumes de la royauté de Yahwé dans l'exégèse moderne', *Le Psautier. Ses origines. Ses problèmes littéraires. Son influence*. ed. R. de Langhe, Louvain, 1962, pp. 133–272; E. Kutsch, *Das Herbstfest in Israel*, Dissertation, Mainz, 1955, (cf. *ThLZ* 81, 1956, cols. 493–495).

[2] Cf. A. R. Johnson, *Sacral Kingship in Ancient Israel*, p. 54 note; S. Mowinckel, *The Psalms in Israel's Worship*, I, p. 151.

F

presence in Jerusalem was the basis of a hope of a transformed world, and his kingship was not only demonstrated in the natural order, but was closely related to his purpose in history.[1] From an early period, therefore, the Autumn Festival in Jerusalem contained a combination of mythological elements, deriving originally from Canaanite religion, together with ideas of Yahweh as the God of the exodus and of Mount Sinai.[2] In this festival the idea of Yahweh's theophany was still of his appearing from Mount Sinai,[3] although in course of time it seems that this idea gave way to that of his coming down direct from heaven.

A fundamental presupposition of this festival was that Yahweh himself, the heavenly king, was present in the sanctuary at Jerusalem. He came from his heavenly realm to appear in glory in the temple on Mount Zion from where he passed judgment on the unrighteous. This is vividly expressed in Ps. xcvi.

> 'Proclaim among the nations, "Yahweh reigns",
>   Surely the world is established, it shall never be moved;
>   He will judge the peoples with equity.
> Let the heavens be glad, and let the earth rejoice;
>   Let the sea roar, and all that fills it;
>   Let the field exult, and everything in it.
> Then shall the trees of the forest sing for joy
>   Before Yahweh, for he comes,
>   For he comes to judge the earth.
> He will judge the world with righteousness
>   And the peoples with his truth.'
>   (Ps. xcvi. 10–13)

The nature of the divine theophany is beautifully described in Psalm xcvii, where Yahweh appears clothed in the mysterious majesty of the storm clouds and wielding the lightning as the weapon of his righteousness:

> 'Yahweh reigns, let the earth rejoice;
>   Let the many coastlands be glad.
> Clouds and thick darkness are round about him;
>   Righteousness and justice are the foundation of his throne.
>
> Fire goes before him,
>   And burns up his adversaries round about.
> His lightnings illumine the world;
>   The earth sees and trembles.

---

[1] Exod. xv. 18.
[2] e.g. Ps. xcv. Cf. A. R. Johnson, *Sacral Kingship in Ancient Israel*, p. 61.
[3] Cf. Ps. lxviii. 8ff., 18 (EVV. 7ff. 17).

> The mountains melt like wax before Yahweh,
> Before the Lord of all the earth.'
>
> (Ps. xcvii. 1–5)

With the doctrine of Yahweh's presence in Jerusalem as the basis of the belief in his judgment of the world from there, must be coupled the belief that his presence was also the defence of the city and the guarantee of its inviolability. This doctrine came to great prominence in Isaiah's time, but it must antedate this prophet and probably goes back to the pre-Israelite inhabitants of the city.[1] It is found most dramatically in Pss. xlvi, xlviii and lxxvi. The main features are expressed in Ps. xlviii:

> 'Great is Yahweh and greatly to be praised,
>   In the city of our God.
> His holy mountain, beautiful in elevation,
>   Is the joy of all the earth.
> Mount Zion, the heights of Zaphon,
>   The city of the great King.
> Within her fortress God
>   Has shown himself a defence.
> For the kings of the earth assembled;
>   They advanced together.
> When they saw it, they were astounded,
>   They panicked, they fled.
> Trembling seized them,
>   Anguish like a woman in childbirth'.
>
> (Ps. xlviii. 2–7 (EVV. 1–6))

Thus deliverance comes from Zion[2] and Yahweh's presence in Jerusalem, which betokens judgment for the nations, is a guarantee of deliverance for his people. The righteous find blessing from Yahweh in his city. This is not limited to victory over hostile armies, but extends also to the bestowal of all blessing and fertility from the temple where Yahweh is to be found.[3] With this we must connect the belief in the fertilizing river which flowed through Zion to bless the land. It is mentioned in Ps. xlvi. 5 (EVV. 4);

> 'There is a river, whose streams make glad the city of God,
>   The holy abode of 'Elyon.'
>
> (Ps. xlvi. 5 (EVV. 4))

---

[1] On this particular aspect of the Jerusalem cult tradition see H. J. Kraus, *Psalmen*, I, pp. 342ff.; J. Schreiner, *Sion-Jerusalem*, pp. 223ff., and J. H. Hayes, 'The Tradition of Zion's Inviolability', *JBL* 82, 1963, pp. 419–426.

[2] Cf. also Pss. xiv. 7; xx. 3 (EVV. 2); liii. 7 (EVV. 6).

[3] Cf. Pss. xxiv. 5; lxv. 5 (EVV. 4); lxviii. 10–11 (EVV. 9–10); cxxviii. 5; cxxxii. 15; cxxxiii. 3; cxxxiv. 3.

This river may have been identified with the spring Gihon which played
a part in the Jerusalem festivals, but its real significance is to be found
in the mythological belief in the river which fructified the garden of
paradise, where God's dwelling was situated.[1] The idea of this river is
vitally related to the belief in the presence of God, for just as in paradise a life-giving river was thought to flow, so Jerusalem was looked upon
as a paradise on earth, a place where God's presence was to be found.

The doctrine of the presence of Yahweh in Jerusalem enjoyed
its greatest prominence in connection with the Autumn Festival,
but it cannot be restricted to it, as though it were only thought to be a
reality on that occasion. It was the conviction of his people that Yahweh was present at all of the festivals in Jerusalem, and all the worship
there was conducted in the belief that he was present to accept the
offerings of his people. It is probable, as A. Arens has argued,[2] that
the daily sacrifices came to be thought of as a renewal of the sacrifice
on Mount Sinai, so that all the daily worship was linked to the idea
of Yahweh's covenant with Israel. When this interpretation arose, however, we do not know. From David's own days there can be no question
that Jerusalem enjoyed a prestige and importance that surpassed that
of any other Yahweh sanctuary. This was a result of the combination
of circumstances which first led to the worship of Yahweh in Jerusalem. The prestige of David, the possession of the ark, as well as the
inheritance of the Jebusite El-'Elyon cultus, all combined to raise
Jerusalem above the level of other shrines.

Throughout the Psalter there is much evidence of the special
relationship between Yahweh and Mount Zion. It is Yahweh's holy
mountain,[3] and, as such, can be identified with Mount Zaphon.[4] The
unique position of Mount Zion, together with the temple, in Israelite
faith, gained for them both a special affection in the hearts of those who
were privileged to worship there. The loyal citizen of Judah could find
no higher honour than to approach God in the sanctuary:

'O God, thou art my God, I seek thee;
My soul thirsts for thee;

---

[1] Gen. ii. 10–14; Cf. Rev. xxii. 1–2. Mention of this river in Jerusalem, and of its
life-giving powers, is found in Ps. lxv. 10 (EVV. 9); Isa. xxxiii. 21; Joel iv. 18 (EVV.
iii. 18); Ezek. xlvii. and Zech. xiv. 8. H. J. Kraus, *Psalmen*, I, p. 344, suggests that
the 'river' in Jerusalem may be connected with the 'spring' which first fertilized
the created world, mentioned in Gen. ii. 6. For the translation of Hebrew *'ēḏ* as
'spring' (EVV. 'mist') see W. F. Albright, *Recent Discoveries in Bible Lands*, New
York, 1955, p. 66.

[2] A. Arens, *Die Psalmen im Gottesdienst des Alten Bundes*, Trier, 1959, pp. 111ff.

[3] Pss. ii. 6; iii. 5 (EVV. 4); xv. 1; xliii. 3; xlviii. 2 (EVV. 1); xcix. 9. Cf. 'Mountain
of Yahweh' Ps. xxiv. 3.

[4] Ps. xlviii. 3 (EVV. 2).

My flesh longs for thee.
As in a land that is dry, exhausted and waterless.
So I have seen thee in holy power,
Beholding thy power and thy glory.'
(Ps. lxiii. 2–3 (EVV. 1–2))

The blessings which this brought were not only, nor even mainly, of a mystical or spiritual nature, but encompassed the whole round of daily needs and requisites. For the ancient Israelite material and spiritual were inextricably interwoven aspects of life, and the worship of Yahweh was believed to bring with it the benefits that were sought by an agricultural people.

The special symbolism of Mount Zion, by which it represented the whole of Yahweh's land, and, in theory at least, the whole earth, gave an added significance to participation in the worship there. To worship in Yahweh's house was to participate in the outflow of divine blessing to Israel, and to the land on which Israel was privileged to dwell as Yahweh's 'sojourners'.[1] Those who worshipped in Yahweh's house knew that they would continue to share in the blessings of Yahweh towards Israel, and would thereby be enabled to dwell securely upon their land.[2] Therefore, it was a particular privilege to be sought after, to dwell (i.e. worship) in the temple, because this carried with it the benefit of continuing as a member of Yahweh's people on Yahweh's land:

'One thing have I asked of Yahweh,
    That will I seek after;
That I may dwell in the house of Yahweh
    All the days of my life;
To see the beauty of Yahweh,
    And to inquire in his temple.'
(Ps. xxvii. 4)

The assurance that such worship gave was of the continued experience of Yahweh's goodness and kindness:

'Only goodness and kindness,
    Will pursue me all the days of my life;

---

[1] Heb. *Gērîm*. Lev. xxv. 23; Ps. xxxix. 13 (EVV. 12). For the significance of this concept in Israel see K. L. Schmidt, 'Israels Stellung zu den Fremdlingen und Beisassen und Israels Wissen um seine Fremdling- und Beisassenschaft', *Judaica* I, 1945, pp. 269–296.

[2] Cf. Exod. xxxiv. 24 (J):
'For I will expel nations before you, and enlarge your borders; neither shall any man desire your land, when you go up to appear before Yahweh your God three times in the year.'
On this important feature of the temple and its worship see my article, 'Temple and Land: a Significant Aspect of Israel's Worship'. pp. 18ff.

> And I will dwell[1] in Yahweh's house,
> Throughout a long life.'
>
> (Ps. xxiii. 6)[2]

Because this worship entailed such a high privilege, it could not be granted lightly, or indiscriminately, but was limited to those who showed by their lives and conduct that they were loyal to the covenant of Yahweh:

> 'Who shall go up to the hill of Yahweh?
> And who shall stand in his holy place?
> He who has clean hands and a pure heart,
> Who does not take an oath by what is false,
> Nor swear to a lie.'
>
> (Ps. xxiv. 3–4)[3]

One of the priests, acting as 'door-keeper', was entrusted with the important task of declaring the conditions of entry into Yahweh's temple, so that no undesirable person should come into the presence of God, or be regarded as one of his covenant people. In practice such a function was largely an admonitory one, since the requirements demanded were hardly subject to investigation. Such 'entrance-*tôrôṯ*' were a part of a liturgical celebration for all who shared in the worship of the temple.[4] None the less the intention was urgent and real, in seeking to show that sinners would be banished from Yahweh's land:

> 'For thou art not a God who delights in wickedness;
> An evil person may not sojourn with thee.'
>
> (Ps. v. 5 (EVV. 4))

[1] Reading *weṣibtî* with most commentators.
[2] Cf. Pss. lxi. 5 (EVV. 4); lxv. 5 (EVV. 4); lxxxiv. 5 (EVV. 4), and perhaps also Pss. v. 5 (EVV. 4); xci. 1, 9. The language of Pss. xxiii. 6 and xxvii. 4 is not a 'sublime cult-mysticism', as von Rad has argued (' "Gerechtigkeit" und "Leben" in der Kultsprache der Psalmen', *Ges. Stud. zum. A.T.*, p. 241). Nor is it applicable only to the Levitical temple personnel (so H. Graetz, J. P. Peters, S. Mowinckel). It is relevant to every Israelite, who, by 'dwelling' in the temple for worship, was thus assured that he would continue to dwell in Yahweh's land. The point of connection is found in the symbolism of Mount Zion as representing Yahweh's land, and there is no need to resort to any other kind of symbolism as B. D. Eerdmans does ('Sojourn in the Tent of Jahu', OTS I, 1942, pp. 8ff.). Eerdmans suggested that an Israelite left a memorial pillar (Heb. *yaḏ*), cf. 2 Sam. xviii. 18, in the temple to represent his person.
[3] Cf. Ps. xv.
[4] For the form and purpose of the entrance-liturgies see S. Mowinckel, *Psalmenstudien V*, pp. 57ff., 187ff.; *The Psalms in Israel's Worship*, I, pp. 177ff.; Le Décalogue, pp. 141ff.; K. Galling, 'Der Beichtspiegel. Eine gattungsgeschichtliche Studie', *ZAW* 47, 1929, pp. 125–130; K. Koch, 'Tempeleinlassliturgien und Dekaloge', *Studien zur Theologie der alttestamentlichen Überlieferungen*, ed. R. Rendtorff and K. Koch, Neukirchen, 1961, pp. 45–60. J. L. Koole ('Psalm 15—

The righteous Israelite, on the other hand, knew that in Yahweh's house there was a 'fountain of life' and a 'river of delights'. Through his temple Yahweh blessed his land and his people with a wealth of richness, comprising both material and spiritual benefits:

'How precious is thy kindness, O God!
  The children of men take refuge in the shadow of thy wings.
They feast on the abundance of thy house,
  And thou givest them drink from the river of thy delights.
For with thee is the fountain of life;
  In thy light do we see light.'

                    (Ps. xxxvi. 8–10 (EVV. 7–9))

'Blessed is he whom thou dost choose and bring near,
  To dwell in thy courts!
We shall be satisfied with the goodness of thy house,
  Thy holy temple!'

                    (Ps. lxv. 5 (EVV. 4))

All, therefore, who worshipped in Yahweh's temple experienced the benefit of living in his land, so that they could even be said to be 'planted' in Yahweh's house:

          'The righteous shall flourish like a palm tree;
            Like a cedar in Lebanon he shall grow.
          Those who are planted in Yahweh's house
            Shall flourish in the courts of our God.
          They will still be fruitful in old age;
            Luxuriant and fresh shall they be.'
                    (Ps. xcii. 13–15 (EVV. 12–14))

The worship of the temple was centred upon the belief that during its ceremonies Yahweh himself was present, and the benefits that such worship conferred were not simply of a spiritual, or mystical, nature. There seems in fact to be very little evidence of a purely mystical 'dwelling' with Yahweh. The blessings that the Israelite sought were of a practical, as well as a spiritual, kind. Especially he desired fertility in his fields and herds, with deliverance from pesti-

---

ein königliche Einzugsliturgie?', OTS XIII, Leiden, 1963, pp. 98–111) has argued that Psalm xv was not an entrance liturgy for ordinary worshippers, but was a liturgy used in the royal accession to the throne. Many of Koole's objections to the interpretation as a temple entrance-liturgy disappear in the light of the above arguments, whilst the application to the king introduces many difficulties.

lence and war, and all that threatened the enjoyment and security of his land. It was to these ends especially that the temple cult was directed, and the presence of Yahweh on his holy mountain was thought to be a firm assurance that his goodness and kindness would continue to be with Israel.

We can discern in this relationship between the cult of the temple and the life of Israel in its broader aspects, that participation in such worship came to be regarded as vital for every true Israelite. The cult, therefore, especially in its most elaborate expression in the Jerusalem temple, served as a unifying influence within the nation, creating a sense of nationhood and oneness, which, without it, would have been lacking.[1] For the individual Israelite the true expression of his faith, and the badge of his membership of the community of Israel, was to enjoy the privilege of sharing in its corporate worship. His faith was learnt in the temple, and his loyalty to it was shown by his attendance at the festivals. To have neglected his obligations to do this would have been tantamount to a rejection of Yahweh as his God.

The entire ideology of the Jerusalem temple centred in the belief that, as his chosen dwelling-place, Yahweh's presence was to be found in it, and that from there he revealed his will and poured out his blessing upon his people. When we press to find out how this presence was conceived, we find that it was dominated by the idea of Yahweh as the God of the exodus and Mount Sinai.[2]

The far-reaching religious changes and innovations of the Davidic–Solomonic era went side by side with important changes in Israel's political structure, which resulted in the formation of an Israelite state. The old amphictyony of twelve tribes gave place under the monarchy to a state organization which overrode the borders and privileges of individual tribes, and the covenant between Yahweh and the house of David gave a new sanction and authority to the monarchy as a permanent institution. The united empire, however, was short-lived, and after the death of Solomon and the disruption of the state into the two separate kingdoms of Israel and Judah, only in the southern Kingdom was the adherence to a belief in a covenant between Yahweh and the Davidic dynasty maintained. The particular temple-theology of Jerusalem was therefore the prerogative of Judah, whilst the north sought as far as possible to separate itself from any

---

[1] Cf. H. Ringgren, *The Faith of the Psalmists*, London, 1963, p. 23.
[2] For possible references and allusions to the ark in the Psalms, cf. G. Henton Davies, 'The Ark in the Psalms', *Promise and Fulfilment*, ed. F. F. Bruce, Edinburgh, 1963, pp. 51–61; 'Ark of the Covenant', *IDB*, I, p. 225b.

religious attachment to the south. There is no firm evidence that the northern kingdom honoured its rulers with similar elaborate rites as did Judah.[1] Rather the lack of a strong and stable dynastic succession speaks against any widely recognized acceptance of the divine authority of the kings of the northern State. Neither did any northern shrine rise to a pre-eminence that could rival Jerusalem.

Jeroboam showed himself conscious of the danger of pilgrimages to Jerusalem by his subjects, and so he established his own royal sanctuaries at Bethel and Dan, where bull-calf images, adopted from the old-established Canaanite cults, were set up by Israel.[2] These bull-calves must be interpreted as pedestals on which the invisible Yahweh was thought to stand.[3] Thus they were not so very dissimilar in intention from the carved cherubim which stood in Solomon's temple, although the Jerusalem historians strongly objected to them. The worship of Bethel, as 1 Kings xii. 28 shows, was firmly linked to the tradition of the exodus.

We are much less well informed how the presence of God was conceived in the northern kingdom than we are for the corresponding worship of Judah. The Book of the Covenant, which originated in a northern milieu, preserves for us the old law of the altar,[4] and demands that each Israelite should go up three times in every year 'to see the face of Yahweh'.[5] The occasions that are stipulated show that the festivals were those of an agricultural community, which makes it almost certain that such festivals originally came into Israel as borrowings from the Canaanites. The Book of Deuteronomy also preserves for us many features of the traditions and practices of northern Israel, and its law-code connects the Feast of Unleavened Bread with the Passover, and associates this combined feast with the

---

[1] Cf. A. Alt, 'Das Königtum in den Reichen Israel und Juda', *KSGVI*, II, 1953, pp. 118ff.; G. Widengren, *Sakrales Königtum im Alten Testament und im Judentum*, pp. 34ff., seeks to find in the Samaritan liturgy traces of an earlier royal rite of the Autumn Festival at Bethel, in which the king played a prominent part. This is possible, but hardly justified by Widengren's evidence. Cf. S. Mowinckel, *He That Cometh*, Oxford, 1956, p. 72 note.

[2] 1 Kings xii. 28.

[3] H. Th. Obbink, 'Jahwebilder', p. 268. These bull-images may well have been at one time associated with the god Bethel, who was a form of the 'bull El'.

[4] See above p. 40.

[5] Exod. xxiii. 17. This is the original meaning of the phrase which the English versions, following an early Jewish re-interpretation, read as 'to appear before Yahweh'. The change in meaning was achieved by reading an active verb (Heb. Qal) as a reflexive (Niph'al), in order to avoid what was felt to be a crude and imperfect idea of the divine presence at the sanctuary. There is no doubt, therefore, that the sanctuaries were at one time thought of as Yahweh's abodes, where the Israelites came before his presence. Cf. also the law of the slave who, if he is to become a permanent slave, is to be brought to the sanctuary, 'before God' (Exod. xxi. 6).

exodus.[1] It is possible, therefore, that the Passover was held in particular regard in the northern kingdom, as a festival recalling Israel's
origins.[2]

That Yahweh was believed to be present in the sanctuaries of
northern Israel is quite clear, and the popular acceptance and understanding of this belief came under the severe criticism of the prophets
Amos and Hosea, who both prophesied against north Israelite
shrines. To these and other prophetic criticisms we must now give
our attention.

[1] Deut. xvi. 1–8.
[2] A. C. Welch, *The Code of Deuteronomy. A New Theory of its Origin*, London,
1924, pp. 62ff.; but cf. now J. B. Segal, *The Hebrew Passover from the Earliest
Times to A.D.* 70, London, 1963, pp. 94, 204, 209ff.

CHAPTER VI

THE PROPHETIC REACTION AND THE DEUTERONOMIC REFORM

T H E conviction that Yahweh's presence had been promised to Israel in the covenant, and was made actual in its worship, is fundamental to a right understanding of Israel's cult, and, without this idea, the particular importance of Jerusalem becomes unintelligible. In the northern kingdom, where, after the disruption, a repudiation of the cult-tradition of Judah was to be expected, we have seen that Jeroboam took steps to counter any attachment that his subjects might have felt towards Jerusalem. Nevertheless here also the revival of the use of the bull-calf symbols meant that the presence of Yahweh with Israel was believed to be a reality manifested in its worship. Yahweh's blessing for his people was made effective by his dwelling in their midst, and the departure of this divine presence would have meant the loss of the security and prosperity of his people. The idea of this divine presence in the cult was explained and justified on the basis of a symbolism which had its origin in Canaanite mythology, although this was now related to Yahweh as the God who had brought his people out of Egypt. The danger of such a cultic symbolism was that it fostered the idea that Yahweh's gifts to Israel were unconditional, and were rendered by his permanent association with Israel's shrines. In particular the Jerusalem temple could become a token of a divine guarantee to bless Israel, irrespective of the people's conduct and loyalty to him. In brief, the cult could be divorced from the tradition of the covenant, and so obscure the fact that Yahweh was its Lord, who made demands on Israel, as well as offered benefits to it. Israel could feel itself so sure of the immanent presence of Yahweh that it forgot his transcendent lordship. That this danger was not a mere possibility, but did in fact have a deep and harmful effect on the popular attitude of Israel, is evidenced by the criticism of Israel's worship made by the prophets.[1]

The canonical prophets protested against false ideas of the presence of Yahweh in Israel's cult, and insisted upon the demands of the

---

[1] For the attitude of the prophets to the cult see my *Prophecy and Covenant* (SBT 43), London, 1965, chapter 5.

covenant law. Amos, who prophesied at Bethel in the northern kingdom, accepted that Yahweh dwelt on Mount Zion, and asserted that from Jerusalem his voice was to be heard:

'Yahweh roars from Zion,
  and utters his voice from Jerusalem.'
(Amos i. 2)[1]

The popular belief that the presence of Yahweh was with Israel could only be a reality if the people sought good and not evil.[2] In fact, however, they had demonstrably failed to do so, with the consequence that Yahweh's presence would mean judgment and not blessing.[3] With this we must connect Amos's oracle regarding the day of Yahweh, in which he declared that this would bring disaster, and not happiness.[4] Yahweh's dramatic intervention would mean the punishment of evil, so that the sinful people could only anticipate his judgment.

Hosea too proclaimed the presence of Yahweh as the Holy One in the midst of his people,[5] but he rejected the worship of the sanctuaries.[6] He repudiated the entire cult of Israel as being nothing other than a thinly masked imitation of the immoral cult of Canaan. The belief that fertility and prosperity could be brought to the land through the blessing of the Baals at their sanctuaries was rejected. It was Yahweh, and not the Baals, who gave to Israel the produce of its land.[7]

The prophet who stands out most of all as the messenger of Jerusalem is Isaiah, for whom Mount Zion, with its tradition of Yahweh's dwelling there, had a very special significance. This particular prominence of Jerusalem and its temple in Isaiah's prophecies can be traced back to his call vision, which took place in the temple. Earlier attempts of commentators to interpret the vision as a special revelation to the prophet of the divine court in heaven are rendered unnecessary when we bear in mind the correspondence that was believed

---

[1] These words are sometimes denied to Amos, but their authenticity is defensible as a general introduction to the oracle Amos i. 2–ii. 16. See A. Bentzen, 'The Ritual Background of Amos i: 2–ii: 16', OTS VIII, Leiden, 1950, p. 96.

[2] Amos v. 14.

[3] Amos v. 17.

[4] Amos v. 18–24. The origins of this concept of the Day of Yahweh are still contested. See S. Mowinckel, *Psalmenstudien* II, pp. 221ff.; *The Psalms in Israel's Worship*, I, pp. 116ff.; G. von Rad, 'The Origin of the Concept of the Day of Yahweh', *JSS* 4, 1959, pp. 104ff.; *Theologie des A.T.*, II, München, 1960, pp. 133ff.; On the relationship between the Day of Yahweh and Israelite eschatology see my *Prophecy and Covenant*, chapter 6.

[5] Hos. xi. 9.

[6] Hos. iv. 15–19; viii. 5; x. 1–2, 5; xii. 12 (EVV. 11); xiii. 2.

[7] Hos. ii. 10f. (EVV. 8f.).

to exist between the earthly and the heavenly realms. Through the doors of the earthly building the way of access was open to the throne of Yahweh himself, who dwelt in the splendour of heaven.[1] In the vision of Micaiah-ben-Imlah,[2] with which Isaiah's vision must necessarily be compared, Yahweh is said to be seated on his throne with all the host of heaven standing beside him on the right hand and on the left. The seraphim which Isaiah saw form a part of this heavenly host who surrounded Yahweh's throne. In his vision Isaiah saw the reality for which the Jerusalem temple existed. To him was given to know the truth of Yahweh's dwelling on Zion in which others in the nation believed, but which to them usually remained hidden.

The full meaning of Mount Zion as the place where Yahweh's presence is known and revealed becomes explicit in Isaiah's prophecy in Isa. ii. 2–4,[3] where it is to become the spiritual centre of the universe:

'It shall come to pass in future days,
    That the mountain of Yahweh's house,
Shall be established as the highest of the mountains,
    And shall be raised above the hills.
And all nations shall flow to it,
    And many peoples will come and say:
"Come, let us go up to the mountain of Yahweh,
    To the house of the God of Jacob;
That he may teach us his ways
    And that we may walk in his paths."
For out of Zion shall go forth instruction,
    And the word of Yahweh from Jerusalem.
He shall judge between the nations,
    And shall educate many peoples;
And they shall forge their swords into mattocks,
    And their spears into pruning knives.
Nations shall not raise the sword against each other,
    Nor shall they learn war any more.'
                    (Isa. ii. 2–4)

---

[1] S. Mowinckel, *Psalmenstudien* II, p. 153 note, suggested that Isaiah's call came during the autumn Enthronement Festival, celebrating Yahweh's kingship. For a fuller elaboration of this view see I. Engnell, *The Call of Isaiah*, (*UUÅ* 1949, 4), Uppsala, 1949, pp. 28ff.

[2] 1 Kings xxii. 19ff.; cf. also Yahweh's heavenly court in Job i. 6–12, ii. 1–7.

[3] = Mic. iv. 1–4. The authorship of this oracle can better be ascribed to Isaiah than to Micah, but the passage is full of traditional Zion themes so that it is difficult to tell how far Isaiah himself may be quoting from older material. Cf. G. von Rad, 'Die Stadt auf dem Berg', *Ges. Stud. z.A.T.*, p. 215; H. Wildberger, 'Die Völkerwallfahrt zum Zion. Jes. ii, 1–5', *VT* 7, 1957, pp. 62–81.

In this passage we find an abundance of allusions to the traditional hope of Jerusalem, as the place where Yahweh's presence is to be found. We are already familiar with the expression of such a hope in the temple festivals, especially as these are reflected in the Zion Psalms. From an early period, as we have seen, the presence of Yahweh in Jerusalem as the divine king, was the basis of a hope of a changed world in which the lordship of Yahweh would be acknowledged by all nations. The mythological origin of this was to be found in an identification of Mount Zion with Mount Zaphon, so that it was regarded as a cosmic mountain, whose summit reached above the stars. In this Yahwistic re-interpretation of the myth, the unique size and significance of Mount Zion are pictures of a future hope, yet to be fulfilled. From this mountain Yahweh's *torah* would be proclaimed to all peoples leading to a new manner of life among the nations. The result of this exaltation of Mount Zion is shown as a new age of peace and happiness for all mankind.

A similar expectation of a transformed world is to be found in another oracle[1] which, however, is most probably not from Isaiah himself, but from a later writer:

> 'None shall do harm or act corruptly
> ,   In all my holy mountain;
> For the earth shall be full of the knowledge of Yahweh,
>   As water covers the sea.'
>
> (Isa. xi. 9)[2]

Here again traditional mythological material has been fashioned into a prophecy of future bliss, when the world will be restored to the conditions of paradise. Yahweh's holy mountain must refer to the whole land of Palestine, if not to the whole world, which is signified by Mount Zion as a world-mountain.[3]

One of the major features of the Zion traditions, as witnessed in the Psalms, is that concerning the defeat of the nations outside Jerusalem. Yahweh's presence implies a judgment upon evildoers, among both gods and men, and in Israelite faith this particularly meant the destruction of the forces of foreign nations which threatened her.[4]

---

[1] Isa. xi. 1–9. S. Mowinckel, *He That Cometh*, pp. 17, 19, 20, regards this prophecy as post-exilic, probably from Zechariah's time.

[2] In Num. xiv. 21 the earth is said to be filled with 'the glory of Yahweh', and in Hab. ii. 14 we find that this has become 'the knowledge of the glory of Yahweh'. The theme was probably traditional in the Jerusalem temple cult. Cf. also 2 Cor. iv. 6.

[3] Cf. Ps. lxxviii. 54; Isa. xiv. 25; lvii. 13.

[4] See above p. 71.

Isaiah adopted this theme in his interpretation of the political events of his day. He described the Assyrian armies as continuing their victorious march until they were brought to a halt outside the walls of Jerusalem, when Yahweh himself would inflict a crushing defeat upon them.[1] The manner in which this was to be accomplished is vividly described by Isaiah in Isa. xxxi. 4–5, where it is not any human instrumentality, but the personal action of Yahweh which secures the victory and guarantees protection to Jerusalem:

'For thus has Yahweh said to me,
  As a lion or a young lion growls over his prey,
  And when a band of shepherds is summoned against him,
  Is not terrified by their shouting
    Or daunted at their noise,
So Yahweh of Hosts will come down
  To fight upon Mount Zion and upon its hill.
Like birds hovering, so Yahweh of Hosts
  Will protect Jerusalem;
He will protect and deliver it,
  He will spare and rescue it.'

(Isa. xxxi. 4–5)

This theme, that Mount Zion is to be the place where Yahweh will defeat the nations, reappears several times in pre-exilic prophecy.[2] In the Isaianic passage that is quoted above the counterpart to this defeat of the foreign nations is the assertion that Jerusalem itself will be inviolate, because Yahweh is in the midst of it, guaranteeing the city's protection. In the biographical narrative of Isaiah's part during Sennacherib's seige of Jerusalem,[3] this belief is placed right at the fore of the prophet's message. He is said to have assured Hezekiah that Yahweh would defend Jerusalem, and that the Assyrians would be unable to enter it.[4] The actual course of events is difficult for the historian to unravel, but for the development of Israel's religion the important fact is that the traditional hope of Jerusalem was thought to have been historically vindicated.[5] Isaiah is associated with this vindication, and, as Mowinckel has argued, the accounts of

---

[1] Isa. x. 27b–34.
[2] Mic. iv. 11–13; Zeph. iii. 8–13; Ezek, xxxviii. 17–23.
[3] 2 Kings xviii. 13–xix. 37 = Isa. xxxvi. 1–xxxvii. 38.
[4] Isa. xxxvii. 33–35; 2 Kings xix. 32–34.
[5] J. Bright, *A History of Israel*, London, 1960, pp. 282ff., argues that there were two campaigns, one in 701 B.C., when Hezekiah surrendered to Sennacherib and one later (*c.* 688 B.C.), in which Jerusalem experienced a remarkable deliverance. The theory of a single campaign is upheld by H. H. Rowley, 'Hezekiah's Reform and Rebellion', *Men of God*, London, 1963, pp. 98–132.

what transpired have been coloured by the traditional belief in Yahweh's direct intervention to protect his dwelling-place.[1] At least the events did nothing to discredit the belief in Yahweh's protection of the city, but rather served to strengthen it. For the inhabitants of Jerusalem the eleventh hour reprieve from the assault by the besieging armies of Sennacherib served to entrench more firmly than ever the belief in the city's safety through its divine protector. Isaiah himself contended vigorously against a faith which placed more trust in Yahweh's dwelling-place than in Yahweh, and his condemnation of the inhabitants of Jerusalem has led to a certain ambivalence in his preaching.[2]

Micah, the contemporary, and perhaps disciple, of Isaiah, also challenged this excessive assurance that Yahweh could be relied upon to defend Zion, no matter how godless its citizens. This merely turned faith into superstition, and made the temple a fetish, and not a sanctuary. Micah foretold that in the face of the injustice and greed of rulers, priests and prophets within the city, Jerusalem would be destroyed:

> 'Therefore because of you,
>   Zion shall be ploughed as a field;
> Jerusalem shall become a heap of ruins,
>   And the mountain of the temple a wooded height.'
>
> (Mic. iii. 12)

Micah therefore resisted the notion that Yahweh's presence in Jerusalem was unconditional, and that the cult in itself was an adequate guarantee of the divine favour. Yahweh was perfectly free to destroy both temple and city if they continued to profane his holy name.

The opposition to the temple and its cult was taken up even more forcibly by Jeremiah, who saw it as a superstitious fetish, which was blinding the people to a true faith in Yahweh. He proclaimed that the temple was quite unable to save the people and that, like that of Shiloh in the past, so this temple also would be destroyed:

'Thus says Yahweh of Hosts, the God of Israel, "Amend your ways and

---

[1] S. Mowinckel, *Psalmenstudien* II, pp. 63, 214. It can no longer be accepted that the doctrine of Jerusalem's inviolability arose out of the events of Sennacherib's campaign. The events themselves can hardly have warranted the extravagance of such a doctrine, which must rather be traced back to the ancient Zion cult. Cf. J. Schreiner, *Sion-Jerusalem*, pp. 219ff., 236ff.

[2] Cf. Isa. i. 27–31; iii. 1–8, 16–26; v. 1–7; xxix. 1ff. The threat of Isa. xxxix. 5–8 is usually thought to be post-Isaianic.

your deeds, and I will let you dwell in this place.[1] Do not trust in deceptive words, saying, the temple of Yahweh, the temple of Yahweh, the temple of Yahweh is this.' "

(Jer. vii. 3–4)

'Go now to my place which was in Shiloh, where I made my name dwell at first, and see what I did to it because of the wickedness of my people Israel. And now, because you have done all these things, says Yahweh, and I spoke to you earnestly, but you did not listen, and when I called you, you did not answer, therefore I will do to the house which is called by my name, in which you trust, and to the place which I gave to you and your ancestors, as I did to Shiloh. And I will cast you out of my sight, as I cast out all your kinsmen, all the offspring of Ephraim.'

(Jer. vii. 12–15; cf. Jer. xxvi. 6)

An interesting feature of this temple speech is not simply that the temple is to be destroyed, but that this carries with it, by implication, the ejection of the inhabitants of Judah from their land. As we have shown, the possession of the temple as Yahweh's dwelling-place on Mount Zion, was regarded as the entitlement to possession of the whole land. Yahweh's sacred mountain in Jerusalem was symbolic of his land, and was the means through which his blessing flowed out to it. The destruction of the temple, and the withdrawal of Yahweh's presence, meant the removal of Judah from its territory. Its source of blessing and security were to be taken away. We notice also that in this important oracle Yahweh is not said to dwell directly in Jerusalem, but his presence is there by means of his name. This, as we shall see, is a reflection of the theology of the Deuteronomic editing of Jeremiah.

Jeremiah is completely adamant that the temple is no guarantee of Yahweh's presence and favour, but insists that he is Lord of all sanctuaries. As in the past he had punished the sins of the people by destroying their sanctuary at Shiloh, so he would do likewise to Jerusalem. Yahweh's presence was holy, and was set in Jerusalem as an act of grace, but in the face of Judah's sins he could no longer continue in the midst of an unholy people. A performance of a cultic act, however conscientious, could be no substitute for obedience to

---

[1] Some versions suggest 'that I might dwell with you' (Heb. $w^e e\check{s}k^e n\hat{a}\ itt^e\underline{k}em$), and this is accepted by G. Fohrer, 'Jeremias Tempelwort, 7, 1–15', *ThZ* 5, 1949, pp. 402f. Fohrer also emends verse 7 to read 'and I will dwell with you' (cf. Vulg. and 8 Hebrew MSS.). Neither emendation is necessary, and the Massoretic text can stand. The connection between possession of the temple and dwelling in the land was basic to the meaning of the temple, and it underlies Jeremiah's argument in verses 3, 7 and 14–15. There is no need to excise verses 5–7, as e.g. A. C. Welch, *Jeremiah: His Time and His Work*, London, 1928, pp. 140ff.

G

the covenant. Neither could the mere fact of the existence of the temple ensure the favour of the God who was invoked there. It was only the intervention of Ahikam-ben-Shaphan that saved Jeremiah from suffering the death penalty for his words.[1]

In a study of the meaning of the temple in Israelite prophecy, M. Schmidt has argued that there existed an inherent tension between the prophetic idea of God, and that exemplified by the temple.[2] For the prophets Yahweh's presence was active and dynamic, both in judgment and salvation, whereas the temple was something static, and so tended to present a notion of the deity as static, and almost passive. We have seen how both Micah and Jeremiah contended against a popular belief in the temple in which it was thought to guarantee the presence and blessing of Yahweh at all times and under all circumstances. It is evident that some at least of the populace of Judah regarded the divine dwelling among them as a charm that guaranteed protection against all disasters. The prophets believed that Yahweh's presence would be actively demonstrated in history, whilst the temple, in contrast, pointed to a divine indwelling that was static and relatively permanent. Thus it is readily intelligible that the temple was threatened with destruction because it had become a positive hindrance to the covenant faith. We must not, however, raise Schmidt's distinction into a general principle as though the prophetic view of God were inevitably distinct from that of the cult. As we have already seen in our study of the Psalter, the Jerusalem cult proclaimed both in word and act the coming of Yahweh to his people to judge evildoers and to vindicate the righteous. This was certainly not an attitude to God which regarded his presence as static. Yet it is apparent that the cult had been abused, and its real meaning was no longer alive in the hearts of the people who participated in it.

The great prophets of Israel and Judah preached to a people who stood under the judgment of Yahweh. Israel had broken the covenant by perpetual disobedience to its demands, and the prophets, as Yahweh's messengers, proclaimed the end of the covenant relationship between Yahweh and Israel. They foretold the coming judgment which would make effective the ending of the older order. In the face of such a doom, the cult, with its promises of salvation and blessing, was turned into a lie, for no cultic rites could heal Israel's

---

[1] Jer. xxvi. 24.
[2] M. Schmidt, *Prophet und Tempel*, Zürich, 1948, esp. pp. 9ff.; cf. also R. Hentschke, *Die Stellung der vorexilischen Schriftpropheten zum Kultus*, pp. 47ff., 61, 71, 102.

wound. Further the prophets, as the spokesmen of the ancient Yahweh traditions of the covenant, were well aware how overladen the
cult had become with accretions borrowed from the Canaanites.
Only in a very imperfect and fragmented way was the covenant
tradition preserved at all in Israel's worship. In this failure and decay
of the cult the Jerusalem temple too must be included.[1]

The prophetic attitude to Israel's worship, and especially to the
worship of the temple in Jerusalem, can be summarized in two pro-
positions. Firstly Yahweh's presence means judgment as well as
blessing. This judgment is not only upon foreign transgressors, but
upon all wrongdoing in Israel as well. Secondly Yahweh's presence
in Israel is a gift of grace bestowed in the covenant, and in the face of
Israel's persistent breach of this covenant Yahweh will abandon his
temple and people. The prophets accused those who used the cult
of making its belief in Yahweh's presence a ground for trusting in
the divine blessing without any accompanying notion of the divine
righteousness. Yahweh could not be subject to the control of men,
no more when this control was thought to be effected by the possession
of a divine dwelling-place, than when it was achieved by the profane
use of images, or the blasphemous invocation of his name.

The prophetic criticism of the cult, focussing ultimately in a
condemnation of the Jerusalem temple, asserted that Israel's worship
did not serve the true interests of the covenant. Instead of making
known the demands of the covenant law, and of revealing the nature
and purpose of Israel's election, the cult obscured it by promising a
false security which knew nothing of the moral conditions of fellow-
ship between Israel and Yahweh. Yet the prophets were not the only
critics of the cult, since within circles drawn from the Levitical cult-
personnel a dissatisfaction and desire for reform, nursed over a
considerable period, were responsible for a far-reaching reform in the
days of Josiah (621 B.C.). Already in the time of Hezekiah some attempt at cultic reform had been introduced in Jerusalem, but its
success was ephemeral[2] Neither in this instance, nor the more
significant attempt in Josiah's day, does the main stimulus appear to
have come from the Jerusalem cult-officials, but from provincial
Levitical groups, whose background lay in the shrines of northern

---

[1] A. Weiser, *The Psalms*, p. 26, argues that the Jerusalem cult, especially in its
Autumn Festival, maintained the genuinely Israelite tradition of Mosaic Yahwism
during the period of the monarchy. This is no doubt true, but the Jerusalem cult
was also much overloaded with features drawn from the Jebusite El-'Elyon cult,
and the genuinely Yahwistic elements must have been very much obscured by them.

[2] 2 Kings xviii. 4. Cf. H. H. Rowley, 'Hezekiah's Reform and Rebellion', pp.
126ff.

Israel.[1] Many of these Levites must have been dispossessed of their means of livelihood with the Assyrian conquest of the northern kingdom in 721 B.C., and its incorporation into the Assyrian empire. Their attention was therefore turned towards Jerusalem, where it was still not too late to hope that a form of worship more truly expressive of the will of Yahweh could be introduced.

The idea of a divine dwelling-place, and with that the existence of a temple, had been adopted by Israel from the Canaanites, and it had its roots in a polytheistic religion, with its distinctive religious symbolism. As a consequence the temple had not easily been assimilated by the Yahwistic faith, with its tradition of the covenant on Mount Sinai, without provoking opposition, and endangering some of the most vital aspects of the religion of Israel. It is not surprising, therefore, that there should have arisen a tension between the understanding of the temple, with its claim to be a source of blessing to the land, and the knowledge of Yahweh as the God of the covenant.

The Jerusalem temple had been greatly indebted to the Jebusite El-'Elyon cultus, and it testified to the belief that Yahweh had chosen Mount Zion for his dwelling-place, upholding its king and defending its inhabitants. Yet a number of great prophetic figures had declared to Israel that the covenant was broken, and Israel stood under sentence of death. The cult was no guarantee of deliverance and blessing, since the covenant was the foundation of all Israel's life and worship, and by its disobedience to the covenant law Israel had forfeited its privileged position. If the temple were to serve the will of Yahweh it had to be given a new interpretation which no longer engendered a false and immoral promise of salvation.

It is a profound and thoroughgoing attempt at such a re-interpretation which took place in Josiah's time with the finding of the Deuteronomic law-book in the Jerusalem temple. How this book came to be in the temple is an unsolved mystery, but certainly it was not a creation of a moment, but represents the result of a long-established tradition of instruction and exhortation by experienced teachers. These were to be found amongst the Levites, who had once

---

[1] Cf. A. Bentzen, *Die josianische Reform und ihre Voraussetzungen*, Copenhagen, 1926, pp. 58ff.; G. von Rad, *Das Gottesvolk im Deuteronomium* (BWANT III, 11), Stuttgart, 1929, pp. 78ff.; *Studies in Deuteronomy*, pp. 60ff.; 'Deuteronomy', *IDB*, I, p. 836a; P. Buis and J. Leclercq, *Le Deutéronome*, Paris, 1963, pp. 15f.

The north Israelite origin of Deuteronomy was apparently first suggested by C. F. Burney, *The Book of Judges*, London, 1918, p. xlvi note. Besides the works of Bentzen and von Rad it was argued by A. C. Welch, *The Code of Deuteronomy. A New Theory of its Origin*, London, 1924, and A. Alt, 'Die Heimat des Deuteronomiums', *KSGVI*, II, 1953, pp. 250–275.

officiated at Israel's sanctuaries, and who undertook a kind of cate-
chetical instruction of the people.[1] These Levites preserved much of
the tradition of the covenant which had been maintained in the great
northern sanctuaries, especially Shechem and Bethel. When these
shrines were lost to the Assyrian conquests in 721 B.C., survivors of
the cult-personnel were able to bring their traditions south into
the kingdom of Judah. Behind their activity, as the fountain-head
of their understanding of Yahwism, was the memory of the pre-
monarchic amphictyony. The great Deuteronomic history-work
(Joshua–2 Kings) shows many points of similar theological interest
and concern as are found in the Deuteronomic law.

These Deuteronomic preachers endeavoured to re-awaken Judah
to the situation of crisis in which it found itself, and to return to a true
Yahwistic cult, untainted by the evils of Canaanite religion. They
preached to a people under the threat of judgment, and sought to call
the nation back to a right understanding of the covenant and its
demands. Behind their work stood the stormy prophetic protests of
the eighth and seventh centuries. As the prophets had criticized and
attacked a false trust in the cult, so the Deuteronomic legislators
sought to implement a similar criticism by providing a truly Yahwistic interpretation of worship.[2] They did this by placing a new
emphasis upon Yahweh's transcendence, stressing that the covenant
of Sinai-Horeb was a gift of grace, and that Israel's obedience was to
be motivated throughout by gratitude and love to Yahweh. Israel
owed its very existence to its election by Yahweh, for no merit of its
own, and its worship was above all to be the necessary response of
grateful hearts. Once and for all the Deuteronomists wished to break
with an attitude to the cult which suggested, even by a misunderstanding, that Yahweh could be subjected to the control of his worshippers. They wished so to stress the divine grace and power that
no room would be left for Israel to think that by its rites and offerings
it exerted any coercion upon Yahweh. Thus for the Deuteronomists

---

[1] P. Buis and J. Leclercq, op. cit., pp. 15f., claim that the Levitical authors of
Deuteronomy lived outside the sanctuaries and did not carry on priestly functions.
This probably overstates the position, although it is likely that the political exigencies
of the northern kingdom prohibited the ready fulfilment of sacerdotal functions by
such Levites.

[2] The relationship between the eighth-century prophets and Deuteronomy is
most probably explicable by an indirect connection. The Levitical authors of
Deuteronomy, and the eighth-century prophets, especially Hosea, were both
dependent on faithful guardians of the old covenant tradition, who had lived outside
the major sanctuaries. Cf. H. W. Wolff, 'Hoseas geistige Heimat', *ThLZ* 81, 1956,
cols. 91ff., and N. W. Porteous, 'Actualization and the Prophetic Criticism of the
Cult,' *Tradition und Situation. Studien zur alttestamentlichen Prophetie*, ed. E.
Würthwein and O. Kaiser, Göttingen, 1963, pp. 97ff.

the basis of morality was gratitude, and the foundation of worship was sincere thanksgiving and praise to God. Yahweh was the sovereign lord of Israel's life, and the giver of all its benefits.

The Deuteronomists, therefore, in accordance with their desire to emphasize the transcendence of Yahweh, lay great stress upon Yahweh as the God of heaven, who exerts his power over all creation.[1] The divine dwelling-place is not to be found on earth, whether it be regarded as Mount Sinai, or Mount Zion. In following out this policy of laying all emphasis upon Yahweh's heavenly nature it is instructive to notice the way in which the Deuteronomic account of the theophany on Mount Sinai is given. This is of quite special interest because already the JE narrative leaves it perfectly clear that Yahweh's abode is in heaven and that he came down to Sinai in order to speak with Moses.[2] As Deuteronomy tells of these events there is no mention at all of a descent by Yahweh from heaven to the mountain:

'And you came near and stood at the foot of the mountain; and the mountain was burning with fire to the heart of heaven—darkness, cloud and impenetrable blackness. Then Yahweh spoke to you out of the midst of the fire; you heard the sound of words, but you saw no form, there was only a voice.'

(Deut. iv. 11–12)

'Out of heaven he let you hear his voice to discipline you, and on earth he showed you his great fire, and you heard his words out of the midst of the fire.

(Deut. iv. 36; cf. also v. 4, 22–23, 26; ix. 10)

There is no suggestion here of a descent of Yahweh in any fashion, but only of the appearance of fire and of a voice out of the fire. Deuteronomy has the same tradition of the revelation to Moses and of the law-giving on Mount Horeb-Sinai as JE also possessed, but the later editors, who could no doubt have accepted the earlier narratives without particular offence to their theological ideas, retell the events in such a way that no room is left for any misunderstanding.

Even more forcibly is the Deuteronomic theology of Yahweh's transcendence brought out in the attitude to Mount Zion and its temple. This is most apparent in the prayer of dedication for the temple which is put into the mouth of Solomon.[3] The whole Deutero-

---

[1] Cf. Deut. iii. 24; iv. 39; x. 14; xxvi. 15.

[2] Cf. Exod. xix. 9, 11, 20; xxxiv. 5.

[3] 1 Kings viii. 23–53. This prayer seems to be a free composition of the Deuteronomistic historian, and must be ascribed to a time subsequent to Josiah's reformation. Nevertheless, its teaching is consonant with the whole Deuteronomic attitude to the cult, and its main features derive from this. It is unnecessary to suppose that the temple had already been destroyed when this prayer was composed.

nomic understanding of the temple, and with that the idea of the divine nature, is brought out very clearly:

'But will God indeed dwell on the earth, behold heaven and the highest heaven cannot contain thee, how much less then, this house which I have built.'

(1 Kings viii. 27)[1]

The repetition of the assertion that Yahweh dwells in heaven is so marked that we can hardly fail to suspect that such statements were composed as a refutation of those who held another view. These were unquestionably all who believed that Yahweh dwelt on Mount Zion in his temple. Such an idea is now fully and firmly rejected by the Deuteronomistic historian. Yahweh is not a God who can be said to dwell anywhere on earth, but his only abode is in heaven. He is transcendent and cannot in any way be regarded as contained within the natural order, nor be worshipped as a link in the chain of natural forces. The Deuteronomists are uncompromising in asserting that Yahweh is superior to the natural order, and is not a part of it.

This entire dedicatory prayer, attributed to Solomon, expresses very effectively the Deuteronomistic re-interpretation of the temple. No longer does the temple symbolize the land to provide a link between the natural and supernatural worlds, whereby the blessing of Yahweh might be poured out upon his land and people. Instead it is a house of prayer, and between the power of God to bless and the needs of men, threatened by famine, pestilence and war, there is always interposed the human cry of repentence and a turning to God in prayer:

'When there is famine in the land, or pestilence, or blight, or mildew, or locust, or caterpillar, or when their enemy lays seige to one[2] of their cities; whatever affliction or sickness there is; whatever prayer, whatever supplication is made by any man, or by all thy people Israel, each one knowing what afflicts his own heart, and stretching out his hands towards this house; then hear thou in heaven thy dwelling-place, and forgive, and act and give to each, whose heart thou knowest, according to his ways; (for indeed thou alone knowest the hearts of all human beings); so that they may reverence thee all the days that they live on the land which thou gavest to our ancestors.'

(1 Kings viii. 37–40)

There is no natural link between God and his world, made effective by the temple and its symbolism; instead the link is a spiritual

[1] Cf. also 1 Kings viii. 30, 32, 34, 36, 39, 43, 45, 49.
[2] Reading with LXX and Syr. Hebrew has 'land'.

one, made effective by the sincere cry of humble men, who turn to Yahweh. This is in accordance with the whole Deuteronomic spirit which opposes any magico-religious way of relationship to God.[1] Rather all stress is laid upon the moral and spiritual factors which condition Israel's communion with Yahweh.[2]

This particular re-interpretation of the temple ideology may well have impressed itself on the minds of the Deuteronomists through their knowledge of the destruction of the famous temples of the northern kingdom. These had not availed to save those who worshipped in them. A very special interest attaches, therefore, to the law which Deuteronomy contains for the centralization of the cultus at 'The place which Yahweh your God has chosen to set his name there'.[3] It is a recognizable fact that this demand for cult-centralization does not dominate all of the Deuteronomic laws, and seems to have arisen at a late stage in the compilation of the work.[4]

The reasons that motivated this demand for centralization are not wholly agreed upon by scholars, and various suggestions have been offered.[5] Certain features which have an important bearing on the subject must be borne in mind. Since the demand for centralization must have been taken up by the Deuteronomists some time in the seventh century B.C., the only Israelite sanctuary which possessed a status commensurate with the requirements of this demand during this period was Jerusalem. Although it was never specifically referred by name in Deuteronomy it seems almost certain that from the start this was the sanctuary which was intended.[6] If only on account of sheer lack of a possible alternative this had to be the

---

[1] Cf. G. von Rad, *Das Gottesvolk im Deuteronomium*, pp. 29ff.

[2] The Deuteronomists were careful to make a distinction between the use of the verb *yāšaḇ* = 'to sit, dwell', and the verb *šāḵan* = 'to pitch tent, dwell'. The former is used of God's heavenly dwelling, whilst the latter is used for his presence on earth. Cf. G. E. Wright, *Biblical Archaeology*, p. 145.

[3] Deut. xii. 1–14.

[4] Cf. G. von Rad, 'Deuteronomy', p. 834a.

[5] The recollection of the single central shrine of the amphictyony has been thought to lie behind such a demand. Cf. G. von Rad, 'Deuteronomy', p. 834a; M. Noth, *A History of Israel*, p. 276; G. E. Wright, 'The Book of Dueteronomy', p. 326a. V. Maag ('Erwägungen zur deuteronomischen Kultzentralisation', *VT* 6, 1956, pp. 10–18), has sought to find the reason for the demand in the status accorded to Jerusalem as Yahweh's chosen sanctuary on account of the miraculous deliverance of the city in 701 B.C. More recently E. Nicholson ('The Centralization of the Cult in Deuteronomy', *VT* 13, 1963, pp. 380–389) has argued that it arose as a consequence of the political necessities of Hezekiah's reign. Whilst such specific situations may have influenced such a demand, A. Bentzen was assuredly correct in asserting that the major shrines inevitably made certain monopolistic claims (*Die josianische Reform und ihre Voraussetzungen*, pp. 69ff., 83ff.). This was especially true of Jerusalem through its association with the Davidic state and kingship.

[6] The Deuteronomistic historians explicitly identify Yahweh's chosen sanctuary as Jerusalem. 1 Kings viii. 15ff., 29.; xi. 36; xiv. 21; 2 Kings xxi. 4, 7.

chosen sanctuary, even supposing that the Deuteronomists would have preferred that it should have been elsewhere. A corroboration of this is found in the fact that Jerusalem was the sanctuary at which the cult was centralized in Josiah's reform. We are faced, therefore, with the strange ambivalence of Deuteronomy, that, whilst it divested the Jerusalem temple of its original meaning, it also demanded that it should be regarded as the only true shrine of Yahweh.

The assertion that the Deuteronomists intended to centralize the entire cult of Yahweh at the temple of Jerusalem, now interpreted in a distinctive way, does not explain, however, why they did so. We have seen that the religious background of the Deuteronomists lay in the northern kingdom, with its strong emphasis upon the Mosaic covenant, and with its memories of the amphictyony. Yet the demand for centralization cannot have derived from this, since, although the amphictyony had a central sanctuary, it made no monopolistic claim to exclusiveness.[1] Neither can such a demand have arisen simply as a political manœuvre, designed to further Hezekiah's rebellion against the Assyrians. Deuteronomy is intensely concerned for a pure cult, divested of any influence from Canaanite religion. The demand for centralization must be in accord with this overall aim.

Our study of the origins of the cult in Jerusalem has shown that from the days of David it made a claim of precedence over that of other Yahweh sanctuaries; a claim which was so far real that Jeroboam I feared that it might wrest his kingdom from him.[2] Solomon's temple was a royal sanctuary, the symbol of the divine authority of the state which Yahweh had put under the hand of the family of David. It maintained the ancient Yahweh traditions of the exodus and the Sinai covenant, and it possessed the ark which had once stood in the temple at Shiloh, the ancient centre of the amphictyony. The Jerusalem cult tradition allowed that only Shiloh had possessed a status commensurate with its own.[3] In the historic succession of Yahweh's chosen sanctuaries the blessing of Shiloh had fallen upon Jerusalem, and from the Jerusalem standpoint no other sanctuary could be regarded as its peer.[4]

Nevertheless this Jerusalem cultic tradition had owed much also to what it had borrowed from the Jebusite cult of El-'Elyon, and it interpreted its own claims by the aid of a mythology which made the

[1] Cf. E. Nicholson, op. cit., p. 383.

[2] 1 Kings xii. 28.

[3] Ps. lxxviii. 60; cf. Jer. vii. 12.

[4] That Jerusalem, because of its association with the Davidic state, had consistently shown strong centralizing tendencies is conceded by A. Bentzen, *Die josianische Reform und ihre Voraussetzungen*, pp. 69ff., 83ff. Bentzen, however, goes on to argue that other (northern) sanctuaries must also have made similar claims.

temple and Mount Zion the symbols of Yahweh's cosmic abode. Yahweh had chosen Mount Zion for his dwelling-place, and from there he sent forth his blessing into the land of Israel. It was this Canaanite-mythological aspect of the Jerusalem cult tradition which was so abhorrent to the Deuteronomists, since it opposed their own ideas of the nature of Yahweh's relationship to Israel. The fact of Yahweh and his relationship to his people formed the two foci of the entire Deuteronomic idea of religion and worship.[1] In order, therefore, to present to the people the meaning of the central sanctuary of Israel in a way acceptable to themselves, the Deuteronomists reinterpreted it, and abolished the ideas and symbolism which had derived from the Jebusites. In so doing they offered a new and effective theology of the temple and its meaning. The terminology of Yahweh's election of his sanctuary was still used, but Mount Zion was never mentioned by name, and the whole idea was greatly modified by the introduction of the further definition that it was to be the place where Yahweh would set his name.[2] Worship at any other sanctuary was forbidden. The earlier traditions of Jerusalem had stressed the notion that Mount Zion was the 'Mountain of Yahweh's inheritance', so that it gave a 'cultic' entitlement to Israel to dwell on Yahweh's land. All this was now abandoned in favour of the purely religious notion that the land was Israel's inheritance which had been given to it by Yahweh through the events of history. Israel had taken the land into its possession by a divinely guided conquest.[3]

Jerusalem, Mount Zion and its temple were all 'demythologized', and in place of the older mythology, by which Yahweh's abode on earth was thought to be united to his abode in heaven, the Deuteronomists offered a theological concept which expressed the manner of Yahweh's dwelling upon earth. This was that of Yahweh's name, which was set in the place which he had chosen. The invocation and public proclamation of the divine name had played a vital part in the worship of early Israel, and now this was elevated still further so that the name of Yahweh was made the vehicle of his presence. It was his *alter ego*, by means of which he made himself present to men, without ever leaving his heavenly dwelling-place.[4] For the first time,

---

[1] G. von Rad, *Das Gottesvolk im Deuteronomium*, p. 21.
[2] Deut. xii. 5, 11, 21; xiv. 23, 24; xvi. 2, 6, 11; cf. 1 Kings viii. 15–21.
[3] Especially Deut. vii. 1ff.; ix. 1ff.
[4] The older ideas of Yahweh's accompanying presence in Israel are to be found in Deuteronomic material: Deut. ii. 7; iv. 7, 37; vii. 21; ix. 3; xxiii. 14; xxxi. 3. These references are not elaborated into the theology of Yahweh's name, but there is no doubt that it is with the doctrine of Yahweh's name set in Israel's sanctuary that the Deuteronomic interpretation of this belief is given.

therefore, we have with the Deuteronomists a strictly theological endeavour to express the reality of Yahweh's presence within Israel, which did not throw in question his heavenly and transcendent nature. In the earlier Jerusalem tradition the meaning of Yahweh's temple and the manner of his dwelling there had been explained on the basis of mythology in which things on earth and things in heaven were believed to be mysteriously related. Deuteronomy now broke with this mythology and replaced it with a theology in which the divine name became the means by which the transcendent Yahweh was present with his people. By this re-interpretation the Deuteronomists hoped to preclude the idea that Yahweh was contained within the natural order, as a part of a natural chain of cause and effect, and to assert beyond question that he was superior to all his creation. His dwelling within Israel was thereby stressed as a gift of grace.[1]

In accordance with this re-interpretation of the meaning of Mount Zion and its temple, the Deuteronomists also set forth a new and simpler meaning for the ark:

'At that time Yahweh said to me, cut for yourself two tablets of stone, like the first, and come up to me on the mountain, and make for yourself an ark of wood. And I will write upon the tablets the words which were on the first tablets which you broke, and you shall put them in the ark. So I made an ark of acacia wood and I cut two tablets of stone like the first and I went up the mountain with the two tablets in my hand. Then he wrote upon the tablets, as on the first writing, the words which Yahweh spoke to you on the mountain out of the midst of the fire, on the day of the assembly. Then Yahweh gave them to me, and I turned and came down from the mountain, and I put the tablets in the ark which I had made; so they remained there as Yahweh commanded me.'

(Deut. x. 1–5)

---

[1] F. Dumermuth, 'Zur deuteronomischen Kulttheologie und ihren Voraussetzungen', *ZAW* 70, 1958, pp. 59–98, has argued that Deuteronomy's name theology was originally applied to the sanctuary at Bethel, where, he believes, much of the Deuteronomic material originated, and whence it was taken to Jerusalem. He supposes that the priests of Bethel came to reject their bull-calf images, because of their Canaanite associations and replaced them by the spiritual notion of Yahweh's name in the sanctuary. This doctrine, therefore, was intended in favour of Bethel and in opposition to Jerusalem, so that it is the former sanctuary that Yahweh has chosen as the abode of his name.

Such a hypothesis fails to carry conviction for lack of evidence, as we have no knowledge that the priests of Bethel ever did reject their bull-calves until it was too late. Although much of Deuteronomy is built upon older northern traditions, it seems clear that their name-theology was an attempt to re-interpret the significance of Mount Zion, in accordance with their own desire to show the transcendent nature of Yahweh. A detailed criticism and rejection of Dumermuth's hypothesis is given by J. Schreiner, *Sion-Jerusalem*, pp. 159ff.

When we bear in mind the significance of the ark as a symbol of Yahweh's presence, where the cherubim-throne of Yahweh was thought to be, we are surprised to find not a word or hint of this in Deuteronomy. The ark has been entirely robbed of any connection with Yahweh's presence, and with his heavenly cherubim-throne.[1] It now became simply a container for the keeping of the law tablets, and had no mysterious significance as a symbol of his presence on earth. Deuteronomy was attempting a complete re-interpretation so far as the ark was concerned, and in their view the ark was, as its name implied, only a container.[2] What it contained was the law, which formed the ethical basis of the covenant relationship between Israel and Yahweh, and the Deuteronomic elaboration of the law was itself ordered to be kept beside it.[3]

Both in their attitude to the temple, and to the ark, therefore, the Deuteronomists had in mind the Jerusalem temple as the place where Yahweh had chosen to set his name. The ancient claim of Jerusalem to be the chosen sanctuary was conceded, but only when its temple and cult had been submitted to a new theological interpretation. The motives for the centralizing of the cult at this one shrine were manifold. Overall the aim was undoubtedly to remove the menace of the Canaanite high-places, with their crude nature worship, by restricting the cult to a shrine over which control could be exercised, and where the covenant tradition was maintained. With their own religious heritage of the northern kingdom, looking back to the days of the amphictyony, the Levitical–Deuteronomic reformers required that such a shrine should possess the ark; a requirement which pointed them to Jerusalem. Further Jerusalem itself had always maintained a claim to absolute precedence over all other Yahweh sanctuaries on the grounds of its royal associations with David and his empire, and its place as the successor of the old amphictyonic order of worship. In the seventh century B.C. the Deuteronomists must have been sufficiently realistic to know that they could not abolish the Jerusalem cult and temple to establish a centralized worship

---

[1] Cf. G. von Rad, *Studies in Deuteronomy*, pp. 39f.

[2] It is very probable that the ark was a container of some kind, and it may have had some function as such, even alongside its place as a symbol of Yahweh's presence. G. Henton Davies, 'Ark of the Covenant', p. 225a, argues that the idea of the ark as a container represents a divergent cult tradition from its interpretation as a symbol of Yahweh's presence. It is wrong, he argues, to suppose that Deuteronomy was presenting a new, demythologized, interpretation. Whilst it is no doubt true that the ark was some kind of container, it is hardly conceivable that the Deuteronomists could have ignored its interpretation as a symbol of Yahweh's presence unless they deliberately intended to do so.

[3] Deut. xxxi. 24–26.

of Yahweh elsewhere. The result was a remarkable marrying together of the old northern traditions with ideas which had long been established in the Jerusalem cult. The Deuteronomists re-interpreted the Jerusalem cultic tradition in accordance with their desire to remove those aspects of Israel's religious life which were Canaanite in origin and significance. Any belief in a permanent association between Yahweh and the land of Canaan, or which fostered a magico-religious understanding of worship, had to be abolished. The result was a new theology of the temple and its meaning for Israel.

That some aspects of the Deuteronomic demands were not acceptable to the priests of Jerusalem does not preclude that the centralization demand was formulated with Jerusalem in mind.[1] The Levitical reformers were in a difficult position since their own religious heritage was in the northern kingdom, which the Assyrians had overrun. Its sanctuaries had been desecrated, and could no longer be revitalized to begin a new phase in the history of Israel's worship. Jerusalem alone was left as a major cult-shrine, and so it was inevitably here that the Deuteronomists sought to introduce their reforms. The short-lived nature of their success must have been partly due to the opposition of the Jerusalem priesthood, who were not prepared to accept all that the Deuteronomists demanded. Nevertheless some features of the reform could not be ignored, and, especially when Jerusalem itself had suffered defeat and destruction, the Deuteronomic theology took on a new significance.

In accordance with this Deuteronomic emphasis upon Yahweh's transcendence we find that any institution, or notion, current in Israel, which might suggest that a bond existed between Yahweh and the phenomena of nature was removed. Yahweh was transcendent to the world which he had created. The symbolism of the cult, which had originated in a mythological and polytheistic milieu was, as far as possible, rejected in favour of an emphasis upon the moral and spiritual requirements which governed the covenant relationship between Yahweh and Israel. Not only was Yahweh protected from the suggestion that he was a part of the natural order, but any kind of magico-religious way of union between him and Israel, or Israel's land, was opposed. In everything the ethical demands of the covenant were set forth as the grounds of Israel's communion with its God. So also the basis of all welfare, in the blessing of the fields and herds, and the

[1] In particular the requirement, that the Levites, who were displaced from the rural sanctuaries, should be allowed to officiate in Jerusalem (Deut. xviii. 6–8), was not accepted (2 Kings xxiii. 9). Cf. G. von Rad, 'Deuteronomy', p. 838a; G. E. Wright, 'The Book of Deuteronomy', p. 325b.

occupation of the land, was conditional upon obedience to the commandments.[1] Thus the relationship between Yahweh and the world of nature took second place to the primary relationship, which was between Yahweh and his people. The whole of Deuteronomy is dominated by the concept of Israel as the people of God, a holy people. Although Yahweh had chosen the place where his name was to dwell, antecedent to this, and as the primary ground which made such a sanctuary necessary, he had chosen Israel to be his people. Thus the verb 'to choose' (Heb. *bāḥar*) came to be used by Deuteronomy of Yahweh's covenant relationship to Israel, which was now set forth as a doctrine of election.[2] A similar stress on the moral requirements of the covenant is found in the new attitude to the land of Canaan as Israel's inheritance. Because Israel is a holy people, chosen by Yahweh in his grace, in order to continue to occupy the land which he has given to them, they must hold fast to the commandments.

The actual success of the Deuteronomists as reformers seems to have been short lived, and the crisis that came into Judah's affairs with the sudden death of Josiah at the hands of Pharaoh Necho led to wholly new developments. In some measure at least the priestly circles of Jerusalem were not willing to follow the Deuteronomic re-interpretations, nor to accede to all the demands of the reformers. The work of the Deuteronomists, however, continued, and extended, so far as their historical work was concerned, beyond the disasters of 597 and 586 B.C., into the period of the exile. With this series of defeats, with their attendant sufferings, the strictures of the Deuteronomists upon the monarchy and the cult attained a historical vindication. Neither the covenant between Yahweh and the Davidic dynasty,

---

[1] Deut. xi. 8ff. Cf. G. von Rad, *Das Gottesvolk im Deuteronomium*, p. 30; 'Verheissenes Land und Jahwes Land im Hexateuch', p. 98; O. Bächli, *Israel und die Völker*, (ATANT 41), Zürich, 1962, pp. 161ff.

[2] Esp. Deut. vii. 6ff. Cf. G. von Rad, *Das Gottesvolk im Deuteronomium*, p. 28; T. C. Vriezen, *Die Erwählung Israels nach dem Alten Testament*, p. 47; O. Bächli, *Israel und die Völker*, pp. 136ff., 165ff. G. E. Mendenhall, 'Election', p. 79a, argues that the use of the term '*bāḥar*' to express the action of Yahweh by which he had brought Israel into a covenant relationship to himself may well have originated in a small group within the nation, before the Deuteronomic reform. In Deuteronomy it was taken up into the vocabulary and literature of the reformers, who found in it a valuable expression of the grace which underlay the covenant. This is a plausible suggestion, but it must not be forgotten that this very verb had already been given a strong religio-political colouring by its use in Jerusalem circles as an expression of Yahweh's will for Jerusalem and the Davidic dynasty. It is quite possible, therefore, that the Deuteronomic reformers adopted it as a counterbalance to the claims of the Jerusalem court and temple. They insisted that Yahweh had not chosen a state, with its political and territorial claims, but a people to live in covenant union with himself. They replaced a theo-political notion, by a purely religious one, as they did also in the case of the term 'inheritance'.

nor the existence of a temple on Mount Zion, had sufficed to save the people from the judgment of God. On the contrary the fearful consequences of apostasy had become manifest in that the king and many of Judah's leading citizens had gone into exile. The temple was in ruins, and with it many of the people had been driven out from Yahweh's land. The idea of any kind of permanent bond between Yahweh and the land of Judah with its temple was completely discredited. In every way the work of the Deuteronomists was vindicated that the grounds of Israel's life and faith must be sought in morality and not myth.

We can see that in the history of the temple of Jerusalem, which had become the focus of Israel's faith in Yahweh's presence in its midst, the Deuteronomic work, both in the law and the history, marks a great watershed. Deuteronomy had broken with a mythological understanding of Israel's cult, and had replaced mythology with theology. There could be no going back on this, and historical events confirmed that Israel's relationship to Yahweh was not something permanently rooted in the natural order, but rather an ethical and spiritual relationship grounded in a covenant of grace.

CHAPTER VII

THE CRISIS OF THE EXILE AND THE PRIESTLY RE-INTERPRETATION OF THE CULT

THE Deuteronomic writers provided in their name-theology a major contribution towards a new understanding of the divine presence in Israel. Their real concern had been to avoid a one-sided doctrine of immanence which reduced Yahweh to the level of a nature-spirit, and which obscured the reality of his freedom to act towards his people in judgment as well as mercy. For the Deuteronomists the covenant between Israel and Yahweh was contingent upon the people's obedience, not unconditional and eternal. A belief in the contingent nature of the covenant had also manifested itself in the oracles of the prophets, and Micah and Jeremiah, had proclaimed that Yahweh would destroy his temple in Jerusalem because it had become the object of a false faith, and thereby a kind of substitute for the living God. The popular cult had lapsed into a self-assured formality, confident in the eternal bond between God and his people expressed in the temple worship, whilst the prophets urged repeatedly that Yahweh was lord of life and history. He could not be subject to the profane control of his people through the rites and offerings which they brought. By destroying the temple Yahweh would abolish this false trust on the part of his people, and re-establish the moral and spiritual demands of the covenant.

The Deuteronomists had sought to save the temple by re-interpreting its meaning and worship in such a way that it preserved the notion of the divine transcendence. Whether or not the mass of the people heeded the warnings of the prophets or the instruction of the Deuteronomists, the events which quickly followed the reformation of Josiah served to demonstrate beyond question that Yahweh's presence in Jerusalem was no guarantee of immunity from disaster. The conquest of Jerusalem by the Babylonian armies in 597 B.C., followed swiftly by a second assault which resulted in the destruction of the temple (586 B.C.), destroyed the myth of the city's inviolability.[1]

---

[1] For the crisis of faith occasioned by the exile see E. Janssen, *Juda in der Exilszeit. Ein Beitrag zur Frage der Entstehung des Judentums* (FRLANT 69), Göttingen, 1956, pp. 58ff.; D. R. Jones, 'The Cessation of Sacrifice after the Destruction of the Temple in 586 B.C.', *JTS* (NS) 14, 1963, pp. 12–31. Jones, however, derives consequences from this event which the present study attributes to other influences.

Had it not been for the prophetic forewarnings, especially those of Jeremiah, we may well consider that Yahwism itself would have been discredited. Yahweh's dwelling-place had been destroyed, his ministers exiled and his people humiliated. Was this not a denial of the presence of Yahweh in Israel's midst?

> 'All who pass on the road
> Clap their hands at you.
> They hiss and shake their heads,
> At the daughter of Jerusalem.
> "Is this the city of which was said,
> The perfection of beauty,
> The joy of all the earth?" '
>
> (Lam. ii. 15)

It was because the nobler spirits of the people could think back upon the words of the prophets that Yahwism was saved from eclipse by its ability to interpret these calamitous events as an act of Yahweh's judgment.

> 'The Lord has scorned his altar,
> Disowned his sanctuary.
> He has delivered into the hands of his enemy
> The walls of her palaces.
> A noise was heard in the temple of Yahweh
> As on a festival day.'
>
> (Lam. ii. 7)

The conquest of Jerusalem and the destruction of the temple were not a denial of the presence of Yahweh in Israel's midst, but a confirmation of it, because the events that had happened were the consequences of his wrath. Thus the crisis in Israel's existence, and of the continued belief in Yahweh, which the exile brought, was overcome by taking heed to the prophetic warnings of judgment. In its turn this crisis served as a confirmation of the prophetic reaction against a misplaced trust in Yahweh's presence in Israel. Jeremiah brought encouragement and hope to the people in exile by a characteristic insistence that Yahweh would be with them in mercy, when the lessons of the exile had been learnt and their hearts were ready for him.

'For thus says Yahweh, "When seventy years are fulfilled for Babylon, I will visit you and I will fulfill my promise to you, and I will bring you

H

back to this place. For I know the intentions which I have concerning you, says Yahweh, intentions of wellbeing and not of harm, to give you a future and a hope. Then you will invoke me, and come and pray to me, and I will hear you. Then you will seek me and find me, when you search for me with a whole heart." '

(Jer. xxix. 10–13)

Jeremiah seems to foresee no rebuilding of the temple, nor any need to do so. For all who lament the loss of the ark he has the promise that all Jerusalem will be called the throne of Yahweh.[1]

Whilst Jeremiah envisaged a return to Jerusalem, he saw no necessity to remake the ark, which had been the chief symbol of Yahweh's presence. The throne of the cherubim, which had been associated with it, would be replaced by the knowledge that all Jerusalem was Yahweh's throne. Henceforth his presence in Israel would be realized by his name set in Jerusalem. In this feature Jeremiah's prophecy reflects the ideas of the Deuteronomistic editors, who shared in the compilation of his book.

From a different standpoint, but with substantially the same interpretation of the destruction of Jerusalem and its temple, we have the prophecies of Ezekiel. This prophet, who was thoroughly imbued with the priestly traditions of Jerusalem, was carried away into exile in 597 B.C., at the time of the first Babylonian conquest. There, in exile, a call to prophesy to his fellow-countrymen came to him in the year 593 B.C. The vision in which this call was experienced[2] took the form of a manifestation of Yahweh, coming from the north, and riding upon his chariot drawn by four strange creatures. These weird celestial beings are identified in a later vision as cherubim,[3] and are accompanied by a stormy wind and clouds with lightning flashing forth continually. In many details, both of elaboration and strangeness, they differ from the carved cherubim that stood in Solomon's temple, but there can be no doubt that this is a visionary description of the celestial chariot, which was symbolized by the cherubim set up over the ark in the $d^e\underline{b}\hat{\imath}r$ of the temple. The differences, which are often quite marked, are due to the ecstatic, visionary, nature of Ezekiel's description, in which certain features of Babylonian imagery have entered. It is unnecessary, therefore, to attempt any kind of

[1] Jer. iii 16f.
[2] Ezek. i. 1–iii. 15.
[3] Ezek. x. 15, 20, 22. This identification of the cherubim of chapter x with the creatures seen in the inaugural vision is generally regarded as secondary. Cf. W. Eichrodt, *Der Prophet Hesekiel 1–18*, pp. 52f., but, more cautiously R. de Vaux, 'Les chérubins et l'arche d'alliance', p. 95.

reconciliation with the description of the furnishings of the *dᵉbîr* of the Jerusalem temple.[1] Ezekiel in his vision saw the very presence of Yahweh in all its majesty coming to him in his distant place of exile. There is no suggestion, therefore, that Yahweh was simply the God of Jerusalem, or only of Palestine, but his power was shown to extend throughout the entire universe.[2]

Ezekiel, who combined in himself something of both priest and prophet, condemned the sins and idolatry of his nation, Israel, and singled out for particular mention the wickedness of those who remained in Jerusalem. He saw, and condemned the idolatrous worship of the seventy elders in the temple,[3] as also the women weeping for Tammuz.[4] This wickedness on the part of the people was driving Yahweh out from his dwelling-place:

'And he said to me, "Son of man, do you see what they are doing, the great abominations which the house of Israel are committing here, to drive me far from my sanctuary?" '

(Ezek. viii. 6)

When the disaster came and the temple was destroyed, the whole course of events was seen and interpreted by the prophet in his exile,[5] and he explained it all to his fellow exiles. Yahweh himself is said to have instigated the destruction of the city by the hands of six executioners:

'Then he said to them, "Defile the house and fill the courts with slain. Go forth!" '

(Ezek. ix. 7)

Yahweh, riding on his cherubim-throne, is said to have abandoned his house and to have departed from the midst of his people:

'Then the cherubim lifted up their wings, with the wheels beside them, and the glory of the God of Israel was over them. Then the glory of

---

[1] H. Schmidt, 'Kerubenthron und Lade', pp. 127–129, claimed that there were actually four cherubim in Solomon's temple. Two remained hidden behind the front pair, and so would not be visible to a lay person looking into the *dᵉbîr* from the main hall of the temple. Such a supposition is beside the point in view of the nature of Ezekiel's description.

[2] B. Stade, *Biblische Theologie des Alten Testaments*, I, Tübingen, 1905, p. 291, claimed that it was from the time of Ezekiel that Yahweh was thought to reside in heaven. Cf. E. Jacob, *Theology of the Old Testament*, London, 1957, p. 255, who claimed that Ezekiel gave a new emphasis to the belief in Yahweh's abode in heaven. These suppositions are unnecessary, for the heavenly nature of Yahweh, and his cosmic rule, were ancient and deeply embedded beliefs in Israel.

[3] Ezek. viii. 5–13.

[4] Ezek. viii. 14–15.

[5] Ezek. ix. 1–xi. 25.

Yahweh went up from the midst of the city, and stood upon the mountain which is on the east side of the city.'

(Ezek. xi. 22–23)

From henceforth it can be said of Jerusalem that Yahweh is not there. In foreseeing the destruction of the temple, Ezekiel is in line with Jeremiah, but Ezekiel, in keeping with his priestly outlook and background, saw such an eventuality as taking place only when Yahweh had withdrawn his presence from the temple. Jeremiah had condemned the temple as a fetish, whilst Ezekiel is careful to describe the departure of Yahweh, which had beforehand given meaning and purpose to the sacred building.

In Ezekiel we find that Yahweh's presence on earth is made possible by his glory. The prophet never states that it is Yahweh himself that he has actually seen, but only his glory.[1] In this way the prophet seems to be in accord with Deuteronomy in refusing to say that Yahweh himself is present on earth. Such an idea would divest Yahweh of his transcendence, and would be altogether too crude an understanding of the divine nature. Yahweh is the God of heaven and earth who cannot be said to be located and confined to this or that place. But, whereas Deuteronomy had spoken of Yahweh's name, as the means of his earthly presence, Ezekiel speaks of his glory. It seems that here Ezekiel is falling back on a particular feature of the Jerusalem tradition of worship. That Yahweh's glory was made manifest in the service of the temple was an ancient belief,[2] which is here exalted to a new significance. It is the mode of the divine presence, and, as such, it has a human form. Yahweh himself does not leave his heavenly dwelling to manifest his presence on earth, but he does this by means of his glory. With the departure of Yahweh's glory from Jerusalem the city is left desolate, and its destruction is interpreted not as the defeat of Yahweh, but as his own will accomplished on the city as a punishment for its sins. The presence of its God is now taken from the people, but, as it was Yahweh's will to depart, so, Ezekiel foretells, is it his will to return. In the meantime,

---

[1] Ezek. i. 28; iii. 12, etc.

[2] Cf. Isa. vi. 3. The idea of the glory of Yahweh cannot only have existed in the Jerusalem temple and it is referred to in the pre-monarchic period, e.g. Exod. xxxiii. 18, 22; Num. xiv. 21–22, Deut. v. 24; cf. 1 Sam. iv. 21–22, but it seems to have assumed a particular prominence in Jerusalem. G. von Rad, *ThWzNT*, II, p. 242, has asserted that the origins of the doctrine of the glory are to be traced back to thunderstorm phenomena. Yahweh, as a storm-god, was thought to reveal himself in the lightning and the thunder. From an early time, however, the glory could not be limited to such natural phenomena and came to have a wider and more spiritual content. Cf. Ps. xix. 2 (EVV. 1).

whilst the people suffer the exile and the desolation of their city, they are not left entirely abandoned. In fact it is those in exile who are able still to know something of the divine presence:

> 'Son of man, your brethren, even your brethren, your fellow exiles, the whole house of Israel, all of them, are those of whom the inhabitants of Jerusalem have said, "They have gone far from Yahweh; to us is this land given for a possession." Therefore say, "Thus says the Lord Yahweh, Though I removed them far off among the nations, and though, I scattered them among the countries, yet have I been a sanctuary to them for a little while[1] in the countries where they have gone." '
>
> (Ezek. xi. 15–16)

Yahweh, the universal God, would be with his own wherever they worshipped him sincerely, and when they truly sought him. It is for the future, however, that Ezekiel's most glowing promises are kept, when Yahweh will bring his people back from exile, and then, to crown his saving work, he will set up his dwelling-place in their midst once again:

> 'I will make a covenant of peace with them; it shall be an everlasting covenant with them; and I will bless[2] them and multiply them, and will set my sanctuary in the midst of them forever. My dwelling-place shall be with them, and I will be their God, and they shall be my people. Then the nations will know that I, Yahweh, sanctify Israel, when my sanctuary is in the midst of them forever.'
>
> (Ezek. xxxvii. 26–28)

As Ezekiel had seen in his vision the ruin of Jerusalem with the departure of Yahweh from his sanctuary, so the restoration of Jerusalem would find its climax in the return of Yahweh to dwell permanently in his rebuilt temple. The crowning hope of the future is the re-establishing of the divine presence in Jerusalem which will make possible all those other blessings which Israel desired, and which set this nation apart from all others. We have seen that the presence of Yahweh in Jerusalem, as it was believed to have been realized in the Solomonic temple, was the basis of a cult-prophetic hope for the future. In Judah's cult, especially in its acclamation of Yahweh as the divine king, the people looked forward to a perfect realization of what that kingship meant in the realms of nature and history. Now Ezekiel introduces a new and important theme. In the present he asserts that Yahweh is not in Jerusalem, but promises a time in the

---

[1] Or 'a little sanctuary'.
[2] Reading with the Targum, instead of the unintelligible 'And I will give them'.

near future when Yahweh will return to this elect city. From being the basis of a future hope, the belief in the divine presence has become an object of that hope itself. The promises of the cult-festivals have been transformed into an eschatology. The older order had collapsed, and Ezekiel now foretold the birth of a new order in which the ancient hopes would find a glorious fulfilment. The return of Yahweh would be the supreme gift which would open the door to all other benefits that Israel could wish for. Although Ezekiel does not say so explicitly in this passage, it is quite clear that it is in terms of Yahweh's glory that this dwelling of Yahweh in the midst of his people was expected.

What this return of Yahweh would mean, and how it was to be made possible without profaning Yahweh's holiness, is detailed for us in the chapters xl-xlviii of Ezekiel's book. These contain a programme for the restored community, outlining the essentials of its social and cultic organization, and they come either from Ezekiel, or from a very close disciple.[1] The whole key to their significance is contained in the name which is to be given to the restored central city of the community 'Yahweh is there'.[2] This is the basis on which a new life of blessing is to be made possible for Israel. The new Israel is to be sanctified so that Yahweh's glory may return, without once again offending him, or profaning his holiness so that he is compelled to withdraw. The practical aim which we can detect in this visionary plan is that of guarding the people against those former sins and defilements which had already brought disaster on the nation, and which would prohibit Yahweh's presence with them. Only by the divine presence could all other gifts be received.

The programme shows that the new community is to be resettled in the land of Israel, and its centre is to be found in a city built on a very high mountain.[3] Within this city, which is to bear the name 'Yahweh is there', Yahweh's temple is to be built, and through the eastern gate of this temple, the glory of Yahweh is to enter.[4] The gate is thereafter to remain perpetually shut, and Yahweh in his glory will dwell in the midst of Israel for ever. In order that no infringements of Yahweh's holiness should any more profane his presence detailed regulations of ministry and worship are stipulated.

---

[1] Many critics have accepted that these chapters come from a disciple of Ezekiel, and the ideas upon which they are based show a close dependence upon those of the great prophet.

[2] Ezek. xlviii. 35.

[3] The emphasis upon the height of this mountain cannot have arisen from the actual size of Mount Zion, but is due to the 'mythological' notion that the divine dwelling-place is higher than all other mountains. Cf. Isa. ii. 2 (= Mic. iv. 1).

[4] Ezek. xliii. 1ff.

The consequences of this divine dwelling in Israel's midst are graphically and clearly presented by the imagery of a stream of water flowing out of the eastern side (the front) of the temple, and making fertile the valley of the Arabah:[1]

> 'And wherever the river[2] goes every living creature which swarms will live, and there will be very many fish, for this water goes there, that the waters of the sea[3] may become fresh; so everything will live where the river goes.'
>
> (Ezek. xlvii. 9)

The imagery of this river goes back to the earlier mythological idea of the river of paradise, which was reflected in certain aspects of Israel's cult, but the substance of this vision is of the supernatural blessing which is to flow out to the land from the temple. Wherever the river goes there is an abundance of 'life', and the temple is the means whereby this 'life', the gift of Yahweh to his people, is poured out upon them. The temple is the place where Yahweh's presence is to be found, and as a result of this divine indwelling in its midst, Israel is to experience the richness of the divine blessing in its land.

Ezekiel, as 'the father of Judaism', is the prophet of restoration and hope, and the central feature of this hope is that Yahweh, by means of the glory which effects his presence, will return to Israel and once again make his abode in Jerusalem.

Among the captives of Judah there was also another prophet whose name is unknown to us, but whose prophecies were appended to those of Isaiah of Jerusalem, and are contained in Isaiah xl-lv. In the dark days of exile, and apparently subsequent to the ministry of Ezekiel, he arose to stir the hearts of the people to prepare for a return to Judah. In a startling oracle he pictures Yahweh himself leading his people in triumph through the desert back to their homeland:[4]

> 'For you shall not depart in haste,
>   Nor shall you go in flight;
> For Yahweh will go before you,
>   And the God of Israel shall be your rearguard.'
>
> (Isa. lii. 12)

For this triumphant homecoming the desert road was to be miracu-

---

[1] Ezek. xlvii. 1ff.
[2] So LXX, Syr., Vulg. and Targum. The Hebrew has 'two rivers', which seems out of place, but may perhaps be connected with the two rivers of paradise, which we find reflected in Canaanite mythology as the two rivers where El has his abode.
[3] Cf. Syr.
[4] Isa. lii. 7–12.

lously made straight and level.[1] Deutero-Isaiah viewed Yahweh's deliverance of his people and their restoration to their own land as the sign of the divine kingship. It was Yahweh's accession to the throne of the world, and the establishment of his reign.[2] Much of the thought and language of Deutero-Isaiah has been shown to be borrowed from the language of the great Autumn Festival of Jerusalem.[3] There is a strong faith in the presence of Yahweh with his people, and in this deep experience of the supreme and only God, who had created all things and who governed history, there seems to be little place for an earthly temple; yet Deutero-Isaiah saw the rebuilding of the temple as one of the chief objects of the return home.[4] The existing plight of Israel was exemplified in the destruction of the sanctuary,[5] which had come about because of the nation's sin. In contrast to this unhappy present the future would bring a reversal of Israel's fortunes, when the fullness of its salvation would be made visible in the rebuilt temple and in the richly ornamented city of Jerusalem.[6] To it all the peoples of the world would make their pilgrimage, bringing their gifts and seeking to do homage to the people of God.[7]

With this prophet the nation itself, which had survived from the old southern kingdom of Judah, is frequently termed 'Jerusalem', or 'Zion'. The entire nation is meant, but both by reason of the narrow geographical limits of the land, and also because of the immense theological significance of the city, the name of the ancient city and sacred hill have become synonymous with the nation itself.

Deutero-Isaiah prepared the hearts of the people for the restoration of a national life in Judah, and in the rich imagery of his message he foretold that the return of the people from exile would take place in supernatural circumstances. The supreme blessing would be the return of Yahweh to Jerusalem, when that city would assume its true place as the centre of revelation and worship for all the nations of the world. Deutero-Isaiah, like Ezekiel, assured the exiles of Yahweh's sovereign power to bring them back to their homeland and to bring about a rebirth of the nation. For both prophets the presence of Yahweh with his people is at the centre of their hope.

---

[1] Isa. xl. 1ff.
[2] Isa. lii. 7.
[3] S. Mowinckel, *Psalmenstudien II*, pp. 256f. This is not conceded by N. H. Snaith, *The Jewish New Year Festival*, London, 1947, pp. 200f., 206f., and H. J. Kraus, *Die Königsherrschaft Gottes im Alten Testament*, pp. 99ff.
[4] Isa. xliv. 28.
[5] Isa. xliii. 28.
[6] Isa. liv. 11–14.
[7] Isa. xlv. 14–17; xlix. 18, 22–23.

The exile occasioned a crisis of tremendous magnitude in the life of Judah, and an independent political and religious existence of the nation was brought to an end for a considerable period. But for the teaching of the prophets it seems that faith in Yahweh itself would have been discredited, for the two pillars of Judah's religious life had both fallen. These were the belief in a covenant between Yahweh and the house of David, and the special position of Jerusalem as Yahweh's chosen dwelling-place. That Judah was able to accept the removal of the Davidic monarch, and the destruction of the temple as the will of Yahweh is a miracle of faith. Some at least of the people were able to interpret these events as the expression of a divine purpose which reached beyond these disasters, and pointed to a new life of hope for Israel. That only a minority of the nation grasped this renewal of hope does not occasion surprise, but it is to those who did that the restoration of Judah owes its being, and it was from them that Judaism took its origin. Thus the meaning and destiny of Israel lay in the hands of a group of exiles who, in penitence and faith, accepted their tragic past as a divine judgment, and sought to rebuild and reconsecrate the nation in accordance with the will of Yahweh. We have seen that the programme for the restored community contained in the prophecies of Ezekiel (xl–xlviii) showed the way, and the exhortations of Deutero-Isaiah gave point and urgency to the call to return and rebuild. Among the exiles, in circles that, like Ezekiel, were rooted in the history and traditions of the Jerusalem temple, a detailed and elaborate programme for the future took shape in the form of the Priestly Writing. To this we must now give our attention, for it represents a synthesis of many earlier ideas and symbols of Yahweh's presence, and re-mints them into a theological whole of impressive and compelling grandeur.

The Priestly Writing is a historical work setting out the history and life of the people of God from creation until the eve of the entry of Israel into Palestine. This history has a didactic aim, and, at various points in the narrative, extensive regulations are given with particular regard to Israel's faith and cult. It is these 'legal' sections which earned for the Priestly Writing from earlier critics the title of the Priestly Code, but such a nomenclature obscures the genuinely historical nature of the work. The clear historical outline, with its characteristic genealogical structure, has made it the 'backbone' of the present pentateuch, into which it has been woven.[1]

---

[1] For the contents of the Priestly Writing see the standard introductions to the Old Testament.

The writer, or writers, who were responsible for this comprehensive theological document had behind them traditional material, partly in documentary form, which they were able to utilize and edit to form one whole.[1] It seems beyond question that much of this inherited material which was at the disposal of the Priestly writers concerned the moral and cultic regulations of the Jerusalem temple, so that the belief in Yahweh's dwelling in Jerusalem forms a presupposition which governed the aim of the regulations. The largest continuous block of such inherited material is to be found in the Holiness Code,[2] with its emphasis:

> 'You shall be holy, for I, Yahweh your God am holy.'
>
> (Lev. xix. 2)

A particularly interesting feature of this Holiness Code, so far as the doctrine of the divine presence is concerned, is that it makes the divine dwelling within Israel conditional upon obedience to the commandments:

> 'If you walk in my statutes, and keep my commandments and do them . . .
> I will set my tabernacle in your midst, and will not abhor you; and I
> will walk among you and be your God, and you shall be my people.'
>
> (Lev. xxvi. 3, 11, 12)[3]

Yahweh's presence is the supreme blessing for Israel, and the benefits that are promised in the intervening verses 3–10 find their fitting climax in the promise that Yahweh himself will dwell in Israel. In fact the aim of the whole Holiness Code was to make possible such a continued dwelling with the nation. The Priestly writers have inherited this doctrine, and in the light of the exile, it has assumed a

---

[1] G. von Rad, *Die Priesterschrift im Hexateuch* (BWANT IV, 13), Stuttgart, 1934, advocated a theory of two main sources P[a] and P[b]. The pre-history of some of the material in the Priestly Writing has now been subjected to a form-critical examination. See R. Rendtorff, *Die Gesetze in der Priesterschrift* (FRLANT 62), Göttingen, 1954; K. Koch, *Die Priesterschrift von Exodus 25 bis Leviticus 16: eine überlieferungsgeschichtliche und literarkritische Untersuchung* (FRLANT 71), Göttingen, 1959.
   For the theology of the Priestly Writing see G. von Rad, *Die Priesterschrift im Hexateuch*, pp. 166ff., and *Old Testament Theology*, I, pp. 232ff.; K. Elliger, 'Sinn und Ursprung der priesterschriftlichen Geschichtserzählung', *ZThK* 49, 1952, pp. 121–143; K. Koch, 'Die Eigenart der priesterschriftlichen Sinaigesetzgebung', *ZThK* 55, 1958, pp. 36–51.
[2] Lev. xvii–xxvi. For a form-critical approach to the Code see H. Graf Reventlow, *Das Heiligkeitsgesetz formgeschtichlich untersucht* (WMANT 6), Neukirchen, 1961; R. Kilian, *Literarkritische und formgeschichtliche Untersuchung des Heiligkeitsgesetzes*, Bonn, 1963.
[3] This making of Yahweh's presence conditional upon Israel's obedience cannot have been without influence on the growth of a legalistic spirit, in which Yahweh's gifts were promised on condition of observance of the law.

more critical importance. Yahweh had made evident in the events of history his refusal to continue to dwell in the temple of Jerusalem, in the face of the disobedience of his people. The aim for the future, as Ezekiel's programme had already outlined, must be to re-fashion the life and worship of Israel in order to make possible the return of Yahweh's presence so that Israel might once more, in the fullest sense, become his people.

The Priestly Writing then is a product of the exile in which the traditions of the past were reflected upon in the light of the history of Israel and Judah, and, in view of the lessons of this history, a programme was made for the restoration of the community. This programme itself takes the form of a historical narrative in which, at the appropriate points, the revealed will of God is declared. The date when this Priestly Writing was first completed as an integral whole, has often been put by critics some time during the fifth century B.C., perhaps about 450 B.C. In the light of a closer examination of its contents and purpose there seems every probability that an earlier date is demanded, and M. Noth is more likely to be correct in arguing that the work was substantially complete before the dedication of the rebuilt temple of Jerusalem in 515 B.C.[1] The Priestly Writing may be termed a theological reconstruction of the temple, as distinct from its purely material refurbishing.

The method of the entire work is to get back to the true origins of Israel, and to lay bare the real basis of the nation's life. To this end greatest importance is attached to the work of Moses, who is presented as the mediator of the divine will to Israel, setting him above all other human figures who played their part in Israel's story. Behind Moses, however, the Priestly Writing goes back to Abraham and finds the origins of Israel in certain promises made by God to this patriarch. The work as a whole is built on the theory of two covenants, the first of which was made with mankind through Noah,[2] and the second with Abraham,[3] of which circumcision was the sign and seal.[4] This latter covenant is a covenant of promise, which finds its fulfilment in the existence and nationhood of Israel. Thus the new

---

[1] M. Noth, *Exodus*, p. 17.
[2] Gen. ix. 8–17.
[3] Gen. xvii. 1–14.
[4] The claim of J. Wellhausen, *Prolegomena to the History of Ancient Israel*, pp. 338ff., 385, that the Priestly work is built around four covenants does not seem to be substantiated, for the injunction to the first human couple cannot properly be termed a covenant, and instead of a covenant at Mount Sinai, what we have is the fulfilment and actualizing of the covenant of promise to Abraham. The actual term 'covenant' is not used in connection with Mount Sinai by the Priestly authors.

feature that is introduced with Moses at Mount Sinai is not a new covenant, but the ratification and fulfilment of the covenant with Abraham.[1] The relationship between the age of the patriarchs and that of Moses is one of promise and fulfilment.

We are able to discover what the Priestly Writing considered to be the basis of Israel's life if we examine the promises of the covenant with Abraham, and from this we can see the main aim of the authors for the restoration of Israel. The assurance of a divine promise to the patriarchs is given in the earlier histories of the pre-Mosaic period. Both the J and E narratives inform us of a promise to Abraham in which the patriarch was assured that his descendants would become a great nation, and would inherit the land of Canaan.[2] When we consider the Priestly account of the covenant with Abraham we discover that a significant addition has been made:

'Behold my covenant is with you, and you shall be the father of a multitude of nations.

And I will establish my covenant between me and you and your descendants after you throughout their generations for an everlasting covenant, to be God to you and to your descendants after you. And I will give to you, and to your descendants after you, the land of your sojourning, all the land of Canaan, for an everlasting possession; and I will be their God.'

(Gen. xvii. 4, 7–8; cf. Exod. vi. 7–8)

The divine promise 'I will be their God' must be interpreted here, not merely in the sense of a formal covenant relationship, but in a sense that is of crucial importance for the Priestly authors, that Yahweh will himself dwell in the midst of Israel.[3] The threefold basis of Israel's existence is a triple promise of God: the nationhood of Abraham's descendants, the possession of the land of Canaan and the divine presence in Israel. All three of these had been seriously thrown in question by the disasters of 597 and 586 B.C. Israel, at least that part of it which mattered most for the Priestly writers, was no longer a nation but was in exile; it had been dispossessed of its land and the temple had been destroyed and Yahweh's presence

---

[1] Cf. W. Zimmerli, 'Sinaibund und Abrahambund', *Gottes Offenbarung*, pp. 207ff. G. von Rad, *Die Priesterschrift im Hexateuch*, pp. 175ff., suggested that P eliminated the Sinai covenant because it could offer nothing new, but in his *Old Testament Theology*, I, p. 135, he suggests that there may have been an account of the covenant on Sinai which has fallen out, when the story was worked into JE.

[2] Gen. xiii. 14–17 (J); Gen. xv. 1–6 (E).

[3] W. Zimmerli, 'Sinaibund und Abrahambund', p. 212.

withdrawn. All that was left for Israel was to fall back upon the divine promise, so that whilst in the present it possessed nothing, it might yet in the future possess all things. God's covenant was an everlasting covenant and his word could not fail. The aim of the Priestly Writing is therefore a threefold one, to show how Israel might yet again become a nation, possess its land and receive the divine presence in its midst.[1] It achieves this aim by a re-telling of the story how Israel first became a nation and received the blessing of the divine presence in its midst together with a land where they could dwell. It shows that the grace of God was at work in all these steps, and that all these promises had been fulfilled when Israel obeyed the word of Yahweh.

Because Israel was not, in the estimate of the Priestly authors, a nation whilst in exile, and because also they wished to stress the nature of the community as built around the encounter with Yahweh, who dwelt in their midst, they do not term Israel a 'people' (Heb. 'am), but an 'assembly' (Heb. 'ēḏâ).[2] How this community, led by Moses, was brought to the borders of Canaan forms the climax of the Priestly narrative.[3] The concern of our present study is with the Priestly doctrine of the presence of Yahweh in Israel's midst, and our task is to show how this was thought to have been realized, and what form it adopted.

The form which the divine presence took is clearly and consistently presented in the Priestly work. Yahweh comes down from heaven in a cloud which contains his glory.[4] This glory in the cloud is the vehicle and mode of the divine presence within Israel, and, as such, is a development of the same tradition which we have found in Ezekiel.[5] Yahweh himself does not cease to be the transcendent lord of the universe and to dwell in heaven, but he sends forth his glory to be with his people. Where the Deuteronomists had spoken of the name, as the mode of the divine presence on earth, the Priestly

---

[1] We cannot reduce this threefold aim to an emphasis upon one as K. Elliger ('Sinn und Ursprung der priesterschriftliche Geschichtserzählung', pp. 121ff.) seeks to do. He singles out the re-possession of the land as the main object of the work.
[2] Cf. L. Rost, *Die Vorstufen von Kirche und Synagoge im Alten Testament*, (BWANT IV: 24), Stuttgart, 1938, pp. 38ff.
[3] Num. xxxiii. 1–xxxvi. 13.
[4] Exod. xvi. 7, 10; xxiv. 16; xxix. 43; xl. 34ff.; Lev. ix. 6, 23; Num. xiv. 10; xvi. 19; cf. Lev. xvi. 2.
[5] E. Jacob, *Theology of the O.T.*, p. 81, claims that the doctrine of the glory in Ezekiel is the result of a current of thought which developed independently of that which is found in the Priestly Writing. Cf. G. von Rad, *ThWzNT*, II, pp. 243f. The differences, however, may well be due to the visionary-prophetic character of the one, contrasted with the more strictly theological purpose of the other. Behind the whole concept of the glory and its association with a cloud we can discern an origin in the cult.

authors speak of his glory. This glory is very much a theological concept, and has not the same personal form as we found in Ezekiel, but none the less it is out of the midst of the cloud that the voice of Yahweh is said to have been heard.[1] The Priestly narrative first introduces us to this mode of Yahweh's presence in Exod. xvi. 7, 10, when the Israelites are still on their way to Mount Sinai. On the mountain itself it is by a descent of this cloud that Yahweh is reported to have met with Moses,[2] and delivered to him the instructions for Israel's cult.[3]

These instructions for Israel's worship are the key to what the Priestly authors regarded as the new feature that entered into Israel's life from its encounter with God on Mount Sinai. They concern the design, building and furnishing of a tabernacle (Heb. *miškān*), together with the consecration of its priesthood from the sons of Aaron. It has for long been an accepted point of criticism that this Priestly account of the tabernacle draws a great deal on memories and traditions of Solomon's temple,[4] and that what it in fact presents us with is a description of a temple, under the guise of a portable tent sanctuary. In accordance with their intention of falling back on the foundations of Israel's existence with Abraham and Moses, they refrain from describing an edifice which could only have existed when the people were permanently settled in their own land. Instead, with the knowledge that in Israel's early days there had existed a portable tent shrine, the tent of meeting, they describe in detail a building which has all the furnishings of a temple, whilst remaining a portable tent.[5] Sometimes this is called the tent of meeting, and sometimes the tabernacle. This is the shrine, built according to the instructions which God himself has given through Moses, in which Yahweh's

---

[1] Exod. xxiv. 16.

[2] Exod. xxiv. 15–18a.

[3] Exod. xxv. 1–xxxi. 18a.

[4] J. Wellhausen, *Prolegomena to the History of Ancient Israel*, pp. 39ff., calls the tabernacle a fiction which had no existence before Solomon's temple.

[5] G. Henton Davies, 'Tabernacle', *IDB*, IV, pp. 504aff., argues that the tabernacle of P is an ideal elaboration of an ancient doctrine and its accompanying institutions. He claims that its features provide one of the missing links between the old tent of meeting and the temple of Solomon, and that the Priestly account may well reflect features of the sacred tent set up by David (2 Sam. vi. 17). In any case it is clear that the Priestly writers have presented a theological development of an ancient institution, and the only question in debate concerns the extent of their idealizing. Just how many features of their tabernacle had ever existed in the ancient tent is a question which it is quite impossible to answer. It greatly exceeds the evidence, therefore, when M. Haran ('Shiloh and Jerusalem: the Origin of the Priestly Tradition in the Pentateuch', *JBL* 81, 1962, pp. 14–24) argues that the tabernacle, and indeed the whole Priestly tradition, derive from the ancient sanctuary of Shiloh.

glory, and thus Yahweh's very presence, will come to take up its abode in the midst of Israel:

'And let them make for me a sanctuary, that I may dwell in their midst. According to everything which I show you concerning the pattern of the tabernacle, and the pattern of all its furniture, so you shall make it.'

(Exod. xxv. 8–9)

'And I will dwell among the people of Israel, and will be their God. And they shall know that I am Yahweh their God, who brought them out from the land of Egypt that I might dwell among them; I am Yahweh their God.'

(Exod. xxix. 45–46)

In these verses it is perfectly clear that for Yahweh to be the God of Israel means that he dwells in their midst, and that the means to the realization of this is the building of the tabernacle. This is the new feature that entered into Israel's life from Mount Sinai. These verses are in fact the motive clauses for the entire cult and worship of Israel, which exists simply that Yahweh might dwell with his people, and that by doing so he might bless them.[1] Israel only becomes Israel when Yahweh dwells in its midst, and so the birth of the nation can be traced back to Mount Sinai. All that went before this is promise, and the fulfilment of this promise is described when the instructions that Moses has received are carried out, and the work is finished:[2]

'Then the cloud covered the tent of meeting, and the glory of Yahweh filled the tabernacle. And Moses was not able to enter the tent of meeting, because the cloud dwelt upon it, and the glory of Yahweh filled the tabernacle. Throughout all their journeys, whenever the cloud was taken up from over the tabernacle, the people of Israel would go onward; but if the cloud was not taken up, then they did not go on till the day that it was taken up. For throughout all their journeys the cloud of Yahweh was upon the tabernacle by day, and fire was in it by night, in the sight of all the house of Israel.'

(Exod. xl. 34–38)

It is from this moment, when Israel's cult is functioning properly and Yahweh's glory comes to dwell with them, that its destiny is fulfilled and it can truly be said to be the people of God. For the Priestly authors, from the standpoint of their own time, this example

[1] M. Haran, 'The Nature of the "Ohel Mo'edh" in Pentateuchal Sources', p. 62 note; cf. also K. Koch, 'Die Eigenart der priesterschriftlichen Sinaigesetzgebung', pp. 48ff.
[2] Exod. xxxv. 1–xl. 33.

from the past was intended as a model by which Israel could re-mould its worship according to the will of God, and thus again in the future become his people. The description of the tabernacle is intended as a building programme for the future of the exiled Judeans, who knew that the glory had departed, and that the temple lay in ruins.

It is the doctrine of the Priestly Writing that Israel's true existence is only possible when Yahweh's glory is dwelling in its midst, and that this can only be achieved when Israel possesses a tabernacle. It was unimportant to the authors that in their own time they expected the tabernacle to take the more permanent form of a temple, for in this respect they were governed by the historical nature of their writing and the conditions that pertained to the original situation on Mount Sinai. What kind of dwelling was it that these writers were thinking of? The title 'tabernacle' (Heb. *miškān*) is important, for it is a noun formed from the verb 'to dwell' (Heb. *šākan*). The normal verb 'to dwell' in Hebrew means literally 'to sit down' (Heb. *yāšab*), and this is the verb used when Yahweh is said to be 'enthroned' over the cherubim, and which was originally employed to describe his 'dwelling' in Israel.[1] Besides this another verb, meaning literally 'to pitch tent' (Heb. *šākan*) was in use, and, in early writings where the 'dwelling' of Yahweh is mentioned, no particular effort seems to have been made to distinguish between the use of the two.[2] Deuteronomy, however, when it came to describe the dwelling of Yahweh's name on earth, distinctly preferred to use *šākan*,[3] reserving *yāšab* for Yahweh's dwelling in heaven.[4] Their belief was that the only place where Yahweh could be said to 'dwell' (*yāšab*) was heaven, and that on earth his name only 'tented', or 'tabernacled' (*šākan*).[5] This development, in which a quite special technical theological sense was imparted to the verb 'to tabernacle' (Heb. *šākan*), came to a new importance in the Priestly Writing. The authors are perfectly explicit that the manner in which Yahweh's presence abides in Israel is by his glory 'tabernacling' there. The very shrine where this occurs is thence called a tabernacle (Heb. *miškān*), and takes the form of a tent. This seems to represent a deliberate attempt to derive a theology

---

[1] 2 Sam. vii. 6; 1 Kings viii. 12–13.
[2] Cf. the parallelism of the ancient oracle 1 Kings viii. 12–13, where no real distinction between the meaning of the two verbs seems intended.
[3] Deut. xii. 5, 11; xiv. 23; xvi. 2, 6, 11.
[4] 1 Kings viii. 27, 30, etc.
[5] For the development of the verb *šākan* in this technical, theological sense see F. M. Cross, 'The Tabernacle', pp. 66–67. Cf. also G. E. Wright, *Biblical Archaeology*, p. 145.

out of an old cult-institution. Israel had once possessed a sacred tent, and, in the Jerusalem cult tradition, the description of its sanctuary as a tent continued to be employed. This is evidenced by some psalms where the temple is referred to as a tent,[1] and it was no doubt encouraged by the fact that the Canaanites had also described a sanctuary as a *miškān*.[2] The Priestly authors now endeavoured to draw a distinctive theological significance out of the use of such a word. Yahweh's presence could no longer be thought of in terms of a fixed 'dwelling' among his people, for that would have suggested altogether too permanent a bond on Yahweh's part, and would be open to the misunderstanding that his true dwelling was not to be found in heaven. For the Deuteronomists the preference for the use of the verb *šākan*, to describe the manner of Yahweh's presence on earth through his name, seems to have been motivated by the need to guard against a false and misleading notion of the divine dwelling on earth. With the Priestly Writing, however, two further factors have entered in; one is that Yahweh's presence took up its abode in Israel in a tent, and this etymologically makes *šākan* a very suitable verb to describe the divine dwelling there; the other is that the Priestly authors were conscious of a gap in the history of Yahweh's presence in Israel, occasioned by the exile. For almost three-quarters of a century the temple of Jerusalem, which, from the Priestly viewpoint, was the heir of the old Mosaic tent, had lain desolate and Yahweh's glory had not 'tented' there. To make this intelligible, and to show that the divine glory was not permanently bound to one place, but only settled impermanently on earth, these authors found a very suitable expression in the verb 'to tabernacle'.[3]

The manner of Yahweh's dwelling in Israel is therefore expressed by the Priestly writers as an impermanent 'tabernacling' on earth by means of the cloud of the divine glory. This cloud immediately recalls to us the idea of Yahweh's theophany in the old tent of meeting, and of his appearing in the temple worship. Yahweh's presence

---

[1] Pss. xv. 1; xxvii. 5, 6; lxi. 5 (EVV. 4).

[2] See above p. 58.

[3] The importance of the impermanence of such a dwelling, and its basis in a theophany, is well attested by the Septuagint translators, who were even more careful to avoid any suggestion that Yahweh dwelt permanently on earth. In Deuteronomy, where the Hebrew verb *šākan* is used to describe the placing of Yahweh's name in the sanctuary, the Septuagint translators paraphrased as 'I will be invoked', thus avoiding altogether any suggestion that Yahweh's presence was on earth. In Deut. xxxiii. 16, where Yahweh's dwelling (Heb. *šākan*) 'in a thorn bush' (That this should probably be 'Sinai', see above p. 19), is mentioned, the Septuagint translates as 'appeared'. The same Greek verb is also used in Exod. xxv. 8 (P), to describe Yahweh's dwelling (Heb. *šākan*) in the tabernacle.

I

was manifested by his coming to his people, and his appearing in a theophany, recalling the covenant celebrations on Mount Sinai. The idea of Yahweh's dwelling in Israel was justified on the basis of his coming and appearing to them, so that some tension can really be sensed as to whether this presence was permanent, or only a temporary theophany,[1] the Priestly Writing set the idea of the theophany in the forefront of its doctrine of the divine presence, but in doing so has made it into a semi-permanent phenomenon.[2] We might indeed speak of a 'sustained theophany', for this is in fact what is intended:

> 'For throughout all their journeys the cloud of Yahweh was upon the tabernacle by day, and fire was in it by night, in the sight of all the house of Israel.'
>
> (Exod. xl. 38)

In this way, by making the cloud into a permanent concept of the divine presence, the Priestly Writing has fashioned a synthesis of earlier ideas of the presence on earth. Their conclusion is that the cloud of the theophany is not merely a temporary manifestation of the divine glory, but is a permanent mode of his activity, and as such, is the way in which he comes to settle within Israel. This abiding in Israel, however, is neither unconditional nor unchangeable, but is only a 'tabernacling', and may be withdrawn in the face of national disobedience. Therefore although the cloud is a permanent mode of Yahweh's being and action, its stay on earth may be only temporary, or at least interrupted.

Within the tabernacle which the Priestly authors describe, the

---

[1] See above p. 63.

[2] G. von Rad, 'Zelt und Lade', p. 125, feels the difficulty in the tension between the Priestly description of Yahweh's theophany in the cloud, and the assertions of Yahweh's dwelling in Israel. In his *Old Testament Theology*, I, p. 239 note, he regards the promises of Yahweh's dwelling (Exod. xxv. 8; xxix. 45f.) as merely retaining an old mode of expression which the Priestly authors themselves have replaced by their 'appearance-theology' of Yahweh's cloud-theophany. This he is able to stress because of his distinction between 'dwelling-temples' and 'theophany-temples'. This cannot be accepted, most especially because the promises of Yahweh's tabernacling presence are fundamental to the Priestly Writing as the motive clauses of the entire cult. This is partly admitted elsewhere by von Rad (*Studies in Deuteronomy*, p. 40), when he notes that there are exceedingly frequent indications in the Priestly Writing that cult activities take place 'before Yahweh' (cf. Num. xvi. 3). Von Rad claims, however (*Old Testament Theology*, I, p. 239 note) that this is more frequent in secondary texts (P^s). The resolution of the difficulty is to be found in the special sense that the authors have imparted to the verb *šākan*, and in the particular kind of semi-permanent presence which they envisage. Cf. E. Jacob, *Theology of the O.T.*, p. 73 note, who regards the Priestly concept of the cloud as an attempt to make a permanent presence out of an occasional one. K. Koch, *Die Priesterschrift von Exodus 25 bis Leviticus 16*, p. 45, sees two traditions woven together in the Priestly doctrine of the cloud.

most important item of furniture is the ark,[1] although it is not quite as we have come to know it from the earlier accounts. It is overlaid with gold, and on top of it is placed a golden cover,[2] which is the place where the divine glory is located, and which perhaps reflects a knowledge that Yahweh's throne was thought to be above the ark. It is upon this cover over the ark, placed at its two ends, that the cherubim are now to be situated. These are wrought of gold, and seem now to be little more than ornaments. It is from above the cover of the ark, and between the two cherubim, that the very presence of Yahweh is to be found:

'There I will meet with you, and from above the ark-cover, from between the two cherubim that are upon the ark of the testimony, I will speak with you all that I will command you in regard to the people of Israel.'
(Exod. xxv. 22)[3]

This ark is termed 'the ark of the testimony', and the Priestly authors show a particular fondness for words from the two Hebrew roots *yāʿad* = 'to meet' and *ʿûd* = 'to testify'.[4] These writers not only delight in the assonance of such words, but seem to hint at a mysterious connection between the meanings of what were originally two separate verbal roots. If, as is usually the case, we take this 'testimony'[5] to refer to the law tablets, which the Deuteronomists claimed were put in the ark, then we have in the Priestly Writing a synthesis of interpretations of the ark. It is a container for the law-tablets, but also it is connected with Yahweh's cherubim-throne, and it is over the ark that his glory is to be found. Thus the older view of the ark, and its Deuteronomic re-interpretation are united in the Priestly account. It has been suggested,[6] however, that the 'testimony' does not refer to the law-tablets, but was thought to be some written seal of the divine promise to dwell with Israel. In this case the tradition of the law-tablets, contained in the ark, has undergone a change at the hands of these authors, and the whole weight of their theology of the sanctuary is directed towards the divine dwelling there. All is interpreted in the light of the promises of God; the

---

[1] Exod. xxv. 10–22.
[2] Heb. *kappōreṯ*; EVV. 'mercy-seat'.
[3] Cf. Exod. xxix. 42, 43; xxx. 36; Lev. xvi. 2.
[4] E.g. the nation is an assembly (Heb. *ʿēdâ ⋀ yāʿad*); the tabernacle is a 'tent of meeting' (Heb. *'ōhel mōʿēd ⋀ yāʿad*); the ark is the 'ark of the testimony' (Heb. *ʿᵃrôn hāʿēdûṯ ⋁ ʿûd*), and it is here that Yahweh 'meets' (Heb. *yāʿad*) with Israel.
[5] Exod. xxv. 16, 21.
[6] L. Rost, 'Die Wohnstätte des Zeugnisses', F. *Baumgärtel Festschrift* (Erlanger Forschungen A:10), Erlangen, 1959, pp. 164f. Rost compares the Egyptian royal protocol.

nationhood of Israel, the possession of the land and the divine presence in its midst. The ark, according to the Priestly account, is to be
set inside the tabernacle when it has been made, showing that the
ark and the tent of meeting were regarded as inseparable. One
additional point is worthy of notice; in Exod. xxx. 26 the ark, like the
tabernacle, is commanded to be anointed with oil, to consecrate it for
its sacred purpose. It is not regarded as holy in itself, but simply as a
material object which is made for a divine purpose, and through
which the holiness of the glory of Yahweh might be shed abroad
among the people. This concept of holiness which radiates out from
the presence over the ark is a remarkable aspect of the whole Priestly
approach to the cult. It affects both persons and objects which come
into contact with the sanctuary. Everything is part of a single unified
whole, and the foundation pillar of the entire cult is the promise
of the divine tabernacling over the ark.

When we look at the Priestly interpretation of the doctrine of
Yahweh's presence with Israel, and compare it with earlier ideas on
the subject, we become aware of a very significant change of emphasis.
No longer is the presence of Yahweh associated with a particular
place at all, but instead it is related to a cultic community. Even
Deuteronomy had spoken of 'the place where Yahweh will choose
to set his name', and Ezekiel's programme for the restoration of
Israel leaves it beyond doubt that he is thinking of a new temple
in Jerusalem, as the abode of Yahweh's glory. But the Priestly
Writing has no mention of a particular place, except that Yahweh
speaks with Israel from above the cover of the ark, from between the
two cherubim. The ark, with its cover and cherubim, is not a place,
however, but a piece of cult-furniture, which, like the tabernacle
in which it is set, is portable and moves about with the people. The
last vestiges of a Canaanite idea of the divine presence, linked to an
earthly dwelling-place through which the land is blessed, have now
disappeared. In its place we have a very distinctive and original Israelite theology of Yahweh, as the God of heaven, who sends forth his
glory to tabernacle among his people, and who sanctifies and blesses
them from the centre of their camp. The ancient words of the
prophet Nathan have taken on a new and living significance for
Israel:

'I have not dwelt in a house since the day I brought up the people of
Israel from Egypt to this day, but I have been moving about in a tent for
my dwelling.'

(2 Sam. vii. 6)

Yahweh's presence, in the Priestly theology, was never committed irrevocably to dwell in Jerusalem, but was ever the gift of his grace to Israel, whenever they were obedient to the conditions which he himself had given. These conditions are simply: the right sanctuary, the right cult and cult-furnishings, and the right priesthood. The Priestly writers were intent on showing Israel the way which could again in the future lead to their becoming a nation, with possession of the land of Canaan, and with Yahweh's glory in their midst.

Alongside of this change of emphasis in the doctrine of Yahweh's presence, we can discern also a changed attitude to the cult. This is particularly important in view of the fact that it is to the Priestly Writing that we owe a great deal of our knowledge of the details of Israel's cultic regulations. The earlier worship of Israel, like that of the Ancient Near East in general, believed very much in the immediate efficacy of cultic acts. Ritual and sacrifice carried their meaning and effectiveness within themselves, so that in the individual act of worship the Israelite believed that his needs of forgiveness and divine blessing were realized. The dramatic nature of ritual was an attempt to 'actualize' what it symbolically proclaimed. With the Priestly Writing, although this previous attitude is certainly not absent, we can see that the different aspects of Israel's cult are 'theologized' to make them fit into one unified whole.[1] Many features have become symbolic of theological truths, and this is apparent in the disposition of the sanctuary and its furnishings. It is also apparent in the rituals, and in the way, for example, that both the tabernacle and all its furnishings, as well as its priesthood, need anointing with oil before they can be used.[2] They are none of them holy in themselves, but are made so by divine action, so that the holiness of Yahweh's glory, in the centre of the Israelite camp, may be conveyed outwards to the people, whilst being protected from any profane contact. This 'theologizing' of the cult is also apparent in the insistence that Moses received the instructions for the tabernacle directly from Yahweh, and was careful to carry out precisely the injunctions given.[3] The true sanctuary and the true way of worship are known only to God, and it is as an act of his grace that he has revealed them to Israel.[4] All Israel's worship therefore is a response to grace, to make possible

---

[1] Cf. M. Haran, 'The Complex of Ritual Acts Performed inside the Tabernacle', *Scripta Hierosolymitana*, VIII, 1961, p. 295.

[2] Exod. xxx. 22–33.

[3] Exod. xxv. 8–9; xxxix. 32, 43; xl. 16.

[4] Possibly the Priestly authors found support for this view in the ancient notion of a heavenly temple, of which the temple on earth was a copy.

the supreme act of grace that Yahweh's glory tabernacles in its midst. There is no suggestion anywhere that by its worship Israel can exercise any coercion upon God.

The Priestly account of Israel's origins and former splendour, containing as it does so many explicit regulations for life and worship, was intended as a paradigm of the future. It was meant not simply as an example, but as a programme to be fulfilled, so that Israel might once again enter into its ancient heritage. Because it bears this programmatic character, and provides a theological basis for the reconstruction of Israel, with a new temple and a re-consecrated priesthood, it certainly gains greatly in meaning and significance if it is to be dated before the dedication of the rebuilt temple in 515 B.C. At this time the exiles were first re-establishing themselves in Judah and seeking to rebuild Jerusalem. It would be remarkable if those who believed so passionately in the worthwhileness of such a task, as the Priestly writers so undoubtedly did, were not amongst the foremost to set to work to achieve it. Nevertheless whenever we date the appearance of the work, the re-thinking and re-planning which it contains are a monument of the devout exiles in Babylon, who could not have completed so large a task in a short space of time. The actual date of its appearance is not so very important beside the fact that it provides a theological basis for the entire work of reconstructing the life and worship of Israel.

CHAPTER VIII

THE PRESENCE OF GOD IN THE POST-EXILIC COMMUNITY

AFTER the exile the Jewish community had to face a great many set-backs and disappointments before they could rehabilitate the temple worship, and establish a stable social life. Those who were mainly responsible for the undertaking of such a task were those who had suffered exile, and had endured the hardships of the long journey home. To these people the carelessness and indifference of the people already living in Judah was blameworthy in the extreme. The inspiration for a return to Jerusalem had been given by Deutero-Isaiah, whose stirring message had foretold supernatural blessing for the homecoming Jews. Yahweh himself would go before them, and the triumphant arrival in Jerusalem would be the signal to all nations that he was King over all. The peoples of the earth would come to Jerusalem, acknowledging Yahweh's lordship and that Israel was his servant-people. The tribute of all these peoples would be brought to Mount Zion, where they would share with Israel in the salvation of the one true God. The actual circumstances in Jerusalem for the homecoming exiles were vastly different from these prophetic hopes, and disappointment and despondency would be a wholly understandable reaction on their part. It is plain from the book of Haggai[1] that the rebuilding of the temple, to which Deutero-Isaiah and Ezekiel had both looked forward, was not the first task to which the returning people set themselves, even though the account of the edict of Cyrus[2] had made the restoration of worship in Jerusalem the basic motive of the return. The depressing conditions of Judah, and the arduous struggle even to make a living appear to have overwhelmed the desire for a new house of God.

In spite of this initial setback the hope of Yahweh's glorious return, and of a miraculous transformation of Judah's sad plight, was not abandoned, but only deferred. If we accept that the work of the compilers of the Priestly Document was completed at this time, then it shows how much earnest thinking was going on to consider under

---

[1] Hag. i. 1–14.
[2] Ezra i.

what conditions Yahweh's return would take place. It gave expression
to a renewal of the vision and faith of Israel, showing that the faithful remnant must fulfil the demands of Yahweh in order to enter into
its spiritual heritage, and to take possession once again of the land of
Canaan.

The meagre fulfilment of the great hopes of the returning exiles,
and the delay in Yahweh's coming, must soon have been felt as
problems, and were no doubt regarded as results of the negligence of
the people to obey the word of God. The great prophets of the exile,
as well as their Priestly colleagues, had seen the rebuilding of the
temple on Mount Zion as the foremost task that awaited fulfilment.
Nevertheless this intention had not been translated into action
when the exiles first returned home. Not until 520 B.C. did the prophet Haggai emerge to challenge this remissness on the part of the
people. Only when the temple had been rebuilt could the glorious
presence of Yahweh bless the people:

‘ "Go up to the hills and fetch wood and build the temple, that I might
take pleasure in it, and that I might appear in glory, says Yahweh." ’

(Hag. i. 8)

Haggai encouraged the people of Jerusalem, under the leadership
of Zerubbabel-ben-Shealtiel and Joshua-ben-Jehozadak, to take
steps to rebuild the ruined temple, prophesying that after a great
shaking of the world and all its peoples, the promised honour would
be given to Israel and the treasures of the nations would be brought
to it in tribute. The splendour of the rebuilt temple would exceed
that of its predecessor.[1]

Haggai's contemporary, Zechariah, proclaimed a similar message,
assuring the harassed Judean community that in the near future the
promise would be fulfilled and Yahweh would return to Jerusalem:

'Sing and rejoice, O daughter of Zion,
  For behold I am about to come,
And I will dwell in your midst, says Yahweh.
And many nations shall join themselves
  To Yahweh in that day,
  And shall be my people;
And I will dwell in your midst,
  And you shall know that Yahweh of Hosts
  Has sent me to you.'

(Zech. ii. 14–15 (EVV. 10–11))

[1] Hag. ii. 1–9.

The same promise is reiterated in Zech. viii. 3:

> 'Thus says Yahweh,
> I will return to Zion[1]
> And I will dwell in the midst of Jerusalem,
> And Jerusalem shall be called the faithful city,
> And the mountain of Yahweh of Hosts, the holy mountain.'
> (Zech. viii. 3; cf. also Zech. i. 16)

Thus both Haggai and Zechariah took up the deferred hope of the returned exiles and promised that in the near future, when the temple was rebuilt and true worship re-established, then the glowing hopes of Deutero-Isaiah would be fulfilled. Yahweh would come in glory to his people, and in consequence all nations would recognize Israel's greatness and would bring honour to Jerusalem; the sorrows and hardships of the struggling Jewish community would be miraculously overcome and joy and blessing would be given to them. But the temple was rebuilt, and no miraculous return occurred. Zerubbabel, the hoped-for messiah,[2] disappears from history in unknown circumstances. Perhaps he suffered a violent end. The return of Yahweh, which Ezekiel and Deutero-Isaiah had foretold, was still delayed, even though a new temple had been erected for him. The promise of the fullness of the divine presence on earth remained a central feature of the eschatological hopes of the post-exilic community. Some may have abandoned all hope of it, but others steadfastly kept faith that it would come. The prophet known as Malachi, after denouncing the unworthy worship of his contemporaries, assured his people that God would come to his temple:

> 'Suddenly the Lord whom you are seeking will enter his temple;
> And the messenger of the covenant in whom you delight.[3]
> Behold he is about to come, says Yahweh of Hosts.'
> (Mal. iii. 1)

---

[1] The tense of the Hebrew verb here and in i. 16 is striking, since the perfect requires a significance in the future. The Septuagint takes as a future, which may be justified by regarding the Hebrew as a prophetic perfect/universal tense. I hazard the suggestion that it could be translated 'I have repented concerning Zion (Jerusalem)' in both cases. Cf. Joel ii. 14 for *šûḇ* used of Yahweh in this sense.

[2] Hag. ii. 23.

[3] R. C. Dentan, 'Micah', *Interpreter's Bible*, VI, p. 1137, regards this line as a paranthetical note inserted by a commentator to interpret the coming in terms of a messenger, and not of God himself. This is not necessary, for there is no reason why the prophet himself should not have so interpreted the promise of the divine coming. Cf. S. R. Driver, *The Minor Prophets* (Century Bible), n.d., Edinburgh, pp. 318f.

Malachi uses the promise as a warning to the people. Instead of heralding in the day of blessing, as the people anticipate, this divine coming will only bring confusion upon them. The presence of God will mean the purging of the people from sin.

In this way the hope of the exilic prophets that when Israel was allowed to return to Jerusalem and to rebuild the temple, then Yahweh would return to it and bestow upon his people supernatural blessings, was thought to have been delayed. The life of the Judean community was not miraculously transformed. The temple was rebuilt and much of the programme outlined in the Priestly Writing was implemented, yet its crowning promise, that the presence of God would be in Israel's midst remained in the realm of eschatological hope. It was not fulfilled in the present but would be so in the future.[1] This sense of unfulfilled promise regarding the post-exilic temple is well reflected in Rabbinic literature, perhaps accentuated all the more strongly by the destruction of the beautiful Herodian temple in A.D. 70. The dissatisfaction, however, is felt in regard to the entire history of the temple since its rebuilding in the late sixth century B.C. The doctrine grew up that five things were lacking in the second temple that had existed in the first.[2] What these five things were varied slightly in Rabbinic belief, but significant among them are the Shekinah, the Rabbinic concept of the divine presence, and the holy spirit. In other words the most vital feature of all was lacking. Just how old this dissatisfaction with the second temple was in Jewish thought we do not exactly know, but apparently it existed from the very time of rebuilding. Men could refurbish the material structure, but only God could graciously bestow his presence if and when he so willed. The temple was not thereby robbed of all significance, as we know that it played a very considerable part in post-exilic Jewish life, but it stood as a witness to a promise that had not yet been fulfilled. This is wholly in line with the increasing emphasis placed in post-exilic times upon the transcendent aspects of the divine nature.

---

[1] Many features of the Jerusalem traditions which were associated with the pre-exilic Autumn Festival in Jerusalem re-appear in the eschatological hopes of Judaism. Cf. especially Zech. xii.–xiv.

[2] See J. Abelson, *The Immanence of God in Rabbinical Literature*, London, 1912, pp. 261, 267, and the references given there. Most important are Midrash Numbers Rabba 15 : 10 where we are told that five things were stored away from the first temple, viz. the ark, the candlestick, fire, the holy spirit and the cherubim; see also Talmud Yoma 21b where we are told that in five things the first sanctuary differed from the second; viz. the ark, the ark-cover, the cherubim (these three taken as one), the fire, the Shekinah, the holy spirit and the Urim and Thummim. Cf. also Yoma 52b where they are the ark, the manna, water, Aaron's rod and the chest of the Philistines.

God was the universal Lord, who could not be confined to one time or one place. Nevertheless alongside this there went a very real sense of his nearness among men, expressed in ways other than through temple rites, although these also played their part. In fact the doctrine of the divine presence on earth had become transcendentalized, so that nothing short of a supernatural transformation of the world was adequate as the expression of Yahweh's coming. All that men knew and experienced of God with them in the present was as nothing in the face of the ultimate reality, when God would fully come to them. The present gave a partial view, the future would see the whole. No wonder that some Jewish and Christian writers transferred the whole hope of the divine presence in a perfect temple on Mount Zion to the realm of heaven. It was no longer realizable in this world, and so the promise of the divine dwelling with Israel was not felt to be truly fulfilled on earth. It was applied to another, heavenly world. There the true Jerusalem existed, with the true temple and the ark. Thus the doctrine of a heavenly temple and of a heavenly Jerusalem became a feature of some Jewish circles.[1] Jerusalem itself had now taken on a kind of supernatural dimension; it had become a symbol for faith.[2] The earlier notions of the centre of the world, the place where all nations would find their destiny, and most of all, of the divine presence with men, all had their part in making Jerusalem a symbol of the ultimate fulfilment of the religious aspirations of Judaism. As such it has passed over into Christian faith and tradition. The influence of Platonic thought in the Hellenistic age served to strengthen such ideas by its doctrine that things on earth are merely copies of realities in heaven, but as we have shown, the belief in a heavenly temple had existed in some form in Israel for centuries.

The Jewish community therefore came to hold to a diversity of beliefs regarding the divine presence. God was experienced in the present, but the hope was cherished that in the future men would enjoy the divine presence in all its fullness either in this world, when Yahweh returned to Israel, or in the next, where the true Jerusalem was.

The book where we find the fullest re-assertion of the divine

[1] Ascension of Isa. vii. 10; Wisdom of Solomon ix. 8; Apocalypse of Baruch iv. 2–6; Testament of Levi iii. 4. Cf. also the Testament of Dan. v. 12–13 and note also in the New Testament Galatians iv. 26; Heb. xii. 22; Rev. iii. 12; and xxi. 1–xxii. 5. For the whole subject see K. L. Schmidt, 'Jerusalem als Urbild und Abbild', *Eranos Jahrbuch* 18, 1950, pp. 207–248.
[2] See N. W. Porteous, 'Jerusalem-Zion: the Growth of a Symbol', *Verbannung und Heimkehr*, ed. A. Kuschke, Tübingen, 1961, pp. 235–252.

presence in the temple, as we have known it in pre-exilic Israel, is
Joel. The prophet asserts quite categorically that Yahweh is in Zion,
dwelling in the temple, without offering any interpretative explanation.[1]

This is the fullest return to the pre-exilic attitude to the temple
that we possess. It is not therefore surprising that A. S. Kapelrud
argues that the book contains pre-exilic prophecies (c. 600 B.C.), that
have been written down after the exile (fourth to third centuries
B.C.).[2] Certainly as far as its doctrine of Yahweh's presence in
Jerusalem is concerned it better fits the period before the exile rather
than after, but it would not be at all surprising if, after the rebuilding
of the temple, some Jews resurrected the old attitudes and ideas.
Indeed it would be surprising if it were otherwise when we remember
that the psalms of the first temple were still being sung, even if in a
different context of worship. The older ideas could easily take hold
again of the minds of some people. There was apparently a certain
mixture of beliefs regarding the temple and the divine indwelling
there. The older beliefs and promises were retained, even though
some of them needed to be interpreted in new ways.

The work of the Chronicler is a good illustration of this diversity of
inherited ideas which continued to live on in Judaism. The work gives
a history of the Davidic dynasty and of Jerusalem from the age of
David himself. Yet in spite of this over-riding interest it appears not
to possess a systematic doctrine of the divine presence and dwelling-
place on earth. In this it is quite unlike either Deuteronomy or the
Priestly Writing. In spite of a great interest in Jerusalem and its
temple, there is no clear-cut doctrine of Yahweh's abode which has
motivated the work. Instead we find that the ideas which the author has
drawn from his sources re-appear in his own work. We are thus faced
with what is virtually a synthesis of earlier thought and doctrine on
the subject, without any attempt being made to resolve the tensions,
or to eliminate the difficulties.

We find that Yahweh is a God who is in heaven;[3] Solomon's
dedicatory prayer for the temple repeats the Deuteronomic emphasis
of 1 Kings viii,[4] and in 2 Chron. vii. 1 fire is said to have come down
from heaven to consume the burnt-offering and the sacrifices. On

---

[1] Joel ii. 27; iv. 16f. (EVV. iii. 16f.)
[2] A. S. Kapelrud, *Joel Studies*, (*UUÅ*, 1948: 4), Uppsala, 1948, especially pp.
179ff. G. W. Anderson, *A Critical Introduction To The O.T.*, London, 1959,
pp. 145ff, after consideration of Kapelrud's claim, argues that probability still
favours a post-exilic date for the composition of the work.
[3] 2 Chron. vi. 18, 21 etc.
[4] 2 Chron. ii. 6; xx. 5; xxx. 27.

the other hand the temple is still the place which was built for Yahweh to dwell in,[1] so that Yahweh could be called the God of Jerusalem.[2] The plan of the temple is stated to have been handed over by David to Solomon,[3] whilst David himself is said to have received it 'from the hand of Yahweh'. This is of interest in that it is in line with the Priestly doctrine that Moses received the details of the tabernacle from Yahweh. The true plan for a temple is known only to God. David, the founder of the dynasty, is regarded as the true cult-founder, rather than Solomon who merely carried out his father's instructions. In this section, which is most probably a composition of the Chronicler himself, it is striking that never once is the temple stated to be for Yahweh to dwell in. The site of the temple is now given as Mount Moriah,[4] and it is to be a house for the name of Yahweh, thus following the Deuteronomic expression.[5] After the dedication of the temple the divine glory fills it.[6]

The ark is variously presented by the Chronicler. In 1 Chron. xiii. 6 it is related to the presence of Yahweh who is enthroned on the cherubim. This is probably also the sense of 1 Chron. xvii. 5 where Yahweh, prior to the building of the temple, is said to have dwelt in both a tent (Heb. *'ōhel*) and a tabernacle (Heb. *miškān*). We may also compare 1 Chron. xv. 1; xvi. 1 where David is said to have pitched a tent for the ark. The ark is thus in some way related to the divine presence, but yet, following the Deuteronomic statement, it is said to have been empty except for the law tablets.[7] In 1 Chron. xxviii. 2 the ark is regarded as the footstool of God. The main theological emphasis in the Ezra-Nehemiah narrative is to stress the divine transcendence, and this was most probably already present in the Chronicler's sources, so that he is again merely re-echoing the views of others. We shall investigate these further below.

The Jews who had suffered the exile, and who played so vital a part in the post-exilic religious life of Judea and the formation of Judaism, could not return to Jerusalem with the same attitudes and beliefs with which the exiles had gone forth. Not even their enthusiasm could restore the conditions that had pertained before Jerusalem had been destroyed. They could rebuild the temple, but they could not restore to it the prestige and significance which it had

[1] 2 Chron. vi. 2; xxxvi. 15.
[2] 2 Chron. xxxii. 19; cf. Ezra i. 3 which perhaps reflects the pagan attitude.
[3] 1 Chron. xxviii. 11–20.
[4] 2 Chron. iii. 1; cf. Gen. xxii. 2.
[5] 2 Chron. ii. 4; vi. 6, 10, 20; vii. 16; xxxiii. 4, 7.
[6] 2 Chron. v. 14; vii. 1, 2.
[7] 2 Chron. v. 10; vi. 11.

previously enjoyed. The exile marks the water-shed in Israelite-
Jewish history and thought, and not least is this marked in the attitude
adopted towards the divine dwelling-place and the belief in Yahweh's
presence upon earth. For half a century and more Jewish life and
worship had continued without a temple, and during those years
the religious leaders had lived far away from Jerusalem and Mount
Zion. The expatriated Jews in Babylon had learnt to worship as best
they could in their own homes and settlements; the voice of prophecy
had not been denied to them, and in Deutero-Isaiah it had risen to its
most powerful expression. The lessons of the past were brought home
to the people very plainly by those who had been schooled in the
Deuteronomic doctrines, and by those whose work we see in the
Priestly Writing. The years spent in Babylon are full of tremendous
significance for the understanding of the Jewish religion, and were
creative of a new outlook and hope. That those years were spent
away from the temple is a key feature to be reckoned with in the new
religious and theological attitude which emerged. The synagogues,
which became so vital an aspect of Judaism, must certainly have had
their earliest origin in this period.

The people had come to experience that the divine presence
could be with them even when no temple existed. Jeremiah had
taught them so,[1] and Ezekiel had seen the presence of Yahweh in
his call-vision by the river Chebar.[2] The existence of regular Sabbath
worship, which was practised by the faithful nucleus of the exiles,
if not by the majority, could not have left the people with the feeling
that God had utterly deserted them. The Jerusalem tradition had
always placed some stress upon the universal and cosmic aspects of
Yahweh's nature, and the prophets had insisted that God had dealings
with all nations. For those who were mature enough not to be carried
away by the strange magnificence of Babylonian culture and ideas,
the new surroundings could mean a widening of their spiritual
horizons. The years of exile served to strengthen the conviction that
Yahweh was not limited either to one country or to one place. Thus
their experience, reflected upon in the light of their historic faith,
pointed inevitably to the conclusion that a temple was not essential
for the worship of Yahweh, the God of Israel. He was the only God,
who had created both the heavens and the earth. His dwelling was
in the heavens;[3] what need was there then for another temple? At
least one prophetic voice gave expression to such thoughts;

[1] Jer. xxix. 13–14.   [2] Ezek. i. 1–iii. 15.
[3] Isa. lxiii. 15.

'Thus says Yahweh:
  Heaven is my throne
  And the earth is my footstool;
  What is the house which you would build for me,
  And what is my resting-place?
  All these things my hand has made,
  And so they are all mine,[1] says Yahweh.
  But to this man I will look,
  He who is humble and unassuming,
  And trembles at my word.'

                    (Isa. lxvi. 1–2)[2]

The emphasis upon the divine transcendence, expressed most
particularly by asserting Yahweh's heavenly nature, is a prominent
characteristic of the post-exilic community.[3] Possibly behind this
attitude there has been some influence from Persian thought, which
laid great stress on the transcendence of Ahura Mazda, and which led
Jewish writers to affirm the superiority of Yahweh by mentioning
him as the God of heaven. We find a similar emphasis in the Book of
Daniel.[4] Although there is no need to deny that some influence has
come from other religions, yet it remains basically true that these
developments within Judaism were wholly in line with indigenous
trends of thought. They are in fact only what we should have expected to arise from earlier Israelite assertions of divine transcendence
in the Deuteronomic and Priestly circles. This emphasis continued
to be a marked characteristic of Jewish theology, and we find reflections of it in the New Testament with such phrases as 'the Kingdom

---

[1] Reading with the Septuagint and Syriac '$w^e l\hat{\imath}$ $h\bar{a}y\hat{u}$' instead of '$wayyihy\hat{u}$'.

[2] J. Muilenburg, *Interpreter's Bible*, V, New York–Nashville, 1956, pp. 758ff.,
regards the passage Isa. lxvi. 1–16 as a single unit to be dated *c.* 538–520 B.C. He
refers it to the rebuilding of the temple in Haggai's time, but does not consider that
it expresses an out-right rejection of all temples as such. Even so it is plainly far
removed from the popular pre-exilic attitude to the temple. Note, however, that in
verse 6 Yahweh speaks in judgment from the temple (in heaven ?). Isa. lxvi. 17–24
is probably the addition of a redactor, but in these verses the holy mountain of
Yahweh is the centre to which all nations will one day come in order to present
themselves before Yahweh, and that they might also have their priestly representatives officiating before him there.

[3] Ezra i. 2; Neh. i. 4, 5; ix. 12, 13, 27, 28. The record of the 'Heilsgeschichte',
attributed to Ezra (Neh ix. 5–37), was probably taken over by the Chronicler from
an extra-canonical poetry collection. So K. Galling, *Chronik, Esra, Nehemiah*
(ATD 12), Göttingen, 1954, p. 239. It is of interest for our present study in that it
asserts that Yahweh heard the cry of his people from heaven (ix. 27–28), and that
he came down to Sinai (ix. 13), but spoke to the people from heaven. (Contrast the
Priestly account.) No mention at all is made of the election of Jerusalem, or of the
divine dwelling there.

[4] Dan. ii. 18, 19, 28, 37; cf. also Dan. ii. 11. O. Eissfeldt ('Ba'alšamēm und
Jahwe', pp. 183 note and 192 note) sees behind these references the rivalry between
Baal-Shamem (Zeus Olympios) and Yahweh in the time of Antiochus Epiphanes.

of Heaven' and 'our Father who is in heaven'. Not unnaturally it
encouraged the belief in mediating powers, either in the form of
angels, or as personified divine attributes hypostatically regarded;
e.g. Word, Wisdom and Spirit. An examination of these is not
possible in this present study, but it may be claimed that they all
imply a belief in the divine transcendence. They were called in to help
bridge the gulf created by too great a stress on the divine dwelling
in heaven, and a corresponding weakening of the sense of his dwelling
on earth. A doctrine of mediating powers, or of intermediary angelic
beings, is an attempt to keep a strict monotheism and yet to provide
an adequate basis for worship in the belief in the proximity of God.
We find in later Rabbinic theology a resort to the doctrine of the
Shekinah as an attempt to define theologically how God may be
present in the world without ceasing to be other than the world.

It would be wrong, however, to regard the major theological
trend of post-exilic Judaism as a removal of God from his world.
Whilst the exile opened the way for an enlarged idea of God, it also
provoked renewed thought as to the manner and mode of his presence with men. In human experience in suffering and exile, as well
as in the wider view of the providential rule of history, Israel knew
that God was still their God and that he could still be with them.
Thus alongside the emphasis upon God's transcendence there went
an assurance that he could still be present in and with those who
loved him:

> 'Whither shall I go from thy spirit?
> Or whither shall I flee from thy presence?
> If I ascend to heaven, thou art there.
> If I make my bed in Sheol, thou art there.'
>   (Ps. cxxxix. 7–8)

This is surely a post-exilic psalm, and such ideas do not stand
isolated in that time. The experience of the divine presence, without
the mediation of either a temple or any of the usual cult apparatus
had been real to the exiles, and was not forgotten thereafter. There
was in many ways a spiritualizing and even humanizing of the belief
in God's presence. Alongside the theology of transcendence, therefore, it is no accident that we also find an accompanying presentation
of the divine spirit present with the restored Israel. Such ideas were
not new at this time, but they gained a new importance. The exile,
which on one hand had led to the belief that God's presence had
departed from the temple since God was greater than any building,

also pointed to the real experience that God was to be found wherever men sought him with a whole heart. We find in Hag. i. 13 that
Yahweh asserts by the prophet that he is with the people, before any
work on the restoration of the temple had begun, and in ii. 5 this
is explained as the spirit of God abiding with the people. Zechariah
similarly proclaimed that it was through the spirit of God that Zerubbabel would be empowered to complete the work of rebuilding the
temple:

'This is the word of Yahweh to Zerubbabel;
"Not by power, nor by force,
But by my spirit," says Yahweh of Hosts.'
(Zech. iv. 6)

The whole vision of Zech. iv. with its seven-branched lampstand fed
by the oil of two olive trees, is interpreted as the spirit of God flowing
to the community through the two anointed ones; i.e. Zerubbabel
and Joshua.[1] There is no doubt at all therefore that the post-exilic
Jewish community did have a real experience of the divine presence,
usually interpreted in terms of the spirit, even though they held to
the promise that they would experience the full and complete enjoyment of it in the future.[2] A notable feature, which represents a real
advance is that this presence was thought of more and more in terms
related to human life and activity. God did not dwell in buildings
made of stone and bricks, but in the hearts of those who were humble
and sincere in seeking him.[3] Thus a real fulfilment was found of the
prophecies of Jeremiah[4] and Ezekiel,[5] even though this was less than
the fuller experience that was still anticipated. This spiritualizing of
the idea of the divine presence arose directly out of experience, which
was naturally already felt in pre-exilic times, but which had been
sharpened and clarified by the destruction of the temple. The
Qumran sectaries combined a regard for the promises concerning
the temple with a more personal understanding of the divine presence
by describing their community as a 'sanctuary' and a 'holy of holies'.[6]
In later Rabbinic thought we similarly find this idea of the divine
immanence, especially in its personal aspects.[7] God was present
where there were hearts willing to receive him, and in this the Rabbis

---

[1] Zech. iv. 14.
[2] Cf. L. H. Brockington, 'The Presence of God', ET 57, 1945/6, pp. 21–25.
[3] Isa. lvii. 15; lxvi. 2; cf. John iv. 21–24; Acts xvii. 24.
[4] Jer. xxxi. 31ff.
[5] Ezek. xxxvi. 26f.
[6] Cf. H. Kosmala, *Hebräer-Essener-Christen* (Studia Post-Biblica I), Leiden, 1959, pp. 363ff.
[7] Cf. J. Abelson, *The Immanence of God in Rabbinical Literature*, pp. 126ff.

K

were simply continuing the teaching of their predecessors. Only with this belief could the insistence upon the transcendence of God have remained supportable; without it Rabbinic Judaism would have run out into deism. At the same time it left open the belief in a coming of Yahweh in supernatural power and splendour in the future. This would fulfil the imperfect experience of God in the present.

The faith of the post-exilic community was marked by a renewed interest in the temple, and the recovery of much of its significance. In the diaspora, as well as in Palestine, it became a symbol of hope and loyalty.[1] In many ways it served to preserve the best of the past and to create afresh the sense of awe and wonder when men are confronted with the holy God. But in their lives and worship apart from the temple, faithful Jews knew that God was with them, and this experience was not essentially different from the experience of God on Mount Zion. The spirit of God was not restricted in location, or governed by spatial limitations. He was present with all who were of a truly humble disposition. Thus the promises of the return of God's presence to dwell in the midst of Israel, as Ezekiel had foretold and as Deutero-Isaiah had so confidently described, were kept for the future and even transferred altogether to another realm as a description of heaven. In heaven existed the true Jerusalem and the true temple where men would enjoy the presence of God. The old belief in God's dwelling in the temple had first lost its mythological background when the Deuteronomists had introduced their theology of Yahweh's name. Subsequently the deepened sense of God's nature, and the more spiritual awareness of how he came to men, combined together to give Judaism a new understanding of the divine presence. Nevertheless it still left the problem, 'Will God in truth dwell on the earth?' The old answers were no longer valid and Judaism resorted to its eschatology to provide the solution, or gave up altogether seeking the answer in this world, and averred that only in heaven would the ancient promises be fulfilled.

[1] Cf. Dan. vi. 11 (EVV. 10).

CHAPTER IX

CONCLUSION

THE foregoing study of the ideas current in ancient Israel about the nature and mode of God's presence on earth has attempted to trace the development of the conception, and to demonstrate that underlying the apparent diversity of expressions on the subject there is a fundamental unity. In particular we have endeavoured to show the vital importance for the development of Israel's religion of the conquest of Jerusalem, and the building of a temple there. The continuing need to define the nature and location of the divine presence was a vitally important factor for Israelite theology, because such a notion expressed an essential fact about the nature and purpose of God. Yahweh was a God who had not only called Israel to be his people, and bound them to himself by a covenant, but he had promised within this covenant to dwell among them, so that this divine presence would distinguish Israel from all other nations upon the earth.[1] Throughout the pages of the Old Testament we can see that this conviction of Yahweh's dwelling in the midst of Israel forms a unifying theme, in which we are able to trace a certain historical development of ideas. In this process there was a continuing effort at interpretation and re-interpretation until a group of theological concepts were employed to give expression to the idea. In the last centuries of the Old Testament period we find a multiplicity of ideas on the subject, together with a sense of tension between what had been promised, and what was fulfilled in the immediate present. Such a tension was all the more felt because of the great emphasis upon the transcendence of God, which coloured Jewish theology and interpretations of history. The promises of Yahweh's presence became an essential part of Jewish theology, leading to the formation of the doctrine of his Shekinah, as well as colouring their eschatological hope. In the New Testament, with the claim of Christianity to be the true Israel of God, and to be the heir of the Old Testament promises, the earlier notions of the divine presence in Israel took on a new meaning and significance in the light of the Incarnation and the gift of the Holy Spirit. It is worth while then for us to attempt to place

[1] Exod. xxxiii. 16; Ezek. xxxvii. 28.

135

the ideas about Yahweh's presence in Israel into a co-ordinated whole, and to lay bare the convictions that underly them.

A prominent tendency of nineteenth-century attempts to reconstruct the history of Israel's religion was to see an evolution in which Yahweh, originally a nature-spirit of Mount Sinai, developed into the transcendent Lord of the universe.[1] Others have regarded the belief in Yahweh's 'tabernacling' presence on earth as a late emergence in Israel.[2] The present work started out with the conviction that early Israel's experience of Yahweh, in accordance with the religious experience of the surrounding nations, showed him to be both transcendent and immanent, so that we cannot regard it as satisfactory either to derive a transcendent God out of an immanent one, or to make an immanent God out of a transcendent one. Neither theory of development does justice to the fact that from the beginning of Israel's sacred story Yahweh is shown as manifesting both transcendent and immanent aspects in his nature. Such too was true of the gods of Canaan, although here a belief in divine immanence tended to predominate. This was partly because the gods themselves were deified aspects of nature, or natural phenomena, and more especially because such gods were thought to be accessible by the use of symbols of their persons and abodes. The earthly dwelling-places of such gods were regarded as related to their true, 'mythological' dwellings, and to be the means by which the blessing and fertilizing powers of the gods were poured out upon the land. Inevitably such gods were treated as part of a natural process, and so all stress was placed upon their immanence in nature. Theoretically transcendence and immanence were combined and the tension overcome, by a cultic symbolism.

Israel's earliest faith in God was a faith in Yahweh who had delivered them out of Egypt, and who had made a covenant with them on Mount Sinai. In his theophany he revealed himself as transcendent to the world of nature and men, and yet by manifesting his presence and declaring his will he had shown himself present with men. Furthermore he was believed to have promised that he would send forth his presence to accompany Israel into their own land. Originally Mount Sinai seems to have been looked upon as Yahweh's abode, but this belief was never allowed to obscure his transcendent nature. At the covenant festival at Shechem, Israel recalled and re-

---

[1] Cf. e.g. B. Stade, *Biblische Theologie des Alten Testaments*, I, pp. 103f., 291.
[2] Cf. the article on Shekinah in *Hastings Dictionary of the Bible*, Edinburgh, 1902, IV, pp. 487–489, by J. T. Marshall.

experienced the wonder of Yahweh's appearing to them, and so in his theophany in the cult, the promise of his accompanying presence was believed to have been fulfilled. Any attempt to reduce Yahweh to the level of a nature-spirit, bound up with the processes of nature was firmly resisted. None the less with the advent of a more settled agricultural life for Israel there was an inevitable tendency to resort to the Canaanite gods who were thought to bless the land and to make it fertile. It was most especially in Jerusalem that a reconciliation with Canaanite ideas was made, where the idea was taken over from the cult of El-'Elyon that Mount Zion was to be identified with Mount Zaphon and formed a divine abode. Mount Zion came thus to be regarded as Yahweh's abode, even though such an innovation was subordinated to the traditional Israelite belief in Yahweh as the God of Sinai. The consequent tendency to regard Jerusalem as a guarantee of divine protection and blessing, led certain prophets, especially Micah and Jeremiah, to react strongly against Yahweh's temple on Mount Zion. They objected to a cult which tended to make Yahweh subject to the control of men, and foretold the destruction of the temple, with the consequent withdrawal of Yahweh's presence from Israel. In an attempt to re-interpret the cult in the light of the prophetic strictures, the Deuteronomists abandoned the notion of a symbolic unity between the earthly and heavenly abodes of Yahweh, and substituted the doctrine that Yahweh sent forth his name, as a mode of his presence, to dwell in the temple. Thus the mythological interpretation of the cult gave way to a theological one, and to a separate concept of the presence of God with his people. In this way Israel sought to protect the doctrine of Yahweh's transcendence and to insist that his dwelling with Israel was a gift of his grace. The destruction of the temple in 586 B.C. confirmed the prophetic criticism of a false trust in it, and led to a crisis in Israel's faith in Yahweh. But for the fact that Israel was able to reconsider the words of the prophets in the light of events, Yahwism itself might have disappeared.

In exile Ezekiel taught the people that Yahweh had only temporarily withdrawn his presence and that he would return to a new and rebuilt Jerusalem. Ezekiel, like the Deuteronomists, however, refused to say that it was Yahweh himself who dwelt on earth, but whereas the Deuteronomists had spoken of the divine name, Ezekiel spoke of Yahweh's glory as the mode of his presence. This was also employed by the composers of the Priestly Writing, who, during the exile, sought to revise and re-interpret Israel's religious heritage as a basis for the restoration of the nation. They outlined a programme in which Yahweh's presence would 'tabernacle' in the midst of Israel. Instead of a divine dwelling-place they substituted a cultic community, where, in a portable sanctuary, Yahweh's glory would appear to the priestly representatives of Israel. This programme remained largely an unfulfilled hope of Israel, and the hope of Yahweh's presence with his people took on a more and more eschatological dimension. At the same time a deepening sense of spiritual communion with God in the present, apart from the temple, led to a fuller understanding of his spiritual presence with all who were loyal to him. The Old Testament period came to an end, therefore, without a full reconciliation of the ideas that had emerged of Yahweh's transcendence and immanence. A fulfilment of Israel's hopes was still looked for when Yahweh would come to Israel in a new way, whilst others came to see in the prophecies about Mount Zion a description of heaven.

From an early stage Israelite religion had had a clear and firm conviction of the divine transcendence, and yet had no less sought to do justice to the belief in Yahweh's presence with his people. The problem arose in its sharpest form around the temple upon which the promises of the divine presence were centred, and where they were thought to be fulfilled. Varied concepts came to be used to explain how Yahweh could indeed dwell on the earth, and these were taken up into an eschatological hope in which Israel looked to the future for the full manifestation of Yahweh's dwelling with men. In this way a clear path was made for the central assertion of Christianity; the Incarnation of God in Christ. God had indeed dwelt, or 'tabernacled', on earth as a full revelation of his being,[1] but this was not by means of any material object, nor by a divine attachment to one place, but through a human personality the only adequate temple for God on earth. Jesus was the true temple in which the fullness of the divine Being dwelt. Here divine immanence and transcendence are reconciled in the person of one who is the perfect union of the human and the divine. It is illuminating then to observe that the claim of Jesus to build a new temple, supplanting the old, was a leading feature of the criticism levelled against him by his Jewish contemporaries.[2] We find that it was a similar insistence upon a

---

[1] John i. 14.

[2] Mark xiv. 58; Matt. xxvi. 61; John ii. 18–22; cf. Mark xiii. 2. For a brief survey of the synoptic material concerning Jesus' supersession of the temple and its cult see E. Lohmeyer, *The Lord of the Temple*, Edinburgh, 1961. Cf. C. F. D. Moule, 'Sanctuary and Sacrifice in the Church of the New Testament', *JTS* (NS) 1, 1950, pp. 29–41.

Christian understanding of the temple which provoked bitter opposition against Stephen by the Jewish authorities, and which led to his martyrdom.[1] The ancient promises that God would dwell with his people were eagerly taken up by Christians and applied to the Church, the Body of Christ, in which God dwelt by the Holy Spirit.[2] The major difference between the new fulfilment and the old promise is that whereas the Old Testament had spoken of a dwelling of God among men, the New Testament speaks of a dwelling of God within men by the Holy Spirit. We can see that both for the New Testament and the Old the meaning of the temple was of profound importance for faith, because the temple was an important witness to the presence of God with men. The Old Testament was conscious of the inadequacy of its concepts in describing the manner of God's dwelling in the temple, and the New Testament proclaims the truth that was already beginning to be felt in the Old, that only human personality can provide a fit dwelling-place for God on earth. The Christian doctrine of the Trinity, proclaiming that God has taken human nature and dwelt among men, and that through the Holy Spirit given through Christ, he indwells human life so as to be truly present with men, completely supersedes any need for a material temple. This is not to be taken to imply that the Christian doctrine of the Trinity was already found in the Old Testament, nor that there was any conscious formulation of such a doctrine there. It is true, however, that the Old Testament is aware of a problem created by its faith in the presence of Yahweh with his people; a problem which we might describe as that of a tension between immanence and transcendence. Such a problem takes a new form and finds a new solution in the New Testament doctrines of the Incarnation and the Trinity.[3]

As so often in religious matters, experience outran the current ideas and concepts, and Israelite thinkers were continually striving to find an adequate expression for their knowledge and experience of God. In the coming of Christ, the inadequacy of human language and concepts was shown up in its most acute form. Nevertheless the difficulty was not entirely new, and the way towards a resolution of the problems had already been prepared in Israel's efforts to interpret theologically its experience of God. Those concepts which had already been employed to describe God's presence on earth were

---

[1] Acts vii. 48–50. Cf. M. Simon, 'Saint Stephen and the Jerusalem Temple', *Journal of Ecclesiastical History* 2, 1951, pp. 127–142; and *St. Stephen and the Hellenists in the Primitive Church*, London, 1958, pp. 5off.

[2] 1 Cor. iii. 16; vi. 19; cf. Rev. xxi. 22.

[3] Cf. F. M. Cross, 'The Tabernacle', p. 68.

pressed into service to describe the new event of the Incarnation, and that event compelled a new interpretation of the whole doctrine of God. Thus by a trinitarian formula the early Christian theologians were expressing a truly biblical doctrine of God. The spiritually minded in ancient Israel had long felt the difficulty of doing justice in theological thought to both the transcendent aspect of the deity, and to his immanence on earth. Christian theology resolves the tension between the two in its trinitarian faith. The doctrine of the Trinity does not mark the emergence of a totally new problem, but proposes a Christian solution to a problem already existent in the faith of Israel.

LIST OF ABBREVIATIONS

AJSL	*American Journal of Semitic Languages and Literatures*
Ac.Or.	*Acta Orientalia*
ARW	*Archiv für Religionswissenschaft*
ATANT	Abhandlungen zur Theologie des Alten und Neuen Testaments
ATD	Das Alte Testament Deutsch
BA	*The Biblical Archaeologist*
BASOR	Bulletin of the American Schools of Oriental Research
BKAT	Biblischer Kommentar: Altes Testament
BWANT	Beiträge zur Wissenschaft vom Alten (und Neuen) Testament
BZAW	Beihefte zur Zeitschrift für die alttestamentliche Wissenschaft
CBQ	*Catholic Biblical Quarterly*
ET	*Expository Times*
Ev. Th.	*Evangelische Theologie*
EVV	English versions
FRLANT	Forschungen zur Religion und Literatur des Alten und Neuen Testaments
HAT	Handbuch zum Alten Testament
HTR	*Harvard Theological Review*
HUCA	*Hebrew Union College Annual*
IDB	*The Interpreter's Dictionary of the Bible*, New York-Nashville, 1962
IEJ	*Israel Exploration Journal*
JAOS	*Journal of the American Oriental Society*
JBL	*Journal of Biblical Literature*
JNES	*Journal of Near Eastern Studies*
JSS	*Journal of Semitic Studies*
JTS	*Journal of Theological Studies*
KSGVI	*Kleine Schriften zur Geschichte des Volkes Israel*, A. Alt., I-III, München, 1953, 1959
LXX	The Septuagint
MUSJ	*Mélanges de l'université Saint Joseph*, Beyrouth
MVAG	*Mitteilungen der vorderasiatisch-aegyptischen Gesellschaft*
NRT	*Nouvelle revue théologique*
OTS	Oudtestamentische Studiën
PEQ	*Palestine Exploration Quarterly*
RB	*Revue biblique*
RGG	*Die Religion in Geschichte und Gegenwart*, I-VI (3 Aufl.), Tübingen, 1957–63
RHPR	*Revue d'histoire et de philosophie religieuses*
RSPT	*Revue des sciences philosophiques et théologiques*
SANT	Studien zum Alten und Neuen Testament
SBT	Studies in Biblical Theology
SEÅ	*Svensk exegetisk årsbok*
St.Th.	*Studia theologica*

SVT	Supplements to Vetus Testamentum
Syr.	Syriac
TGUOS	*Transactions of the Glasgow University Oriental Society*
ThLZ	*Theologische Literaturzeitung*
ThSK	*Theologische Studien und Kritiken*
ThWzNT	*Theologisches Wörterbuch zum Neuen Testament*
ThZ	*Theologische Zeitschrift*
UM	*Ugaritic Manual*, C. H. Gordon, (Analecta Orientalia 35), Rome, 1955
UUÅ	*Uppsala universitets årsskrift*
VT	*Vetus Testamentum*
Vulg.	The Vulgate
WMANT	Wissenschaftliche Monographien zum Alten und Neuen Testament
WZ	*Wissenschaftliche Zeitschrift*
ZAW	*Zeitschrift für die alttestamentliche Wissenschaft*
ZThK	*Zeitschrift für Theologie und Kirche*

BIBLIOGRAPHY

ABELSON, J., *The Immanence of God in Rabbinical Literature*, London, 1912.

ABRAHAMS, I., *The Glory of God*, Oxford, 1925.

AHLSTRÖM, G. W., *Psalm 89. Eine Liturgie aus dem Ritual des leidenden Königs*, Lund, 1959.

'Der Prophet Nathan und der Tempelbau', *VT* 11, 1961, pp. 113–127.

ALBRIGHT, W. F., 'The Mouth of the Rivers', *AJSL* 35, 1918/19, pp. 161–195.

'The Babylonian Temple-Tower and the Altar of Burnt-offering', *JBL* 39, 1920, pp. 137–142.

The Archaeology of Palestine and the Bible, New York, 1933.

'The Names Shaddai and Abram', *JBL* 54, 1935, pp. 173–204.

'The Oracles of Balaam', *JBL* 63, 1944, pp. 207–233.

Revue of B. N. Wambacq, *L'épithète divine Jahvé Sᵉba'ôt*, *JBL* 67, 1948, pp. 377–381.

'The Psalm of Habbakuk', *Studies in O.T. Prophecy*, ed. H. H. Rowley, Edinburgh, 1950, pp. 1–18.

'Baal-Zephon', *Bertholet Festschrift*, Tübingen, 1950, pp. 1–14.

'A Catalogue of Early Hebrew Lyric Poems (Psalm 68)', *HUCA* 23, Part 1, 1950/51, pp. 1–39.

Archaeology and the Religion of Israel[3], Baltimore, 1953.

Recent Discoveries in Bible Lands, New York, 1955.

From the Stone Age to Christianity[2] New York, 1957.

'The High Place in Ancient Palestine', *Strasbourg Congress Volume* (SVT IV), Leiden, 1957, pp. 242–258.

'Some Remarks on the Song of Moses in Deuteronomy xxxii,' *Essays in Honour of Millar Burrows*, Leiden, 1959, pp. 3–10 (Rep. from *VT* 9, 1959, pp. 339–346).

The Archaeology of Palestine (rev. ed.), London, 1960.

ALFRINK, B., 'Der Versammlungsberg im äussersten Norden', *Biblica* 14, 1933, pp. 41–67.

ALLEGRO, J. M., 'Uses of the Semitic Demonstrative Element Z in Hebrew', *VT* 5, 1955, pp. 309–312.

ALT, A., 'Der Gott der Väter', *KSGVI*, I, 1953, pp. 1–78.

'Die Staatenbildung der Israeliten in Palästina', *KSGVI*, II, 1953, pp. 1–65.

'Das Grossreich Davids', *KSGVI*, II, 1953, pp. 66–75.

'Das Königtum in den Reichen Israel und Juda', *KSGVI*, II, 1953, pp. 116–134.

'Verbreitung und Herkunft des syrischen Tempeltypus', *KSGVI*, II, 1953, pp. 100–115.

'Die Heimat des Deuteronomiums', *KSGVI*, II, 1953, pp. 250–275.

'Zelte und Hütten', *KSGVI*, III, 1959, pp. 233–242.

'Jerusalems Aufstieg', *KSGVI*, III, 1959, pp. 243–257.

'Micah 2, 1–5. GĒS ANADASMOS in Juda', *KSGVI*, III, pp. 373–381.

AMSLER, S., *David, roi et messie. La tradition davidique dans l'Ancien Testament* (Cahiers théologiques 49), Neuchâtel, 1963.

ANDERSON, G. W. *A Critical Introduction to the Old Testament*, London, 1959.

ANDERSEN, K. T., 'Der Gott meines Vaters', *St.Th.* 16, 1962, pp. 170–188.

ARENS, A., *Die Psalmen im Gottesdienst des Alten Bundes*, Trier, 1959.

ARNOLD, W. R., *Ephod and Ark* (Harvard Theological Studies III), Harvard, 1917.

BÄCHLI, O., *Israel und die Völker* (ATANT 41), Zürich, 1962.

BARR, J., 'The Problem of Israelite Monotheism', *TGUOS* 17, 1959, pp. 52–62.

'The Meaning of Mythology in Relation to the O.T.', *VT* 9, 1959, pp. 1–10.

'Theophany and Anthropomorphism in the O.T.', *Oxford Congress Volume* (SVT VII), Leiden, 1960, pp. 31–38.

BARROIS, G. A., 'Temples', *IDB*, IV, pp. 560b–568a.

GRAF BAUDISSIN, W. W., 'El Bet-el Genesis 31[13], 35[7]', *Vom Alten Testament* (BZAW 41), Giessen, 1925, pp. 1–11.

BEAUCAMP, E., 'La théophanie du Psaume 50 (49)', *NRT* 81, 1959, pp. 897-915.

BENTZEN, A., *Die josianische Reform und ihre Voraussetzungen*, Copenhagen, 1926.

BEYERLIN, W., *Die Kulttraditionen Israels in der Verkündigung des Propheten Micha* (FRLANT 72), Göttingen, 1959.

Herkunft und Geschichte der ältesten Sinaitraditionen, Tübingen, 1961.

BIRKELAND, H., 'Hebrew *Zā* and Arabic *Dū*', *St.Th.* 2, 1948, pp. 201–202.

BRIGHT, J., *A History of Israel*, London, 1960.

BRINKER, R., *The Influence of Sanctuaries in Early Israel*, Manchester, 1946.

BROCKINGTON, L. H., 'The Presence of God', *ET* 57, 1945/6, pp. 21–25.

'Presence', *A Theological Word Book of the Bible*, ed. A. Richardson, London, 1950, pp. 172–176.

BROWN, J. R., *Temple and Sacrifice in Rabbinic Judaism*, Evanston, 1963.

BUBER, M., *Moses*, London, 1946.

The Prophetic Faith, New York, 1949.

BÜCKERS, G. H., 'Zur Verwertung der Sinaitraditionen in den Psalmen', *Biblica* 32, 1951, pp. 401–422.

BUDDE, K., 'Imageless Worship in Antiquity', *ET* 9, 1897/8, pp. 396–399.

'Die ursprüngliche Bedeutung der Lade Jahwes', *ZAW* 21, 1901, pp. 193–197.

'War die Lade Jahwes ein leerer Thron?', *ThSK* 79, 1906, pp. 489–507.

BUIS, P. and LECLERCQ, J., *Le Deutéronome*, Paris, 1963.

BURNEY, C. F., *The Book of Judges*, London, 1918.

BURROWS, E., 'Some Cosmological Patterns in Babylonian Religion', *The Labyrinth*, ed. S. H. Hooke, London, 1933, pp. 87–110.

BURROWS, M., *An Outline of Biblical Theology*, Philadelphia, 1946.

CAQUOT, A., 'Le Psaume 47 et la royauté de Yahwé, *RHPR* 39, 1959, pp. 311-337.

'La prophétie de Nathan et ses échos lyriques', *Bonn Congress Volume* (SVT IX), Leiden, 1963, pp. 213–224.

CASSUTO, U., 'The Palace of Baal', *JBL* 61, 1942, pp. 51–56.

CAUSSE, A., 'Le mythe de la nouvelle Jérusalem de Deutéro-Esaïe à la IIIe Sibylle', *RHPR* 18, 1938, pp. 377-414.

CHILDS, B. S., *Myth and Reality in the Old Testament* (SBT 27), London, 1960.

CLEMEN, C., *Die phönikische Religion nach Philo von Byblos* (*MVAG* 42, 3), Leipzig, 1939.

CLEMENTS, R. E., 'Temple and Land: a Significant Aspect of Israel's Worship', *TGUOS* 19, 1963, pp. 16–28.

Prophecy and Covenant (SBT 43), London, 1965.

CONGAR, Y. M. J., *The Mystery of the Temple*, London, 1962.

COOK, S. A., *The Religion of Ancient Palestine in the Light of Archaeology*, London, 1930.

CROSS, F. M., 'The Tabernacle', *BA* 10, 1947, pp. 45–68.

CROSS, F. M. and FREEDMAN, D. N., 'The Blessing of Moses', *JBL* 67, 1948, pp. 191–210.

'A Royal Song of Thanksgiving; II Sam. 22–Psalm 18A', *JBL* 72, 1953, pp. 15–34.

'The Song of Miriam', *JNES* 14, 1955, pp. 237–250.

DANIÉLOU, J., *Le Signe du Temple*, Paris, 1942.

'La symbolisme cosmique du temple de Jerusalem chez Philon et Josephe', *Le symbolisme cosmique des monuments religieux*, Rome, 1957, pp. 83–90.

DAVIES, G. HENTON, 'The Presence of God in Israel', *Studies in History and Religion*, ed. E. A. Payne, London, 1942, pp. 11–29.

'An Approach to the Problem of O.T. Mythology', *PEQ* 88, 1956, pp. 83–91.

'Presence of God', *IDB*, III, pp. 874a-875b.

'Ark of the Covenant', *IDB*, I, pp. 222b–226a.

'Tabernacle', *IDB*, IV, pp. 498a–560b.

'Glory', *IDB*, II, pp. 401a–403b.

'The Ark in the Psalms', *Promise and Fulfilment*, ed. F. F. Bruce, Edinburgh, 1963, pp. 51–61.

DEL MEDICO, H. E. L., 'Melchisédech', *ZAW* 69, 1957, pp. 160–170.

DENTAN, R. C., 'The Book of Micah', *Interpreter's Bible*, VI, New York-Nashville, 1956, pp. 1117–1144.

DHORME, E., 'Le nom des chérubins', *Recueil Édouard Dhorme*, Paris, 1951, pp. 671–683.

DIBELIUS, M., *Die Lade Jahves* (FRLANT 7), Göttingen, 1906.

DREYFUS, F., 'Le thème de l'héritage dans l'Ancien Testament', *RSPT* 42, 1958, pp. 3–49.

DRIVER, G. R., *Canaanite Myths and Legends*, (Old Testament Studies 3), Edinburgh, 1956.

DUMERMUTH, F., 'Zur deuteronomischen Kulttheologie und ihren Voraussetzungen', *ZAW* 70, 1958, pp. 59–98.

EERDMANS, B. D., 'Sojourn in the Tent of Jahu' (OTS I), Leiden, 1942, pp. 1–16.

The Hebrew Book of Psalms (OTS IV), Leiden, 1947.

EHRLICH, E. L., *Kultsymbolik im Alten Testament und im nachbiblischen Judentum*, Stuttgart, 1959.

EICHRODT, W., *Theology of the Old Testament*, I, London, 1961.

Theologie des Alten Testaments, II-III⁴, Tübingen, 1961.

EISSFELDT, O., *Baal Zaphon, Zeus Kasios und der Durchzug der Israeliten durchs Meer*, Halle, 1932.

EISSFELDT—*cont.*

'Baalšamēm und Jahwe', *Kleine Schriften*, II, Tübingen, 1963, pp. 171–198.

'Lade und Stierbild', *Kleine Schriften*, II, pp. 282–305.

'Die Wohnsitze der Götter von Ras Schamra', *Kleine Schriften*, II, pp. 502–506.

'Jahwe Zebaoth', *Miscellanea Academica Berolinensia*, Berlin, 1950, pp. 128–150.

El im ugaritischen Pantheon, Berlin, 1951.

'El and Yahweh', *JSS* 1, 1956, pp. 25–37.

'Silo und Jerusalem', *Strasbourg Congress Volume* (SVT IV), Leiden, 1957, pp. 138–147.

'El', *RGG*³, II, cols. 413–414.

'Baal', *RGG*³, I, cols. 805–806.

'Kanaan III: kanaanäische Religion', *RGG*³, III, cols. 1111–1113.

'Lade und Gesetztafeln', *ThZ* 16, 1960, pp. 281–284.

'Der Gott Bethel', *Kleine Schriften*, I, Tübingen, 1962, pp. 206–233.

'Jahwe, der Gott der Väter', *ThLZ* 88, 1963, cols. 481–490.

ELIADE, M., 'Centre du monde, temple, maison', *Le symbolisme cosmique des monuments religieux*, Rome, 1957, pp. 57–82.

Images and Symbols, London, 1961.

ELLIGER, K., 'Sinn und Ursprung der priesterschriftlichen Geschichtserzählung', *ZThK* 49, 1952, pp. 121–143.

ENGNELL, I., *The Call of Isaiah*, UUÅ 1949, 4, Uppsala, 1949.

FENSHAM, F. C., 'Thunder-stones in Ugaritic', *JNES* 18, 1959, pp. 273–274.

FISHER, L. R., 'Abraham and his Priest King', *JBL* 81, 1962, pp. 264–270.

FLIGHT, J. W., 'The Nomadic Idea and Ideal in the O.T.', *JBL* 42, 1923, pp. 158–226.

FOHRER, G., 'Jeremias Tempelwort 7:1–15', *ThZ* 5, 1949, pp. 401–417.

'Der Vertrag zwischen König und Volk in Israel', *ZAW* 71, 1959, pp. 1–22.

FRANKFORT, H., *The Birth of Civilization in the Near East*, London, 1951.

The Art and Architecture of the Ancient Orient, London, 1954.

FREEDMAN, D. N., 'The Name of the God of Moses', *JBL* 79, 1960, pp. 151–156.

FUSS, W., 'II Samuel 24', *ZAW* 74, 1962, pp. 145–164.

VON GALL, A., *Altisraelitische Kultstätten* (BZAW 3), Giessen, 1898.

GALLING, K., *Die Erwählungstraditionen Israels* (BZAW 48), Giessen, 1928.

'Der Beichtspiegel. Eine gattungsgeschichtliche Studie', *ZAW* 47, 1929, pp. 125–130.

Chronik, Esra, Nehemia (ATD 12), Göttingen, 1954.

'Die Ausrufung des Namens als Rechtsakt in Israel', *ThLZ* 81, 1956, cols. 65–70.

'Die Ehrenname Elisas und die Entrückung Elias', *ZThK* 53, 1956, pp. 129–148.

GASTER, T. H., *Thespis*, New York, 1950.

GESE, H., 'Der Davidsbund und die Zionserwählung', *ZThK* 61, 1964, pp. 10–26.

GORDON, C. H., *Ugaritic Literature*, Rome, 1949.

Ugaritic Manual (Analecta Orientalia 35), Rome, 1955.

GRAY, J., 'The Desert God Attar in the Literature and Religion of Canaan', *JNES* 8, 1949, pp. 27–34.

'Cultic Affinities between Israel and Ras Shamra', *ZAW* 62, 1950, pp. 207–220.

'Canaanite Mythology and Hebrew Tradition', *TGUOS* 14, 1950–52, pp. 47–57.

The Legacy of Canaan (SVT V), Leiden, 1957.

'The Desert Sojourn of the Hebrews and the Sinai-Horeb Tradition', *VT* 4, 1954, pp. 148–154.

'The Kingship of God in the Prophets and Psalms', *VT* 11, 1961, pp. 1–29.

GRESSMANN, H., *Mose und seine Zeit* (FRLANT 18), Göttingen, 1913.

Die Lade Jahwes und das Allerheiligste des salomonischen Tempels (BWANT III, 1), Stuttgart, 1920.

The Tower of Babel, New York, 1928.

GUNNEWEG, A. H. J., 'Sinaibund und Davidsbund', *VT* 10, 1960, pp. 335–341.

HARAN, M., 'The Bas-Reliefs on the Sarcophagus of Ahiram King of Byblos in the Light of Archaeological and Literary Parallels from the Ancient Near East', *IEJ* 8, 1958, pp. 15–25.

'The Ark and the Cherubim; their Symbolic Significance in Biblical Ritual', *IEJ* 9, 1959, pp. 30–38, 89–94.

'The Nature of the "Ohel Mo'edh" in Pentateuchal Sources', *JSS* 5, 1960, pp. 50–65.

'The Complex of Ritual Acts Performed inside the Tabernacle', *Scripta Hierosolymitana* VIII, Jerusalem, 1961, pp. 272–302.

'Shiloh and Jerusalem: the Origin of the Priestly Tradition in the Pentateuch', *JBL* 81, 1962, pp. 14–24.

'The Disappearance of the Ark', *IEJ* 13, 1963, pp. 46–58.

HARTMANN, R., 'Zelt und Lade', *ZAW* 37, 1917/18, pp. 209–244.

HAUER, C. E., 'Who was Zadok?', *JBL* 82, 1963, pp. 89–94.

HAYES, J. H., 'The Tradition of Zion's Inviolability', *JBL* 82, 1963, pp. 419–426.

HENTSCHKE, R., *Die Stellung der vorexilischen Schriftpropheten zum Kultus* (BZAW 75), Berlin, 1957.

HERBERT, A. S., *Worship in Ancient Israel*, London, 1959.

HERRMANN, S., 'Die Königsnovelle in Ägypten und in Israel. Ein Beitrag zur Gattungsgeschichte in den Geschichtsbüchern des Alten Testaments', *WZ* Leipzig, 3, 1953/4, pp. 51–62.

'Das Werden Israels', *ThLZ* 87, 1962, pp. 561–574.

HERTZBERG, H. W., 'Die Melkisedek Traditionen', *Beiträge zur Traditionsgeschichte und Theologie des A.T.*, Göttingen, 1962, pp. 36–44.

'Der heilige Fels und das Alte Testament', ibid., pp. 45–53.

HOLLIS, F. J., 'The Sun-cult and the Temple at Jerusalem', *Myth and Ritual*, ed. S. H. Hooke, Oxford, 1933, pp. 87–110.

The Archaeology of Herod's Temple, London, 1934.

HOOKE, S. H., *Middle Eastern Mythology*, London, 1963.

HORST, F., 'Zwei Begriffe für Eigentum (Besitz). *NAḤ*ᵃ*LÂ* und ᵃ*ḤUZZÂ*', *Verbannung und Heimkehr*, ed. A. Kuschke, Tübingen, 1961, pp. 135–156.

HUMBERT, P., 'Qânâ en Hébreu biblique', *Bertholet Festschrift*, Tübingen, 1950, pp. 259–266.

HYATT, J. P., 'The Deity Bethel and the Old Testament', *JAOS* 59, 1939, pp. 81–98.

'Yahweh as the God of My Father', *VT* 5, 1955, pp. 130–136.

JACOB, E., *Theology of the Old Testament*, London, 1957.

Ras Shamra et l'Ancien Testament, Neuchâtel, 1960.

JANSSEN, E., *Juda in der Exilszeit. Ein Beitrag zur Frage der Entstehung des Judentums* (FRLANT 69), Göttingen, 1956.

JIRKU, A., 'Neues keilinschriftliches Materiel zum Alten Testament', *ZAW* 31, 1921, pp. 144–160.

JOHNSON, A. R., 'The Rôle of the King in the Jerusalem Cultus', *The Labyrinth*, ed. S. H. Hooke, London, 1935, pp. 73–111.

'Aspects of the Use of the Term Panim in the O.T.', *O. Eissfeldt Festschrift 60 Geburtstage*, Halle, 1947, pp. 155–159.

The One and the Many in the Israelite Conception of God, (rev. ed.), Cardiff, 1961.

The Vitality of the Individual in the Thought of Ancient Israel, Cardiff, 1949.

Sacral Kingship in Ancient Israel, Cardiff, 1955.

'Hebrew Conceptions of Kingship', *Myth, Ritual and Kingship*, ed. S. H. Hooke, London, 1958, pp. 204–235.

JONES, D. R., 'The Cessation of Sacrifice after the Destruction of the Temple in 586 B.C.', *JTS* (N.S.) 14, 1963, pp. 12–31.

JUNKER, H., 'Die Entstehungszeit des Ps. 78 und des Deuteronomiums', *Biblica* 34, 1953, pp. 487–500.

'Der Strom, dessen Arme die Stadt Gottes erfreuen (Ps. 46:5)', *Biblica* 43, 1962, pp. 197–201.

KAISER, O., *Die mythische Bedeutung des Meeres in Ägypten, Ugarit und Israel* (BZAW 78), Berlin, 1959.

KAPELRUD, A. S., *Joel Studies*, UUÅ 1948, 4, Uppsala, 1948.

Baal in the Ras Shamra Texts, Copenhagen, 1952.

'The Gates of Hell and the Guardian Angels of Paradise', *JAOS* 70, 1950, pp. 151–156.

KOCH, K., 'Zur Geschichte der Erwählungsvorstellung in Israel', *ZAW* 67, 1955, pp. 205–226.

'Die Eigenart der priesterschriftlichen Sinaigesetzgebung', *ZThK* 55, 1958, pp. 36–51.

Die Priesterschrift von Exodus 25 bis Leviticus 16. Eine überlieferungsgeschichtliche und literarkritische Untersuchung (FRLANT 71), Göttingen, 1959.

'Tempeleinlassliturgien und Dekaloge', *Studien zur Theologie der alttestamentlichen Überlieferungen*, ed. R. Rendtorff und K. Koch, Neukirchen 1961, pp. 45–60.

KOOLE, J. L., 'Psalm 15—eine königliche Einzugsliturgie?' OTS XIII, Leiden, 1963, pp. 98–111.

KORNFELD, W., 'Der Symbolismus der Tempelsäulen', *ZAW* 74, 1962, pp. 50–57.

KOSMALA, H., *Hebräer-Essener-Christen* (Studia Post-biblica, I), Leiden, 1959.

KRAMER, S. N., *Sumerian Mythology*, Philadelphia, 1944.

KRAUS, H. J., *Die Königsherrschaft Gottes im Alten Testament*, Tübingen, 1951.

'Gilgal', *VT* 1, 1951, pp. 181–199.

Psalmen (BKAT), Neukirchen, 1960.

*Gottesdienst in Israel*², Neukirchen, 1962.

Kuschke, A., 'Die Lagervorstellung der priesterschriftlichen Erzählung', *ZAW* 63, 1951, pp. 74–105.

Kutsch, E., *Das Herbstfest in Israel*, Diss. Mainz, 1955. Cf. *ThLZ* 81, 1956, cols. 493–495.

'Lade Jahwes', *RGG*³, IV, cols. 197–199.

'Die Dynastie von Gottes Gnaden. Probleme der Nathanweissagung in 2 Sam. 7', *ZThK* 58, 1961, pp. 137–153.

Lack, R., 'Miscellanea Biblica. Les origines de Elyon, Le Tres-haut dans la tradition cultuelle d'Israel', *CBQ* 24, 1962, pp. 44–64.

de Langhe, R., *Les textes de Ras Shamra-Ugarit et leurs rapports avec le milieu biblique de l'Ancien Testament*, Paris, 1945.

'Myth, Ritual and Kingship in the Ras Shamra Tablets', *Myth, Ritual and Kingship*, ed. S. H. Hooke, London, 1958, pp. 122–148.

Leslie, E. A., *Old Testament Religion*, New York-Nashville, 1936.

Levi Della Vida, G., 'El Elyon in Genesis xiv: 18–20', *JBL* 63, 1944, pp. 1–9.

Lewy, J., 'The Šulmān Temple in Jerusalem', *JBL* 59, 1940, pp. 519–522.

Lindblom, J., *A Study on the Immanuel Section in Isaiah. Is.vii:1–ix:9*, Lund, 1958.

Prophecy in Ancient Israel, Oxford, 1962.

Lipinski, E., 'Les psaumes de la royauté de Yahwé dans l'exégèse moderne', *Le Psautier. Ses origines. Ses problemes litteraires. Son influence*, ed. R. de Langhe, Louvain, 1962, pp. 133–272.

Lohmeyer, E., *Lord of the Temple*, Edinburgh, 1961.

Løkkegaard, F., 'The House of Baal', *Ac.Or.* 22, 1955, pp. 10–27.

Maag, V., 'Erwägungen zur deuteronomischen Kultzentralisation', *VT* 6, 1956, pp. 10–18.

'Der Hirte Israels. Eine Skizze von Wesen und Bedeutung der Väterreligion', *Schweizerische theologische Umschau*, 28, 1958, pp. 2–28.

'MALKÛT JHWH', *Oxford Congress Volume* (SVT VII), Leiden, 1960, pp. 129–153.

May, H. G., 'The Departure of the Glory of Yahweh' *JBL* 56, 1937, pp. 309–321.

'Some Aspects of Solar Worship at Jerusalem', *ZAW* 55, 1937, pp. 269–281.

'The Patriarchal Idea of God', *JBL* 60, 1941, pp. 113–128.

'The God of My Father—a Study of Patriarchal Religion', *Journal of Bible and Religion* 9, 1941, pp. 155–158, 199–200.

'Some Cosmic Connotations of Mayim Rabbim—Many Waters', *JBL* 74, 1955, pp. 9–21.

'The King in the Garden of Eden. A Study of Ezekiel 28:12–19', *Israel's Prophetic Heritage*, ed. B. W. Anderson and W. Harrelson, London, 1962, pp. 166–176.

McKenzie, J. L., 'Mythological Allusions in Ezekiel 28:12–18', *JBL* 75, 1956, pp. 322–327.

Meinhold, J., 'Die Lade Jahves: ein Nachtrag', *ThSK* 74, 1901, pp. 593–617.

L

MENDENHALL, G. E., 'Election', *IDB*, II, pp. 76a–82a.
'Covenant', *IDB*, I, pp. 714a–723b.
MÖHLENBRINK, K., *Der Tempel Salomos* (BWANT IV, 7), Stuttgart, 1932.
MONTGOMERY, J. A., 'The Highest, Heaven, Aeon, Time, etc., in Semitic Religion', *HTR* 31, 1938, pp. 143–150.
MORGENSTERN, J., 'Moses with the Shining Face', *HUCA* 2, 1925, pp. 1–27. 'The Oldest Document of the Hexateuch', *HUCA* 4, 1927, pp. 1–138.
'The Book of the Covenant', *HUCA* 5, 1928, pp. 1–151.
'The Mythological Background of Psalm 82', *HUCA* 14, 1939, pp. 9–126.
'Psalm 48', *HUCA* 16, 1941, pp. 1–95.
Amos Studies, Cincinnati, 1941.
The Ark, the Ephod and the 'Tent of Meeting', Cincinnati, 1945.
'The King-God among the Western Semites and the Meaning of Epiphanes', *VT* 10, 1960, pp. 138–197.
MOULE, C. F. D., 'Sanctuary and Sacrifice in the Church of the New Testament', *JTS* (N.S.) 1, 1950, pp. 29–41.
MOWINCKEL, S., *Psalmenstudien I-VI*, Rep. Amsterdam, 1961.
Le Décalogue, Paris, 1927.
'Natanforjettelsen 2 Sam. kap. 7', *SEÅ* 12, 1948, pp. 204–213.
Religion und Kultus, Göttingen, 1953.
Der achtundsechzigste Psalm, Oslo, 1953.
'Zum Psalm des Habakuk', *ThZ* 9, 1953, pp. 1–23.
'Psalm Criticism between 1900–1935', *VT* 5, 1955, pp. 13–33.
He That Cometh, Oxford, 1956.
The Psalms in Israel's Worship, Oxford, 1962.
MUILENBURG, J., 'Psalm 47', *JBL* 63, 1944, pp. 235–256.
'Isaiah 40–66', *Interpreter's Bible*, V, New York–Nashville, 1956, pp. 381–773.
MÜLLER, H.-P., 'Die kultische Darstellung der Theophanie', *VT* 14, 1964, pp. 183–191.
NELSON, H. H., 'The Egyptian Temple', *BA* 7, 1944, pp. 44–53.
NEWMAN, M. L., *The People of the Covenant. A Study of Israel from Moses to the Monarchy*, New York–Nashville, 1962.
NICHOLSON, E., 'The Centralization of the Cult in Deuteronomy', *VT* 13, 1963, pp. 380–389.
NIELSEN, E., *Shechem: a Traditio-historical Investigation*, Copenhagen, 1955.
'Some Reflections on the History of the Ark', *Oxford Congress Volume* (SVT VII), Leiden, 1960, pp. 61–74.
NORTH, C. R., 'The Essence of Idolatry', *Von Ugarit nach Qumran* (BZAW 77), Berlin, 1958, pp. 151–160.
NOTH, M., *Das System der Zwölf Stämme Israels* (BWANT IV, 1), Stuttgart 1930.
Überlieferungsgeschichtliche Studien, Rep. Wiesbaden, 1957.
'Jerusalem und die israelitische Tradition', *Ges. Stud. zum A.T.²*, München, 1960, pp. 172–187.
'David und Israel in II Sam. 7', ibid. pp. 334–345.
A History of Israel², London, 1960.
Überlieferungsgeschichte des Pentateuch, rep. Stuttgart, 1960.

Exodus, London, 1962.
'Samuel und Silo', *VT* 13, 1963, pp. 390–400.
NYBERG, H. S., 'Studien zum Religionskampf im A.T.', *ARW* 35, 1938, pp. 329–387.
Studien zum Hoseabuche (UUÅ 1935, 6), Uppsala, 1935.
OBBINK, H. Th., 'Jahwebilder', *ZAW* 47, 1929, pp. 264–274.
OBERMANN, J., 'An Antiphonal Psalm from Ras Shamra', *JBL* 55, 1936, pp. 21–44.
Ugaritic Mythology, New Haven, 1948.
OPPENHEIM, A. L., 'The Mesopotamian Temple', *BA* 7, 1944, pp. 54–63.
OSSWALD, E., 'Mose', *RGG*³, IV, cols. 1151–1155.
Das Bild des Mose in der kritischen alttestamentlichen Wissenschaft seit J. Wellhausen, Berlin, 1962.
PARROT, A., *The Tower of Babel* (Studies in Biblical Archaeology, 2), London, 1955.
The Temple of Jerusalem (Studies in Biblical Archaeology, 5), London, 1957.
PATAI, R., *Man and Temple*, London, 1947.
PATTON, J. H., *Canaanite Parallels in the Book of Psalms*, Baltimore, 1944.
PEDERSEN, J., *Israel I–II*, Copenhagen, 1926.
Israel III–IV, Copenhagen, 1940.
'Canaanite and Israelite Cultus', *Ac. Or.* 18, 1940, pp. 1–14.
'The Phoenician Inscriptions of Karatepe', *Ac.Or.* 21, 1953, pp. 33–56.
PHYTHIAN-ADAMS, W. J., *The Call of Israel*, London, 1934.
The Fullness of Israel, London, 1938.
The People and the Presence, London, 1942.
PIDOUX, G., *Le Dieu qui vient. Espérance d'Israel* (Cahiers théologiques, 17), Neuchâtel, 1947.
POPE, M. H., *El in the Ugaritic Texts* (SVT II), Leiden, 1955.
PORTEOUS, N. W., 'Shalem-Shalom', *TGUOS* 10, 1943, pp. 1–7.
'Jerusalem-Zion. The Growth of a Symbol', *Verbannung und Heimkehr*, ed. A. Kuschke, Tübingen, 1961, pp. 235–252.
'Actualization and the Prophetic Criticism of the Cult', *Tradition und Situation. Studien zur alttestamentlichen Prophetie*, ed. E. Würthwein and O. Kaiser, Göttingen, 1963, pp. 93–105.
PORTER, J. R., 'The Interpretation of 2 Sam. vi and Psalm cxxxii', *JTS* (N.S.) 5, 1954, pp. 161–173.
PRITCHARD, J. B., *Archaeology and the Old Testament*, Princeton, 1958.
(ed.), *Ancient Near Eastern Texts Relating to the O.T.*², Princeton, 1955.
QUELL, G., 'Jesaja 14, 1–23', *F. Baumgärtel Festschrift* (Erlanger Forschungen A:10), Erlangen, 1959, pp. 131–157.
VON RAD, G., *Das Gottesvolk im Deuteronomium* (BWANT III, 11), Stuttgart, 1929.
Die Priesterschrift im Hexateuch (BWANT IV, 13), Stuttgart, 1934.
'Doxa', *ThWzNT*, II, Stuttgart, 1935, cols. 240–245.
'Das formgeschichtliche Problem des Hexateuch', *Ges. Stud. zum. A.T.*, München, 1958, pp. 9–86.
'Zelt und Lade', ibid., pp. 109–129.
Studies in Deuteronomy (SBT 9), London, 1953.
'Das judäisches Königsritual', *Ges. Stud. zum. A.T.*, pp. 205–213.

VON RAD—*cont.*
  'Verheissenes Land und Jahwes Land im Hexateuch', ibid., pp. 87–100.
  'Die Stadt auf dem Berge', ibid., 214–224.
  Old Testament Theology, Vol. I, Edinburgh, 1962.
  Theologie des Alten Testaments, II, München, 1960.
  Genesis, London, 1961.
  'The Origin of the Concept of the Day of Yahweh', *JSS* 4, 1959, pp. 97–
    108.
  'Deuteronomy', *IDB*, I, pp. 831a–838b.
RENDTORFF, R., *Die Gesetze in der Priesterschrift* (FRLANT 62), Göttingen,
    1954.
  'Die Entstehung der israelitischen Religion als religionsgeschichtliches
    und theologisches Problem', *ThLZ* 88, 1963, cols. 735–746.
  'Der Kultus im alten Israel', *Jahrbuch für Liturgik und Hymnologie* 2,
    1956, pp. 1–21.
GRAF REVENTLOW, H., *Das Heiligkeitsgesetz: formgeschichtlich untersucht*
    (WMANT 6), Neukirchen, 1961.
RINGGREN H., *The Faith of the Psalmists*, London, 1963.
ROHLAND, E., *Die Bedeutung der Erwählungstraditionen Israels für die Escha-
    tologie der alttestamentlichen Propheten*, Diss., Heidelberg, 1956.
ROST, L., *Die Überlieferung von der Thronnachfolge Davids* (BWANT III,
    6), Stuttgart, 1926.
  Die Vorstufen von Kirche und Synagoge im A.T. (BWANT IV, 24),
    Stuttgart, 1938.
  'Davidsbund und Sinaibund', *ThLZ* 72, 1947, cols. 129–134.
  'Die Wohnstätte des Zeugnisses', *F. Baumgärtel Festschrift*, (Erlanger
    Forschungen A:10), Erlangen, 1959, pp. 158–165.
  'Die Gottesverehrung der Patriarchen im Lichte der Pentateuchquellen',
    Oxford Congress Volume (SVT VII), Leiden, 1960, pp. 346–359.
ROTH, J., 'Thèmes majeurs de la tradition sacerdotale dans le Pentateuque',
    NRT 80, 1958, pp. 696–721.
ROWLEY, H. H., 'Zadok and Nehushtan', *JBL* 58, 1939, pp. 113–141.
  'Melchizedek and Zadok (Gen. 14 and Psalm 110)', *Bertholet Festschrift*,
    Tübingen, 1950, pp. 461–472.
  The Biblical Doctrine of Election, London, 1950.
  'Hezekiah's Reform and Rebellion', *Men of God*, London, 1963, pp. 98–132.
SCHMID, H., 'Jahwe und die Kulttraditionen von Jerusalem', *ZAW* 67, 1955,
    pp. 168–197.
SCHMIDT, H., *Die Thronfahrt Jahwes am Fest der Jahreswende im alten Israel*,
    Tübingen, 1927.
  'Kerubenthron und Lade', *EUCHARISTERION*, ed. H. Schmidt, I.,
    Göttingen, 1923, pp. 120–144.
SCHMIDT, K. L., 'Israels Stellung zu den Fremdlingen und Beisassen und
    Israels Wissen um seine Fremdling-und Beisassenschaft', *Judaica* 1,
    1945, pp. 269–296.
  'Jerusalem als Urbild und Abbild', *Eranos Jahrbuch* 18, 1950, pp. 207–248.
SCHMIDT, M., *Prophet und Tempel*, Zürich, 1948.
SCHMIDT, W., *Königtum Gottes in Ugarit und Israel* (BZAW 80), Berlin,
    1961.

'*Miškān* als Ausdruck Jerusalemer Kultsprache', *ZAW* 75, 1963, pp. 91f.

SCHNUTENHAUS, F., 'Das Kommen und Erscheinen Gottes in Alten Testament', *ZAW* 76, 1964, pp. 1–21.

SCHREINER, J., *Sion-Jerusalem. Jahwes Königsitz* (Sant 7), München, 1963.

SCOTT, R. B. Y., 'The Pillars Jachin and Boaz', *JBL* 58, 1939, pp. 143–149.

'Jachin and Boaz', *IDB*, II, pp. 780a–781a.

SEGAL, J. B., *The Hebrew Passover from the Earliest Times to A.D. 70*, (London Oriental Series No. 12), London, 1963.

SELLIN, E., 'Das Zelt Jahwes', *R. Kittel Festschrift* (BWAT 13), Stuttgart, 1913, pp. 168–192.

SIMON, M., 'Saint Stephen and the Jerusalem Temple', *Journal of Ecclesiastical History* 2, 1951, pp. 127–142.

'La prophétie de Nathan et le Temple (remarques sur II Sam. 7)', *RHPR* 32, 1952, pp. 41–58.

St. Stephen and the Hellenists in the Primitive Church, London, 1958.

SMEND, R., *Jahwekrieg und Stämmebund. Erwägungen zur ältesten Geschichte Israels* (FRLANT 84), Göttingen, 1963.

Die Bundesformel (Theologische Studien 68), Zürich, 1963.

STADE, B., 'Der Thurm zu Babel', *ZAW* 15, 1895, pp. 157–166.

Biblische Theologie des Alten Testaments, I, Tübingen, 1905.

STAMM, J. J., 'Zum Altargesetz im Bundesbuch', *ThZ* 1, 1945, pp. 304–306.

Der Dekalog im Lichte der neueren Forschung, Bern, 1958.

STINESPRING, W. F., 'Temple, Jerusalem', *IDB*, IV, pp. 534a–560b.

STOEBE, H. J., 'Erwägungen zu Psalm 110 auf den Hintergrund von I Sam. 21', *F. Baumgärtel Festschrift*, (Erlanger Forschungen A:10), Erlangen, 1959, pp. 175–191.

DE VAUX, R., 'Les chérubins et l'arche d'alliance. Les Sphinx gardiens et les trônes divins dans l'ancien Orient', *MUSJ* 37, 1960, pp. 91–124.

Ancient Israel. Its Life and Institutions, London, 1961.

'Arche d'alliance et tente de réunion', *Memorial A. Gelin*, Le Puy-Lyons-Paris, 1961, pp. 55–70.

VINCENT, A., *La religion des Judéo-Araméens d'Éléphantine*, Paris, 1937.

VINCENT, H., 'Le caractère du Temple salomonièn', *Mélanges bibliques rédigés en l'honneur de André Robert*, Paris, 1957, pp. 137–148.

VINCENT, L. H., 'De la Tour de Babel au Temple', *RB* 53, 1946, pp. 403–440.

VOEGELIN, E., *Order and History*, Vol. 1, *Israel and Revelation*, Louisiana, 1956.

VOGT, E., 'The "Place in Life" of Ps. 23', *Biblica* 34, 1953, pp. 195–211.

VOLZ, P., *Das Neujahrsfest Jahwes* (*Laubhüttenfest*), Tübingen, 1912.

VRIEZEN, T. C., *Die Erwählung Israels nach dem Alten Testament* (ATANT 24), Zürich, 1953.

An Outline of Old Testament Theology, Oxford, 1958.

Jahwe en zijn stad, Amsterdam, 1962.

WAMBACQ, B. N., *L'épithète divine Jahvé S^eba'ôt. Étude philologique, historique et éxégétique*, Brussels, 1947.

WEISER, A., 'Abram, Isaak, Jakob', *RGG*³, I, cols. 68–71; III, cols. 902–903, 517–520.

'Das Deboralied', *ZAW* 71, 1959, pp. 67–97.

Introduction to the O.T., London, 1961.

WEISER—*cont.*
The Psalms, London, 1962.
'Zur Frage nach den Beziehungen der Psalmen zum Kult; die Darstellung der Theophanie in den Psalmen und in Festkult', *Glaube und Geschichte im A.T.*, Göttingen, 1961, pp. 303–321.
WELCH, A. C., *The Code of Deuteronomy. A New Theory of its Origin*, London, 1924.
The Psalter in Life, Worship and History, Oxford, 1926.
Jeremiah: His Time and His Work, London, 1928.
Deuteronomy: The Framework to the Code, London, 1932.
Prophet and Priest in Old Israel, London, 1936.
WELLHAUSEN, J., *Prolegomena to the History of Ancient Israel*, Meridian ed., New York, 1957.
WESTPHAL, G., *Jahwes Wohnstätten nach den Anschauungen der alten Hebräer* (BZAW 15), Giessen, 1908.
WIDENGREN, G., *Psalm 110 och det sakrala kungadömet i Israel* (*UUÅ* 1941, 7, 1), Uppsala, 1941.
Sakrales Königtum im A.T. und im Judentum, Tübingen, 1955.
'Early Hebrew Myths and their Interpretation', *Myth, Ritual and Kingship*, ed. S. H. Hooke, London, 1958, pp. 149–203.
WILDBERGER, H., 'Israel und sein Land', *Ev. Th.* 16, 1956, pp. 404–422.
'Die Völkerwallfahrt zum Zion. Jes. ii: 1–5', *VT* 7, 1957, pp. 62–81.
Jahwes Eigentumsvolk (ATANT 37), Zürich, 1960.
WRIGHT, G. E., 'The Temple in Palestine-Syria', *BA* 7, 1944, pp. 66–77.
'The Book of Deuteronomy', *Interpreter's Bible*, II, New York-Nashville, 1953, pp. 311–537.
Biblical Archaeology, London, 1957.
'Cult and History', *Interpretation* 16, 1962, pp. 3–20.
YEIVIN, S., 'Social, Religious and Cultural Trends in Jerusalem under the Davidic Dynasty', *VT* 3, 1953, pp. 149–166.
'Jachin and Boaz', *PEQ* 91, 1959, pp. 6–22.
YOUNG, G. D., *Concordance of Ugaritic* (Analecta Orientalia 36), Rome, 1956,
ZIMMERLI, W., 'Das zweite Gebot', *Gottes Offenbarung. Gesammelte Aufsätze*. München, 1963, pp. 234–248.
'Ich bin Jahwe', ibid., pp. 11–40.
'Sinaibund und Abrahambund', ibid., pp. 205–216.

REFERENCE INDEX

INDEX OF AUTHORS

GENERAL INDEX